Carnegie Commission on Higher Education
Sponsored Research Studies

EDUCATION FOR THE PROFESSIONS OF
MEDICINE, LAW, THEOLOGY, AND SOCIAL
WELFARE
Everett C. Hughes, Barrie Thorne,
Agostino DeBaggis, Arnold Gurin,
and David Williams

THE FUTURE OF HIGHER
EDUCATION:
SOME SPECULATIONS AND
SUGGESTIONS
Alexander M. Mood

CONTENT AND CONTEXT:
ESSAYS ON COLLEGE EDUCATION
Carl Kaysen (ed.)

THE RISE OF THE ARTS ON THE AMERICAN
CAMPUS
Jack Morrison

THE UNIVERSITY AND THE CITY:
EIGHT CASES OF INVOLVEMENT
George Nash, Dan Waldorf, and Robert E. Price

THE BEGINNING OF THE FUTURE:
A HISTORICAL APPROACH TO GRADUATE
EDUCATION IN THE ARTS AND SCIENCES
Richard J. Storr

ACADEMIC TRANSFORMATION:
SEVENTEEN INSTITUTIONS UNDER PRESSURE
David Riesman and Verne A. Stadtman (eds.)

WHERE COLLEGES ARE AND WHO ATTENDS:
EFFECTS OF ACCESSIBILITY ON COLLEGE
ATTENDANCE
C. Arnold Anderson, Mary Jean Bowman, and
Vincent Tinto

NEW DIRECTIONS IN LEGAL EDUCATION
Herbert L. Packer and Thomas Ehrlich
abridged and unabridged editions

THE UNIVERSITY AS AN ORGANIZATION
James A. Perkins (ed.)

THE EMERGING TECHNOLOGY:
INSTRUCTIONAL USES OF THE COMPUTER IN
HIGHER EDUCATION
Roger E. Levien

A STATISTICAL PORTRAIT OF HIGHER
EDUCATION
Seymour E. Harris

THE HOME OF SCIENCE:
THE ROLE OF THE UNIVERSITY
Dael Wolfle

EDUCATION AND EVANGELISM:
A PROFILE OF PROTESTANT COLLEGES
C. Robert Pace

PROFESSIONAL EDUCATION:
SOME NEW DIRECTIONS
Edgar H. Schein

THE NONPROFIT RESEARCH INSTITUTE:
ITS ORIGIN, OPERATION, PROBLEMS, AND
PROSPECTS
Harold Orlans

THE INVISIBLE COLLEGES:
A PROFILE OF SMALL, PRIVATE COLLEGES
WITH LIMITED RESOURCES
Alexander W. Astin and Calvin B. T. Lee

AMERICAN HIGHER EDUCATION:
DIRECTIONS OLD AND NEW
Joseph Ben-David

A DEGREE AND WHAT ELSE?
CORRELATES AND CONSEQUENCES OF A
COLLEGE EDUCATION
Stephen B. Withey, Jo Anne Coble, Gerald Gurin,
John P. Robinson, Burkhard Strumpel, Elizabeth
Keogh Taylor, and Arthur C. Wolfe

THE MULTICAMPUS UNIVERSITY:
A STUDY OF ACADEMIC GOVERNANCE
Eugene C. Lee and Frank M. Bowen

INSTITUTIONS IN TRANSITION:
A PROFILE OF CHANGE IN HIGHER
EDUCATION
(INCORPORATING THE 1970 STATISTICAL
REPORT)
Harold L. Hodgkinson

THE FINANCE OF HIGHER EDUCATION
Howard R. Bowen
(Out of print, but available from University Microfilms.)

ALTERNATIVE METHODS OF FEDERAL
FUNDING FOR HIGHER EDUCATION
Ron Wolk
(Out of print, but available from University Microfilms.)

INVENTORY OF CURRENT RESEARCH ON
HIGHER EDUCATION 1968
Dale M. Heckman and Warren Bryan Martin
(Out of print, but available from University Microfilms.)

*The following technical reports are available from the Carnegie Commission on Higher Education, 2150 Shattuck Ave.,
Berkeley, California 94704.*

RESOURCE USE IN HIGHER EDUCATION:
TRENDS IN OUTPUT AND INPUTS, 1930–1967
June O'Neill

MAY 1970:
THE CAMPUS AFTERMATH OF CAMBODIA AND
KENT STATE
Richard E. Peterson and John A. Bilorusky

MENTAL ABILITY AND HIGHER EDUCATIONAL
ATTAINMENT IN THE 20TH CENTURY
Paul Taubman and Terence Wales

AMERICAN COLLEGE AND UNIVERSITY
ENROLLMENT TRENDS IN 1971
Richard E. Peterson

PAPERS ON EFFICIENCY IN THE MANAGEMENT
OF HIGHER EDUCATION
*Alexander M. Mood, Colin Bell, Lawrence Bogard,
Helen Brownlee, and Joseph McCloskey*

AN INVENTORY OF ACADEMIC INNOVATION
AND REFORM
Ann Heiss

ESTIMATING THE RETURNS TO EDUCATION:
A DISAGGREGATED APPROACH
Richard S. Eckaus

SOURCES OF FUNDS TO COLLEGES AND
UNIVERSITIES
June O'Neill

TRENDS AND PROJECTIONS OF PHYSICIANS IN
THE UNITED STATES 1967–2002
Mark S. Blumberg

THE NEW DEPRESSION IN HIGHER EDUCATION
—-TWO YEARS LATER
Earl F. Cheit

PROFESSORS, UNIONS, AND AMERICAN
HIGHER EDUCATION
*Everett Carll Ladd, Jr. and
Seymour Martin Lipset*

A CLASSIFICATION OF INSTITUTIONS
OF HIGHER EDUCATION

POLITICAL IDEOLOGIES OF
GRADUATE STUDENTS:
CRYSTALLIZATION, CONSISTENCY, AND
CONTEXTUAL EFFECT
Margaret Fay and Jeff Weintraub

FLYING A LEARNING CENTER:
DESIGN AND COSTS OF AN OFF-CAMPUS SPACE
FOR LEARNING
Thomas J. Karwin

THE DEMISE OF DIVERSITY?:
A COMPARATIVE PROFILE OF EIGHT TYPES OF
INSTITUTIONS
C. Robert Pace

TUITION: A SUPPLEMENTAL STATEMENT TO
THE REPORT OF THE CARNEGIE COMMISSION
ON HIGHER EDUCATION ON "WHO PAYS?
WHO BENEFITS? WHO SHOULD PAY?"

THE GREAT AMERICAN DEGREE MACHINE
Douglas L. Adkins

The following reprints are available from the Carnegie Commission on Higher Education, 2150 Shattuck Ave., Berkeley, California 94704.

ACCELERATED PROGRAMS OF MEDICAL EDUCATION, by Mark S. Blumberg, reprinted from JOURNAL OF MEDICAL EDUCATION, vol. 46, no. 8, August 1971.*

SCIENTIFIC MANPOWER FOR 1970–1985, by Allan M. Cartter, reprinted from SCIENCE, vol. 172, no. 3979, pp. 132–140, April 9, 1971.*

A NEW METHOD OF MEASURING STATES' HIGHER EDUCATION BURDEN, by Neil Timm, reprinted from THE JOURNAL OF HIGHER EDUCATION, vol. 42, no. 1, pp. 27–33, January 1971.*

REGENT WATCHING, by Earl F. Cheit, reprinted from AGB REPORTS, vol. 13, no. 6, pp. 4–13, March 1971.*

COLLEGE GENERATIONS—FROM THE 1930s TO THE 1960s, by Seymour M. Lipset and Everett C. Ladd, Jr., reprinted from THE PUBLIC INTEREST, no. 25, Summer 1971.*

WHAT'S BUGGING THE STUDENTS?, by Kenneth Keniston, reprinted from EDUCATIONAL RECORD, American Council on Education, Washington, D.C., Spring 1970.*

THE POLITICS OF ACADEMIA, by Seymour Martin Lipset, reprinted from David C. Nichols (ed.), PERSPECTIVES ON CAMPUS TENSIONS: PAPERS PREPARED FOR THE SPECIAL COMMITTEE ON CAMPUS TENSIONS, American Council on Education, Washington, D.C., September 1970.*

INTERNATIONAL PROGRAMS OF U.S. COLLEGES AND UNIVERSITIES: PRIORITIES FOR THE SEVENTIES, by James A. Perkins, reprinted by permission of the International Council for Educational Development, Occasional Paper no. 1, July 1971.*

FACULTY UNIONISM: FROM THEORY TO PRACTICE, by Joseph W. Garbarino, reprinted from INDUSTRIAL RELATIONS, vol. 11, no. 1, pp. 1–17, February 1972.*

MORE FOR LESS: HIGHER EDUCATION'S NEW PRIORITY, by Virginia B. Smith, reprinted from UNIVERSAL HIGHER EDUCATION: COSTS AND BENEFITS, American Council on Education, Washington, D.C., 1971.*

ACADEMIA AND POLITICS IN AMERICA, by Seymour M. Lipset, reprinted from Thomas J. Nossiter (ed.), IMAGINATION AND PRECISION IN THE SOCIAL SCIENCES, pp. 211–289, Faber and Faber, London, 1972.*

POLITICS OF ACADEMIC NATURAL SCIENTISTS AND ENGINEERS, by Everett C. Ladd, Jr., and Seymour M. Lipset, reprinted from SCIENCE, vol. 176, no. 4039, pp. 1091–1100, June 9, 1972.

THE INTELLECTUAL AS CRITIC AND REBEL, WITH SPECIAL REFERENCE TO THE UNITED STATES AND THE SOVIET UNION, by Seymour M. Lipset and Richard B. Dobson, reprinted from DAEDALUS, vol. 101, no. 3, pp. 137–198, Summer 1972.

*The Commission's stock of this reprint has been exhausted.

THE POLITICS OF AMERICAN SOCIOLOGISTS, *by Seymour M. Lipset and Everett C. Ladd, Jr., reprinted from* THE AMERICAN JOURNAL OF SOCIOLOGY, *vol. 78, no. 1, July 1972.*

THE DISTRIBUTION OF ACADEMIC TENURE IN AMERICAN HIGHER EDUCATION, *by Martin Trow, reprinted from* THE TENURE DEBATE, *Bardwell Smith (ed.), Jossey-Bass, San Francisco, 1972.*

THE NATURE AND ORIGINS OF THE CARNEGIE COMMISSION ON HIGHER EDUCATION, *by Alan Pifer, based on a speech delivered to the Pennsylvania Association of Colleges and Universities, Oct. 16, 1972, reprinted by permission of the Carnegie Foundation for the Advancement of Teaching.*

AMERICAN SOCIAL SCIENTISTS AND THE GROWTH OF CAMPUS POLITICAL ACTIVISM IN THE 1960s, *by Everett C. Ladd, Jr., and Seymour M. Lipset, reprinted from* SOCIAL SCIENCES INFORMATION, *vol. 10, no. 2, April 1971.**

THE POLITICS OF AMERICAN POLITICAL SCIENTISTS, *by Everett C. Ladd, Jr., and Seymour M. Lipset, reprinted from* PS, *vol. 4, no. 2, Spring 1971.**

THE DIVIDED PROFESSORIATE, *by Seymour M. Lipset and Everett C. Ladd, Jr., reprinted from* CHANGE, *vol. 3, no. 3, pp. 54–60, May 1971.**

JEWISH ACADEMICS IN THE UNITED STATES: THEIR ACHIEVEMENTS, CULTURE AND POLITICS, *by Seymour M. Lipset and Everett C. Ladd, Jr., reprinted from* AMERICAN JEWISH YEAR BOOK, *1971.**

THE UNHOLY ALLIANCE AGAINST THE CAMPUS, *by Kenneth Keniston and Michael Lerner, reprinted from* NEW YORK TIMES MAGAZINE, *November 8, 1970.**

PRECARIOUS PROFESSORS: NEW PATTERNS OF REPRESENTATION, *by Joseph W. Garbarino, reprinted from* INDUSTRIAL RELATIONS, *vol. 10, no. 1, February 1971.**

. . . AND WHAT PROFESSORS THINK: ABOUT STUDENT PROTEST AND MANNERS, MORALS, POLITICS, AND CHAOS ON THE CAMPUS, *by Seymour Martin Lipset and Everett C. Ladd, Jr., reprinted from* PSYCHOLOGY TODAY, *November 1970.**

DEMAND AND SUPPLY IN U.S. HIGHER EDUCATION: A PROGRESS REPORT, *by Roy Radner and Leonard S. Miller, reprinted from* AMERICAN ECONOMIC REVIEW, *May 1970.**

RESOURCES FOR HIGHER EDUCATION: AN ECONOMIST'S VIEW, *by Theodore W. Schultz, reprinted from* JOURNAL OF POLITICAL ECONOMY, *vol. 76, no. 3, University of Chicago, May/June 1968.**

INDUSTRIAL RELATIONS AND UNIVERSITY RELATIONS, *by Clark Kerr, reprinted from* PROCEEDINGS OF THE 21ST ANNUAL WINTER MEETING OF THE INDUSTRIAL RELATIONS RESEARCH ASSOCIATION, *pp. 15–25.**

*The Commission's stock of this reprint has been exhausted.

NEW CHALLENGES TO THE COLLEGE AND UNIVERSITY, *by Clark Kerr, reprinted from Kermit Gordon (ed.),* AGENDA FOR THE NATION, *The Brookings Institution, Washington, D.C., 1968.* *

PRESIDENTIAL DISCONTENT, *by Clark Kerr, reprinted from David C. Nichols (ed.),* PERSPECTIVES ON CAMPUS TENSIONS: PAPERS PREPARED FOR THE SPECIAL COMMITTEE ON CAMPUS TENSIONS, *American Council on Education, Washington, D.C., September 1970.* *

STUDENT PROTEST—AN INSTITUTIONAL AND NATIONAL PROFILE, *by Harold Hodgkinson, reprinted from* THE RECORD, *vol. 71, no. 4, May 1970.* *

COMING OF MIDDLE AGE IN HIGHER EDUCATION, *by Earl F. Cheit, address delivered to American Association of State Colleges and Universities and National Association of State Universities and Land-Grant Colleges, Nov. 13, 1972.*

MEASURING FACULTY UNIONISM: QUANTITY AND QUALITY, *by Bill Aussieker and J. W. Garbarino, reprinted from* INDUSTRIAL RELATIONS, *vol. 12, no. 2, May 1973.*

PROBLEMS IN THE TRANSITION FROM ELITE TO MASS HIGHER EDUCATION, *by Martin Trow, paper prepared for a conference on mass higher education sponsored by the Organization for Economic Co-operation and Development, June 1973.* *

The Commission's stock of this reprint has been exhausted.

*Computers and
the Learning Process
in Higher Education*

Computers and the Learning Process in Higher Education

by *John Fralick Rockart*

Associate Professor, Sloan School of Management
Massachusetts Institute of Technology

and *Michael S. Scott Morton*

Professor, Sloan School of Management
Massachusetts Institute of Technology

A Report Prepared for
The Carnegie Commission on Higher Education

McGRAW-HILL BOOK COMPANY
New York   St. Louis   San Francisco
Düsseldorf   Johannesburg   Kuala Lumpur   London   Mexico
Montreal   New Delhi   Panama   Paris   São Paulo
Singapore   Sydney   Tokyo   Toronto

The Carnegie Commission on Higher Education,
2150 Shattuck Avenue, Berkeley, California 94704,
has sponsored preparation of this report as part
of a continuing effort to obtain and present
significant information for public discussion.
The views expressed are those of the authors.

COMPUTERS AND THE LEARNING PROCESS IN HIGHER EDUCATION

This book was set in Palatino by University Graphics, Inc.
It was printed and bound by The Maple Press Company.
The designer was Elliot Epstein. The editors were
Nancy Tressel and Michael Hennelly for McGraw-Hill
Book Company and Verne A. Stadtman and Karen Seriguchi
for the Carnegie Commission on Higher Education. Audre
Hanneman edited the index. Milton J. Heiberg supervised
the production.

Library of Congress Cataloging in Publication Data
Rockart, John Fralick.
Computers and the learning process in higher
education.

Bibliography: p.
Includes index.
1. Computer-assisted instruction. 2. Elec-
tronic data processing—Education. I. Scott Morton,
Michael S., joint author. II. Title.
LB1028.5.R55   378.1'79'445   75-6720

ISBN 0-07-010122-1

123456789 MAMM 798765

To Elise and Mary

Contents

Foreword

Computers are only one of the several electronic devices currently available that can make a potentially significant contribution to instructional technology. Television and audio cassettes, for example, also find increasing application in the classroom. Computers are now familiar on college campuses as multipurpose servants of administrative planners and financial officers, librarians, scholars engaged in quantitative analyses, and some, perhaps too few, teachers. The full range of such current usage was outlined in an earlier book, *The Emerging Technology,* prepared for the Carnegie Commission and the Rand Corporation by Roger Levien. Few advocates of the use of computers for instruction feel, however, that the full range of the computer's potential has as yet been assessed.

It is at this point that John Fralick Rockart and Michael S. Scott Morton take up the subject. By combining what is known about the learning process with what is now the state of the art in computing science, they are able to construct a model which helps us to find out not only what computers can do, but what they cannot do—at least not well—in the instructional process.

Interestingly, the authors conclude, as did the Carnegie Commission in its own report on instructional technology, *The Fourth Revolution,* that computers and other electronic media do have a useful and valuable role to play in instruction but that it is likely to be one of enrichment rather than substitution for instruction offered in conventional ways. They also conclude that instructional uses of the computer will be resisted in some parts of the academy, and may be held back in their development by current financial stringencies felt by colleges throughout the country.

The work of Professors Rockart and Scott Morton may well

help to break down some of this resistance, partly because it takes a realistic view of the possible, and partly because it bases its analysis not only on the capabilities of the technology but also on the ways people learn—a factor too often overlooked even in conventional teaching.

Clark Kerr

Chairman
Carnegie Commission
on Higher Education

May 1975

Acknowledgments

A report of this type involves the work and advice of many people. The topic is both broad and hard to define, and the issue of how to approach it becomes all important. The supportive research climate at the Sloan School of Management, Massachusetts Institute of Technology, has been essential to us in doing this project. It influences those of us engaged in research more than we will probably ever realize. We are much in debt to Deans William F. Pounds, Abraham J. Siegel, and Thomas M. Hill for maintaining this climate.

This project was originally started by Professor Zenon S. Zannetos at the Sloan School. His initiative and appreciation for the technological forces we are all caught up in were solely responsible for our moving into this area. In particular, he led the early efforts at the Sloan School in experimenting with more effective ways to employ the computer in the instructional process. Some of these efforts are reported in detail in Appendix A. We are much indebted to him.

Dr. Clark Kerr and his staff at the Carnegie Commission were instrumental in helping us to focus on the impact of technology on higher education. Funding came from various sources, the Ford Foundation being the principal contributor. The work on the Associative Learning Project, reported in Appendix A, was supported by an Edwin Land Education Grant, the Ford Foundation, and an IBM Grant to MIT for Computation.

Much help came from Professors Charles A. Myers and David A. Kolb as well as a series of hard-working individuals who included Ada Demb, William Kennedy, George Dixon, John Macko, Loren Platzman, Colin Lay, Jim Beville, and John Wagner. Ada, in particular, contributed intellectually to the content and structuring of the final draft. Able secretarial support was provided by Sandra Litchman, Jacqueline Winton, and Sarah Fitzgerald. Karen Seriguchi deserves credit for significant editorial ideas and her patience with us.

Particular acknowledgment is due to Dr. Jarrod Wilcox, who while on the faculty at MIT was responsible for designing and executing the survey reported in Chapter 9. The bulk of this chapter has been taken verbatim from his report, although the conclusions drawn from his data are ours. Mr. Paul Shapiro contributed significantly to Chapter 2 and Mr. John Reid and Miss Ada Demb did the field work for the survey supporting Chapter 7.

Early conversations with Dr. Roger Levien of the Rand Corporation and Henry Chauncy of EDUCOM were most helpful, as were all the professionals active in the field who, without exception, gave freely of their time and advice.

This is an exciting field. The work reported here was conducted by a few people on a modest budget and raises more questions than perhaps it answers. The challenge remains to increase the effectiveness and efficiency of learning at the college level. Technology can play a part, but we are clearly going to have to pay attention to how we deploy our scarce resources—we hope this report will be useful in this process.

*Computers and
the Learning Process
in Higher Education*

1. *Introduction*

In unquestionably the most comprehensive study of computers and higher education to date, R. E. Levien and his colleagues have recently concluded that

The average cost of computer education will be subject to continuous and significant reduction during the coming decades. Within 5 or 10 years the costs attributable to central computer hardware should become insignificant; terminal and communications costs should also reach acceptable levels within that period. The critical cost factors are those associated with instructional materials (software). If wide distribution of those materials is achieved, the amortized cost of production can reach acceptable or even insignificant levels, perhaps a few cents per student hour. . . .

In sum, we believe that the net effect of these trends will be that *instructional use of the computer will be cost-effective in a wide and continually growing range of circumstances in the future* (Levien, 1972, p. 489).

Levien forecasts a terminal-hour charge of less than 75 cents per student by 1980. There is little reason to quarrel with his figures. Most forecasters see a continued decline in the cost of computer hardware of all types. Predictions of central processing unit costs in the period 1980–1985 on the order of 1 percent of current costs are not uncommon. With this technological prognosis and an evaluation of current trends in software development as well as of social and organizational variables, Levien et al. conclude their efforts with a prescription for national policy. They suggest that a "strategy of promoting the natural growth of instructional computer uses through the development of a competitive market for computer-based instructional materials" (ibid., p. 563) should be pursued by concerned educators, government agencies, and individuals in the United States.

A recent report of the Carnegie Commission on Higher Education entitled *The Fourth Revolution: Instructional Technology in Higher Education* is based in part on these findings. Working also from other evidence, it concludes that

1   Higher education (and education generally) now faces the first great technological revolution in five centuries in the potential impact of the new electronics.

2   New technology has already transformed (a) research techniques in many fields and (b) administrative methods on many campuses. It is now (c) affecting large libraries and (d) is entering into the instructional process. . . . The new technology may provide the single greatest opportunity for academic change on and off campus.

3   The experience thus far with the new technology (applied to instruction), however, as compared with the hopes of its early supporters, indicates that it is (a) coming along more slowly, (b) costing more money, and (c) adding to rather than replacing older approaches—as the teacher once added to what the family could offer, as writing then added to oral instruction, as the book later added to the handwritten manuscript.

4   Nevertheless, by the year 2000 it now appears that a significant proportion of instruction in higher education on campus may be carried on through informational technology . . . (Carnegie Commission on Higher Education, 1972, p. 1).

For many, these are heartening words. Computer technology is arriving to assist the process of higher education. More significantly, it promises to be cost effective. Together with other "new technology," it is going to help fulfill the promise of a better future in the world of higher education.

Yet, somehow, the optimism expressed in these reports is not yet wholly shared by the people who will have to implement the computer's role in higher education. As we shall note in some detail later, professors and other educators tend to be somewhat cautious in their beliefs as to the "widespread use" of computer-based education. They are clearly less optimistic than their computer-technologist counterparts. In part, this may be because they lack a clear understanding as to just *what* the computer *should* do in the future of higher education, because a variety of forces are unfavorable to the spread of computer technology; and because many educators/faculty feel that the uses to which the technology has been put thus far touch only one relatively poorly matched aspect of the educational task. We suspect that the truth about the use of computers in higher education lies nearer the pessimism of the educators than the optimism of the technologists. In particular, we shall argue that any given technology is appropriate for certain types of material and quite inappropriate for others—being clear on where computer technology fits the material contributes to an understanding of where its ultimate impact will be.

To date, the studies cited have answered only one of three significant questions concerning computer-assisted education. Only to the question "Can it be cost effective?" do we have an unambiguous answer. For some types of material it is cost effective now. This will be true for more and more material as time goes on.

There are, however, two additional questions that are equally significant in terms of understanding the relation of computers to higher education. The first of these is to ask in what *specific* ways the computer will affect the learning process in higher education. A large number of tasks are performed in the instructional process. Some of these are impervious to computer technology; others will be dramatically affected. Most studies to date have attempted a *general* prognosis, yet it is not possible to predict the overall effect without looking at the components. And it is impossible to understand the directions for both policy guidelines and actions that should be taken without an understanding of the various parts of the learning process and the possible impact of the technology on each. It is clear that the learning process of students is complex and multifaceted. To say merely that the technology of computer-assisted instruction will become inexpensive says little about where it can be used and with what effect. For example, the technology of paper and pencil is extraordinarily inexpensive, but it is powerful in only some portions of the learning process. Similarly, the computer has high leverage points that must be understood if the future is to be assessed with any confidence.

The second additional question that needs to be answered is, How should a faculty member approach the selection of one or more of these types of computer-based instruction for a particular course of study? That is, what does the design and implementation process look like for computer-assisted education?

It is clear that these questions must be answered in order to sharpen the *very* diffuse current image, held by most professors, of computer-based instructional technology. Although the answers will be constantly evolving through time, we firmly believe that the construction of a preliminary approach to these questions is necessary if we are to reach a clearer understanding of the role of technology in higher education.

Structure of the Report

Higher education can be thought of in terms of several major components. As a simplification, we have focused on three broad, obvious classes of participants in the educational setting, namely, the *students*, the *administration*, who, at least in theory, run the university, and the *faculty*, who do the research and teaching. Obviously, none of these groups is self-contained; they overlap with one another, and they each perform the others' functions to some degree.

As Figure 1-1 suggests, the students and faculty have the primary interaction with the content areas that the university

FIGURE 1-1
Components of higher education: organizational structure

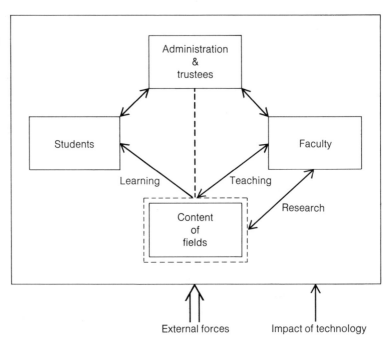

teaches. The university is organized to deliver subject matter to students, and the faculty member in the classroom is the dominant agent. In a fundamental sense, the intellectual content that students are to master is at the core of the whole system. Faculty interaction with this core comes through teaching it, as well as adding to it through research activities. Technology can impact all these interactions—the teaching-learning process, the administration process, and the research process.

This report focuses almost exclusively on the teaching-learning interaction, as we contend that this is at the center of a university's purpose and is the area in which the least innovation has taken place to date. In addition, it is an area in which there exists considerable potential.

These components, then, of content, students, faculty, and administration operate as a system within the organizational structure of the university. As suggested in Figure 1-1, however, there are also external pressures on the system of higher education and, therefore, on the learning-teaching process. These external pressures come from government, the economy, the attitudes of the population, and so forth. One of these pressures is technology.

In this context, technology is important because it can be a very significant actor in higher education today. It can provide added flexibility to the learning process. One can teach differently and add different material because of it. However, technology is not necessarily *the* most important external force. It is one of many, and we attempt to assess the probable impact of technology within the light of these multiple—and very significant—other factors.

Chapter 2 sets the stage for an analysis of the manner in which the technology can be utilized by presenting a model of the fundamental process with regard to educational technology—the learning process. The model presented is based on the work of a particular school of thought with which we find ourselves in agreement. It is a much simplified view of the learning process, and it is not meant as a definitive statement. We find it useful, however, as a basis for organizing the material. The model is provided early in this book because it is integral to our analysis and underscores a fundamental point: Every use of *any* type of methodology in education is based, explicitly or implicitly, on a model of the learning process. Until each of us involved in the process of education clarifies, or at least states, his own model of the learning process, little viable, constructive discussion of the place of *any* technology in higher education is possible. So that our conclusions may be better understood, we make explicit our model of this process. In turn, we suggest that those who draw different conclusions must ask whether these conclusions stem from a different conceptual structure for the learning process or from a different interpretation of the facts within the same conceptual structure.

Although we are focusing on computers, the need to look at this technology with respect to its context is apparent. Computer technology and its potential for education do not exist in a vacuum. Just as one selects his automobile to drive into the city, or his legs to walk next door to borrow a cup of sugar, the choice of a particular type of technology to be utilized in a particular situation will depend not only on the situation but also heavily on the alternatives available and on the attributes of those alternatives with regard to the particular task. Chapter 3 explores the alternatives to computers in the delivery of education—with emphasis on the attributes of each alternative, both positive and negative.

In Chapter 4 we turn to computer technology. This chapter provides a brief discussion of the hardware—for those unfamiliar with computers—and then assesses *current* technological developments with respect to future hardware costs. The discussion is kept simple and is designed to provide a sense of where the technology stands for the professional reader who is not familiar with computer technology.

In addition to hardware technology, however, there is the *courseware* technology—the technology that makes the physical device useful for a student, the technology that lets us put content into the device. An early example of this combination was the first "programmed instruction" effort. Here the hardware technology was primitive (paper and pencil) but the courseware resulted from breaking the course-content material down into pieces and packaging it in a programmed format—a task requiring considerable skill. For our purposes we use *courseware* in the sense implied in this example and we limit it to include only those packages of material that are used in conjunction with some form of hardware technology.

With regard to the use of this hardware and courseware,

there is increasing evidence available today concerning the several modes of computer-based education and their effectiveness in the learning process. Data are available on the number of dollars spent, pedagogic techniques developed, student and faculty acceptance of these techniques, the impact of the techniques on learning, and, perhaps most important, the survival rate of each. Chapter 5 focuses on the state of courseware today and the implications that can be drawn from this state.

Chapter 6 relates the learning model to the available technology. The analysis suggests strongly that there are particular areas where computer assistance to the learning process should be of great value—and that in other areas it would be relatively foolish to push computer technology. In these latter areas, alternate methods of teaching (assisting learning) have a comparative advantage.

In Chapter 7, we move from the theoretical to the actual. The data presented are the results of a survey of all four-year institutions of higher education in Massachusetts. The data provide a snapshot of the current use of computer technology in instruction and are then compared with similar surveys done from 1966 to 1968.

The final section of the book begins in Chapter 8. The previous section defined where computers should be applied and described where they were being applied. We now turn to a look at the factors that will tend to determine whether they will be utilized—and to what extent. Perhaps the most significant forces that influence the future acceptance and use of any technology are the attitudes and behavior of the people involved.

As Figure 1-1 suggests, this is a very large universe. It includes a set of prime actors external to the university, among which are the government (at all levels), the foundations, and the public as a whole. The first two of these influence the direction of education to some extent through regulatory actions, but perhaps most significantly through the provision (or withholding) of funding. The public also has a dual role. On the one hand, it affects the economic climate of higher education by the provision of more or fewer students. On the other, it affects the type of education provided through its attitudes toward education.

There is also a set of internal actors who will have much to say about the future of computers and higher education. There are evident trends in student attitudes and behavior that, we believe, will significantly affect the process. But, undoubtedly, the prime actor is the faculty itself. Its attitudes and behavior will be crucial in the coming decades with respect to *all* aspects of higher education, but most clearly with respect to those involving potential change. We introduce each of these internal environmental factors in Chapter 9 to provide perspective with regard to the relative significance and likelihood of acceptance of the computer in higher education.

Summary Within this structure we are concerned with assessing what the impact of technology will be. This assessment is obviously tentative, but it represents our judgment based on the structure presented, together with extensive reading, visits to sites, and attempts at implementation of various educational technologies here at MIT. The central purpose of this study is to suggest a direction in which higher education should move and to demonstrate the methodology we used to arrive at our conclusions. It is not primarily a survey of current use or current expectations.

We are concerned with universities and four-year colleges, although a large part of the material is relevant for junior colleges and other institutions. And within the areas of computer and four-year institutions, we center on the use of this technology in the *learning* process as opposed to its use in the administrative or research areas.

Even with these limitations, such a study remains an enormous undertaking. What we have produced here is only the beginning of an answer. It will need revision and modification as we learn more, but it is a start that we have found useful in guiding our own thinking.

As professors we are concerned with the specific ways the computer will affect the learning process and the manner in which appropriate types of computer-based instruction are chosen. As researchers in the area of educational technology, we believe we have gained some insights that yield one useful normative model concerning these processes. This has been done through general research in the field, and through the success—and lack of success—of some of our efforts in implementation in the past five years.

In this monograph we report the findings of our study from 1971 to 1974 and in Appendix A some of the results of a larger effort, led by Professor Zenon S. Zannetos. This latter effort was to test some concepts in the use of computer-supported learning (see Scott Morton & Zannetos, 1969). In both these projects, the findings are reasonably clear; the interpretations and extrapolations are debatable. But even though some will argue them, it is time to begin to analyze the implications of the results from the many millions of dollars that have been spent in the field. It is time for the phrase "computer-based education" to be more sharply defined into those segments with great potential and those with relatively little. And it is time to suggest, at least initially, what the place of technology is in higher education and what it is not.

2. The Learning Process

It was argued in Chapter 1 that the impact of technology on higher education has as its very center the subquestion of the impact of technology on learning. In order to discuss the impact of technology on learning, it is important to understand the learning *process*—the manner in which people obtain and assimilate knowledge. If we understand the steps in the learning process—the attributes of each step, on the one hand, and the attributes of the various technologies, on the other—it is possible to ascertain in which steps a particular technology can most successfully impact the learning process. Equally of interest are areas in which a given technology *cannot* usefully play a part or in which it is relatively useless, being heavily dominated by the relevant attributes of other technologies.

The search for a precise model of the learning process is a difficult one. Unfortunately, the majority of the published material with regard to the learning process, while intellectually rewarding, is of little assistance for our purposes. What is needed is an operational statement of the learning process—one that can be acted upon in the design of course materials, the design of a pedagogic strategy—and the assessment of the place of technology in that process.

Everyone who discusses "the impact of technology on higher education" has an *implicit* model of what really goes on in higher education. Most usually, in these discussions, the technology is well described and its "impact" is stated. Yet the implicit model of the process on which the technology is to have "impact" remains unstated. The conclusions, therefore, are hard to pin down—or to refute. The generality of such conclusions provides little guidance for the managers of the education process who seek operational definitions of ways to impact education through technology in the best way.

A precise model, by contrast, enables one to describe and partition the possible impact of various technologies on segments of the learning process. Further, and of equal importance, it enables others to test an author's conclusions about the effects of the technology with reference to the stated model. Finally, a reader can test the author's conclusions against his own model of the learning process—and determine whether differences in perspective are based on differing perceptions of *learning* or differing perceptions of *technology*.

What is important is not whether our particular learning process is "right" or "wrong," but rather that it be stated explicitly and that it be a *useful* base from which to start analysis.

THE STATE OF LEARNING THEORY Over the years learning has been considered primarily the domain of the discipline of psychology. Since the mid-1880s, when the first work on memory was published,[1] there has been a series of attempts at explaining learning phenomena. Unfortunately, many of these attempts have been at or near the level of grand theory and have been in conflict with each other. This led to substantial disagreement over the merits of the different approaches, all of which were hotly debated into the early 1960s.

In the past 10 to 15 years, however, two notable changes have taken place. First, most of the research relating to learning has aimed at developing and clarifying theoretical issues at a much lower level of generality. Second, there have been more concentrated attempts at applying the findings of the learning theorists to practical, especially training, situations.

The changes in the realm of learning theory have been chronicled by Hilgard & Bower (1966). In an attempt to bring some order to the field, Hilgard, in 1948, described the two main groups of theories as being *association* and *field* theories. He stated that

Any naming in this way does some violence to the individual theories, but nevertheless the typical American theories of functionalism, connectionism, and behaviorism have common underlying logic which permits them to be grouped together, and the other theories, stem-

[1]H. Ebbinghaus, *Memory*, 1885, trans. H. A. Ruger and C. E. Bussenius, Teachers College, New York, 1913. Cited in Hilgard & Bower (1966).

ming chiefly from gestalt psychology, have in them a contrasting common ground. The theories here classified as association theories have been labelled *reflex arc* theories and *stimulus-response* theories. The field theories group together various varieties of *gestalt, neogestalt, organismic,* or *sign-significant* theories (Hilgard, 1948, p. 9).

By the mid-1960s whatever of the great debates remained were largely between the two major schools that evolved from the association and field theory groups. These are the schools of stimulus-response (S-R) and cognitive theories. Goldstein, Krantz, & Rains (1965) define these theories in the following way:

In brief, cognition theory asserts that organisms learn *facts about* their environment, they learn "what leads to what," . . . they learn *relations* between parts of their environment. S-R theory, on the other hand, asserts that organisms learn *responses,* they *learn to do* something.

They report that many psychologies now consider the differences between the two schools to be dead issues (ibid., p. v), but they find cognitive theories to be less refined than S-R theories:

In retrospect, it appears that the most significant difference between these two major types of theories lies in the fact that the S-R position is more precisely stated and more highly formulated than the cognitive position. More specifically, it can be said that the most important shortcoming of cognitive theory appears to be its failure to clearly specify (1) the relations between its concepts e.g., cognitions, expectancies, beliefs, and the various antecedent conditions (or independent variables) which determine them, and (2) the relations between concepts and various consequent conditions (or dependent variables) which reveal them in behavior. Many of these theorists have, instead, resorted to thinking of their concepts in terms of a loose model or analogy which appears to endow these concepts with real properties and an independent existence (ibid., p. 2).

To more clearly illuminate the tone of current debate, Hilgard emphatically notes that nowadays *all the theorists accept all the facts.* He finds, therefore, that "the differences between two theories are primarily differences in interpretation (Hilgard & Bower, 1966, p. 9)." He has reported three such current differences between cognitive and S-R theories. It is instructive to infer at the same time the practical consequences to which these differences might lead. These differences and their consequences are:

1 *"Peripheral" versus "central" intermediaries*   S-R theorists believe that physical responses, such as subvocal speech movements and other muscular reactions, are what are involved in thinking and therefore learning. Cognitive theorists consider ideas and other constructs to be what are involved.

The S-R theorists would prefer learning technology which employs as many of the sense organs as possible in the learning process. Rote learning, especially repeating out loud or to oneself would be emphasized. Cognitive theorists would prefer linking material to be learned to past or future desired outcomes or states (ibid.).

2 *Acquisition of habits versus acquisition of cognitive structures*   S-R theorists believe that what is learned is habits. Cognitive theorists believe that what is learned is constructs of thought.

The S-R theorist would prefer learning technology that presents and encourages doing many similar things so that the results are all uniform. More of the same or faster would imply better learning. The cognitive theorist would value finding different ways of putting the same facts together, with little regard for the amount of time involved. Thus the S-R school, in general, would prefer a tutorial or "drill and practice" type of CAI system whereas the cognitive theorist would prefer to give the student access through computer terminals to a system which contained a large data-base and flexible use of models with which to analyze the data (ibid., p. 10).

3 *Trial and error versus insight in problem solving*   S-R theorists believe that experience is all-important in reacting to a new (or familiar) situation because the process of coping with the situation is simply trying past habits in turn until a correct or acceptable response is found. Cognitive theorists believe that understanding the relationship(s) involved will provide the insight required to solve a problem.

The S-R theorist would prefer learning technology which leads the learner from a simple response setting to progressively more complicated ones through a controlled process which keeps the learner in close touch with what is already familiar. Again, author controlled "tutorial" mode of many CAI systems is of this type. The cognitive theorist would favor presenting the learner with progressively less structured concepts to extend and test the latter's ability to create new constructs. This level of presentation can be delivered with many forms of computer courseware as long as the critical requirement of providing considerable user (as opposed to author) control is met (ibid., pp. 10–11).

One reason why S-R theory is more refined than cognitive theory is that its development has been very much based on research with animals. The conditions and responses can be much less complex than for humans. Extrapolation of the results to humans is intellectually risky: for example, the relative weights that would be given to various S-R concepts for post-adolescents or young adults of college age versus children are not obvious. The different technologies that will be discussed in the following chapters vary in their adaptability to the S-R or cognitive approaches to learning. At any given stage in the learning process there are options for the implementation of any given type of material. One must choose the learning model that is "believed" before the technology is chosen for any task.

A third school of learning theory is partially separable from the cognitive and S-R schools. This school is variously called child psychology, child development, or developmental psychology. One of the fundamental differences between it and others is that, at least until the end of adolescence, learning is related to physiological processes. A child's ability to grasp objects, ability to focus and control its eye movements, and ability to understand and express concepts of time and place are all seen as related to its chronological age, its sex, perhaps its race and culture (including diet), and so on.

The work in developmental psychology has also differed from the other schools in that it started out on the basis of observational rather than experimental (as with Pavlov, for example) techniques. This was the method by which Piaget first brought a sense of order into the understanding of a child's pattern of speech and thought.

In recent years, the S-R and cognitive theories have been

"adopted" and put into use by two widely differing groups. Stemming from S-R theory has been the Skinnerian model of the teaching machine. Often named CAI (computer-assisted instruction) and discussed in Chapter 3 as "tutorial," this "fill in the blank correctly and get rewarded" technology has received considerable funding and attention. It is now viewed less optimistically because of the limited area of the learning process it can affect and the other, often less expensive, technologies that compete with it.

Growing from the cognitive school have been many attempts to develop theories of differing cognitive styles and methods of education applicable to these styles. Attempts have been made to further develop cognitive skills in university students. But direct conscious application of the theories of this school of learning theory to education in general has been limited.

THE DILEMMA We have looked at the three major learning theories that have general acceptance today. Unfortunately, their usefulness is dramatically limited when what is desired is a robust, pragmatic, operationally useful model of the university-level learning process.

1 Tested against the question "Understanding this theory of learning, how do I best apply the available technology?" the three major learning theories bear little direct persuasive fruit.

2 These theories suggest only *generalized* approaches to the technology.[2] They leave too few *specific* knobs to turn, they fail to suggest *specific* areas of potential success for learning technology, and they fail to provide guidance for action that can be taken to affect the learning process by the individual professor. Kolb has summarized the pragmatic failures of these theories well:

Because of my early psychological training in learning theory my first impulse was to turn for the answer to these questions to the basic psychological literature on this subject. To my dismay I found that, in spite of the high scientific quality of this work, it was immensely difficult to apply this research on reinforcement theory, discriminative

[2]It is hard to accept, for example, that all learning should be turned over to tutorial-like programmed instruction.

learning and such to the kind of practical decisions involved in the design of university teaching (1971, p. 1).

This same frustration led us to review the work of practitioners in the field of learning, as well as the theorists, in an attempt to elicit a useful learning model. Five sets of critical variables with regard to learning emerged from this search. They are:

- The stages of the learning *process*
- The characteristics of the *material* to be learned
- The characteristics of the *learner*
- The characteristics of the *teacher*
- The learning *environment*

Of these five categories, the first two appeared most significant for our purposes. We return to them in some depth below. The third category, *learner characteristics*, is, as yet, an unsolved area—full of complex and often conflicting clues. It is apparent that there are behavioral, cognitive, and motivational aspects of the learner that must be considered. There is earnest and excellent work being performed at present on each of these subphenomena.[3] In the cognitive area alone, work on "acquisition and retention phenomena," "transfer of training," and "concept formation" has engaged the efforts of many researchers. There is especially interesting work on the differences in human cognitive styles. One would like to incorporate this into a learning model. Yet the translation of the findings in *each* of these areas, much less their *interactions*, into a model of the learner that might assist in guiding an exploration of the impact of computer technology on education is, as yet, an uncertain task. At this stage of our understanding of individual learning differences, we could not include individual learner characteristics in our model.

The fourth category, *teacher characteristics*, also directly affects the learning process. Yet we backed away from the inclusion of these variables in the model for two reasons. First, teachers are no less complex than learners in their approach to the learning-teaching arena. And, similarly, we lack operation-

[3]See, for example, Snyder (1971) and Kolb & Goldman (1973).

ally adequate descriptions—or classifications—of the set of motivations, cognitive processes, and behavioral actions that constitute the role of "teacher." This alone would have led us to eliminate the teacher variable from our learning model. But a second reason added additional weight. There is little doubt that technology is currently engaged in vastly changing the notion of "teacher"—and that, at this time, it would be best to keep this variable (or collection of variables) exogenous to the model.

The final category, *characteristics of the environment*, also affects learning. Social as well as physical environmental characteristics are significant. The Coleman report, for example, concluded that "a pupil's achievement is strongly related to the educational backgrounds and aspirations of the other students in the school" (Coleman et al., 1966, p. 17). The same report concluded that characteristics of the classroom, building, campus, neighborhood, city or county, and region may be assumed to have less effect on learning. But exactly what these physical and social effects are and, more vitally, how they may be classified and utilized in a learning model remain unclear.

The arguments noted above with regard to the teacher variable thus again apply. First, the interacting factors are too complex and not yet well enough described, measured, or categorized to utilize. Additionally, however, the technology applied will *change* the learning environment. Again, both for reasons of lack of operational understanding and because of a desire to model only those relatively *stable* elements of the learning process relatively impervious to the impact of technology, this category of variables was also eliminated from consideration.

We thus limited our modeling of the learning process to two variables—the two that to us seemed (1) significant, (2) operationally describable, and/or (3) least apt to be changed by the impact of the process whose effect we were examining. These two variables are the stages of the learning process and the characteristics of the material to be learned.

THE STAGES OF THE LEARNING PROCESS

The search for an operationally tractable statement of the learning process was not an easy one. We finally felt most comfortable with a model which was developed primarily by behavioral scientists but which, in our view, is generalizable to the learning process in all fields.

This behavioral approach to describing the learning process follows the work of Kolb (1971). Reacting to the frustration of the inapplicability of learning theory for the practical educator and needing something to guide his efforts in the educational process, Kolb turned to the so-called experiential learning model—a model that, adapted somewhat, we have used as the core of our work. Developed primarily out of the experience of sensitivity-training practitioners (Schein & Bennis, 1965), the model has gained increasing acceptance as a framework for the design of learning programs. It has been used in such diverse areas as education (Miles, 1965), the incident process in management training (Pigors & Pigors, 1963), Peace Corps training (Wight, 1969), and self-assessment (Katz, 1970).

In this model, learning is conceived of as a four-stage cycle which translates experience into new concepts (see Figure 2-1). Immediate concrete experience (step 1) is the object of step 2, where the meaning of the experience is embedded and "understood" through observation and reflection. In step 3, these observations are assimilated into a "theory" or conceptual basis from which new implications for action can be deduced. Finally, these implications are tested in the real world in new situations (step 4). In turn, the testing process leads to a need for new concrete experiences themselves—and the loop is closed.

It is important to note that the experiential learning model depends on the learner undergoing some sort of *experience* that

FIGURE 2-1
The experiential learning model

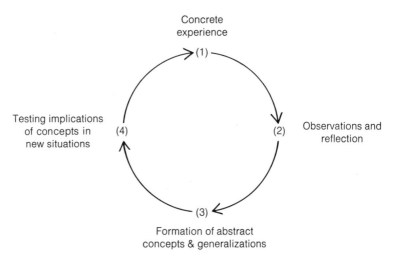

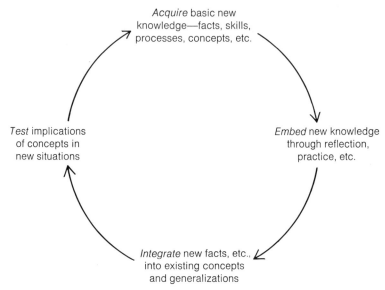

FIGURE 2-2
*A general
learning model*

Acquire basic new knowledge—facts, skills, processes, concepts, etc.

Embed new knowledge through reflection, practice, etc.

Integrate new facts, etc., into existing concepts and generalizations

Test implications of concepts in new situations

provides an initial set of *facts* or *feelings* as input to the learning cycle. It is clear, however, that most of what is learned in college is *not* based on an initial experience,[4] but rather on the acquisition of new *facts* or skills. But the model can be generalized without too much difficulty to this more usual arena of fact, skill, and concept-based learning. In its more general form, the model appears as in Figure 2-2.

The initial stage of this more generalized model is the initial *acquisition of basic components* of knowledge by the student. Here the learner is exposed to, and asked to comprehend, basic data, skills, or concepts that will be put to use in later steps.

The second stage is the "salting away," or embedding, of this knowledge by the learner. In this stage, the student "practices" and ponders his new skills. He may perform homework exercises to see if he has understood the new facts and how to apply them. He may actually use the skills in the performance of a task. Or he may merely think through the facts, skills, or processes he has learned.

The learner then moves to the third stage of this general

[4]Although the acquisition of knowledge through experience is perhaps more widely utilized as a learning mechanism in college than it would at first appear, it is predominant in many behavioral courses, laboratory courses, homework exercises, computer exercises, etc.

model—a stage in which the new ideas assist in the development of a new conceptual grasp of the world. This is an *integrating phase* in which the student moves from the rote acquisition of material to its incorporation and subjugation into more global conceptual structures. It is the stage in which the learning of new things "pays off" in new understanding. New mental models of the universe, or parts of it, are formed. Robust platforms, on the basis of which action can be taken, are constructed.

The testing of these new conceptual structures is the final phase. It is a phase at which the cycle is often broken in formal, university-level education because today there are few pedagogic mechanisms available to the student by which he can test the implications of his new understanding. The richness of the learning process is broken, too, as new conceptual bases are learned and then stored away to gather dust. Stage 4 is clearly more often reached in courses run along experiential lines, in short "executive" programs—or in courses allowing access to a pseudo real-world environment, via simulation models, for example—a point to which we shall return later on.

The general model of the learning process is designed to be used later in this report to help us understand where technology has had, and can have, an impact. Exactly how one interprets the model for its operational implications is partly dependent on the theoretical issues raised earlier—namely, one's standpoint with regard to the stimulus-response, cognitive, and developmental schools. However, we leave this to proceed with our model development.

THE MATERIAL Let us now turn to the second major variable considered in our learning model—the material. Many different categorizations of material can be presented. The problem is to provide a set that is meaningful throughout most disciplines and that can be utilized to describe each learning area in an operationally useful way. One such categorization commonly used in the learning literature we have found to be both applicable to various disciplines and useful in its description of their material:

1 *Facts,* including definitions and other basic information relating to specific single items or ideas.

2 *Skills,* including both procedures and rules and their applications.

3 *Established concepts,* as well as other theories, hypotheses, postulates, or assertions that are well enough established to be of no interest to the current researchers in the field. "Concepts" use "facts" as basic building blocks.

4 *Frontier concepts,* including not only recent developments but also long-standing issues which either have not been, or cannot be, resolved.

For any particular course or department, this breakdown of material can easily be further divided. Category 2, skills, can (perhaps should) be broken down into several highly distinct types of skills. Indeed it is necessary to subdivide these categories further when dealing with a particular course. (For an example of this see Appendix B.)

But across courses and departments, we find that this four-part categorization serves as a good vehicle for understanding the applicability of technology to particular curriculums.

It does not take much imagination or deep thought to hypothesize that the relative emphasis on these four categories of material will vary with particular university departments and with differing degree-level programs (e.g., undergraduate, master's, doctoral). This, in turn, will mean that the type of learning technology that can be effectively employed will also differ. To test this hypothesis, however, as well as the validity of the four-way breakdown, we asked our colleagues at MIT to utilize this categorization in evaluating the material content of their courses.

Categorizing a Curriculum

The Sloan School of Management at MIT offers courses for undergraduate majors, master's students, and Ph.D. candidates. Some students in other MIT departments also enroll for occasional courses or for the equivalent of a minor field, but here we are mainly concerned with management majors at each of these three levels. The Sloan School offers courses in 14 management fields. To approximate the analysis that might be made of a whole university's curriculum, these fields lent themselves easily to a division into three distinct categories: social sciences, disciplines, and professions. The categories and the fields they encompass follow:

Social sciences

   Organization studies

   History and environment

Disciplines

   Economics

   Mathematics/statistics

Professions

   International business

   Finance

   Management information and control

   Management information systems

   Law

   Industrial relations

   Operations management

   Marketing

   Industrial dynamics

   Policy

Of the approximately 75 courses offered in the fall term 1971, the instructors in 40 courses (in 12 of the 14 fields) were asked to rate what they desired undergraduates and master's students to learn from their respective courses. Each instructor was also requested to indicate what a Ph.D. candidate was expected to learn in the instructor's field. The ratings were forced choices in percentages adding to 100 among (1) facts and definitions, (2) skills and procedures, (3) established concepts, and (4) frontier concepts.

Within each of the three field categories (social sciences, disciplines, and professions) and for each category of material, the undergraduate courses were treated as a random sample of course offerings, and the results were averaged together. For the master's students, six out of a total of nine core (required or waivable) courses were covered in the survey, for which the results were averaged and in turn combined with the average rating for the noncore courses in the field. A final average for each category was taken from these field averages. For Ph.D. candidates the ratings within each field were averaged and were then averaged with the results for the other fields within the same category.

This survey was taken to provide an example of the range of material in a given department, and it shows the presence of each type of material at both levels of graduate (though not at undergraduate) education in business management. It should be remembered that the percentages are very rough. They have been rounded to 5-point multiples and made to add to 100. In cases where the total would otherwise not add to 100, the variance of a particular result was considered in making the adjustment.

SOCIAL SCIENCES

Material to be learned	Type of student		
	Undergraduates	Master's students	Ph.D. candidates
Facts and definitions	10%	5%	5%
Skills and procedures	20	40	25
Established concepts	45	25	30
Frontier concepts	25	30	40
TOTAL	100	100	100

These results show that in the social sciences, facts and definitions are considered by faculty in the field to be a very minor part of what students at any level are expected to learn. Skills and procedures constitute about two-fifths of the total for master's students, but only one-fifth to one-fourth for either undergraduates or Ph.D. candidates. Established concepts weigh heavily for undergraduates, but much less so for graduate students. Finally, there is a clearly increasing progression of expectation for a student to learning frontier concepts, from undergraduates through master's students to doctoral candidates.

DISCIPLINES

Material to be learned	Type of student		
	Undergraduates	Master's students	Ph.D. candidates
Facts and definitions	25%	20%	10%
Skills and procedures	30	30	30
Established concepts	45	40	40
Frontier concepts	0	10	20
TOTAL	100	100	100

In the disciplines, while about one-fourth of what the undergraduate is expected to learn is facts and definitions, these become progressively less important for the master's student or Ph.D. candidate. Roughly 30 percent of the total for all three groups is skills and procedures, and 40 to 45 percent is established concepts. Undergraduates are not expected to learn any frontier concepts here, but these amount to one-tenth of what the master's student and one-fifth of what the Ph.D. candidate should know.

PROFESSIONS

Material to be learned	Type of student		
	Undergraduates	Master's students	Ph.D. candidates
Facts and definitions	25%	20%	10%
Skills and procedures	35	25	20
Established concepts	25	35	35
Frontier concepts	15	20	35
TOTAL	100	100	100

Among the professions, facts and definitions form approximately one-fourth of what it is desired undergraduates will learn, one-fifth of the total for master's students, and only one-tenth for doctoral candidates. Skills and procedures were rated about one-third of what undergraduates should learn, one-fourth for master's students, and one-fifth for Ph.D. candidates. Established concepts were seen to be only one-fourth of the total for undergraduates but roughly one-third for all graduate students. Frontier concepts were considered to constitute only 15 percent for undergraduates but 20 percent for master's students and 35 percent for doctoral students.

One of the first observations that can be made about these results is that the portion of what the student is expected to learn that consists of facts and definitions or skills and procedures ranges from not less than 30 percent to as much as 60 percent of the total. At the higher end are the undergraduates in the disciplines and professions; in the middle at 45 to 50 percent are the master's students in all three categories; at the lowest end are the doctoral students, especially in social sciences and the professions.

The areas of facts and definitions and skills and procedures are the ones in which a large amount of research regarding computer assistance was performed in the past. The computer interaction in this area was generally traditional in nature with heavy emphasis on the use of the computer in a tutorial mode.

It may also be seen that established concepts constitute from 25 to 45 percent of what students at all levels are expected to learn. In the social sciences and the disciplines, learning of established concepts is heavier for undergraduates, but in the professions it runs to over one-third of the total material for all graduate students. The area of assisting the learning of established concepts is therefore an important one and one to which computer systems must be applied if they are to impact the bulk of the learning that is taking place. At the Sloan School, the expectations that students will learn frontier concepts is less in general, ranging from a low of 0 percent for undergraduates in the disciplines to 40 percent for Ph.D. candidates in the social sciences.

One of the most significant findings with regard to learning material is the variance in what faculty in different fields expect different students to learn. Although the categories used here are rather crude, a similar exploration could be attempted as a next step in analyzing what the faculty think students should learn throughout a university, in different departments, and in different types of postsecondary schools. This would provide a broader analytic base for estimating the potential applicability of computers to instruction. These first results seem to show that a perhaps surprisingly large proportion of at least one business school's curriculum could be computer-supported in one way or another.

We conclude that the mix of material varies from program to program and subject to subject. This suggests differing potential paybacks from technology applied in the different areas and suggests the technology will have to be radically different in the different areas. Equally significant for our purposes, however, is the fact that this breakdown of the material is a logical one—understandable enough to be used by our faculty for categorization of their material in a particular course.

Our basic learning model, then, has two variables—learning stages and material—that together produce 16 cells, as shown in Figure 2-3. *It is this two-dimensional structure which must be considered when asking where the technology fits in education:* The technology fits in *differing* ways into each of these cells. *The*

FIGURE 2-3
A learning matrix

	Acquisition	Embedding	Integration & generalization	Testing in new situations
Facts and definitions				
Skills and procedures				
Established concepts				
Frontier concepts				

process involved in learning in each of the cells is different, we submit. And the technology utilized must be fitted to these differences.

As we have noted above, the breakdown is still not elaborate enough. The two-dimensional matrix might be expanded to a third dimension to highlight the degree of importance that each cell has for each course or department. This would allow highlighting the targets of opportunity to improve the process of learning in the particular cell.

SOME INTERIM CONCLUSIONS

One cannot think of "computerization" or "technologization" of "learning" as unidimensional without doing a great disservice to the variety of material and the complexities of the learning process, as well as to the departments and programs that exist within the bounds of four-year educational institutions. Technology and the computer in particular must therefore be expected to be utilized in different modes in each area and to have a vastly different impact—and therefore different potential—in each. Some of the cells are almost impregnable by "technology" as we understand it today. Others are ripe for differing types of technology.

We now have before us a learning model divided into 16 cells. The following chapters (1) look at the "technologies" available to assist learning, (2) analyze the learning demands of each of the cells of the learning model, and then (3) attempt to match the appropriate technology to these demands.

3. "Traditional" Methods of Assisting the Learning Process

There are a host of methods and "technologies" for assisting the learner in the process described in Chapter 2. Some of these "technologies" are ivy-covered by tradition. Some of them are quite new. But in any evaluation of learning and technology, *each* must be considered carefully, so that it matches the material and the part of the learning process involved. Figure 3-1 structures the methods of assisting the learning process that will be discussed in this chapter, and it relates these techniques to computer-based learning methods that will be discussed in the following chapters. Five major pedagogic techniques are noted in the first column. The subsequent three columns note, in order, some time-favored manpower-intensive methods of carrying out the particular pedagogic technique; technology-based methods of assisting (or completely carrying out) each technique; and, finally, an outline of available computer-based methods.

In general, teachers have tried to help students to learn in the five major ways noted in column 1. As row 1 notes, a large dose of "learning assistance" has been administered through exposing students to data presented orally or visually. A second method has been to assign reading material to the learner. One variation on these rather passive learning processes (row 3) has been a more active technique of student participation in the learning process through case studies or classroom discussion. A prime pedagogic technique (row 4) involves the assignment to the learner of self-testing material on which he subsequently receives feedback. Written assignments or homework problems to be handed in are the classic formulation of this particular technique. Finally, there is the assignment to the learner of "hands-on" tasks in which he is expected to perform a rela-

FIGURE 3-1   *A categorization of methods to assist learning*

Pedagogical techniques	Dominant traditional methods	Newer noncomputer methods	Computer-based methods
(1) Student "watches, listens," and learns	Lecture	Radio, charts, television, slides, magnetic tape cassettes, films, videotape	Computer-based programmed instruction
(2) Student "reads material" and learns	Textbooks	Paper programmed instruction, self-study modules	Computer-based programmed instruction
(3) Student takes active oral participation in learning	Case studies, class discussions (including seminars)	"Voting machines"	
(4) Student performs "written self-testing" and receives feedback	Written assignments	"Voting machines," paper programmed instruction	Drill and practice, problem solving
(5) Learner performs "hands-on" investigation of phenomena	Library investigation, laboratory experiments, real-world experience		Simulation models, games, inquiry, problem solving

tively original investigation of particular phenomena. This last has usually involved the collection and analysis of data often resulting in a presentation of the findings. Techniques 1 to 3 tie directly to the "acquisition" phase of the learning model presented in Chapter 2. The fourth technique is used for "embedding," and the last for embedding, integrating, or testing purposes. It is clear where teaching emphasis has been in the past!

In this chapter we first present the learning-assistance methods noted in column 2—the traditional methods of carrying out each pedagogic technique in column 1 that utilize little more in terms of "technology" than the printed page, chalk, blackboards, and typewriters. We then turn to more technology-based methods of supporting each pedagogic technique. Note that, together with the non-computer-based methods shown in column 3, we now have a portfolio of *competing* approaches for carrying out the five major pedagogic techniques noted.

THE NON-TECHNOLOGY-BASED TRADITIONAL METHODS OF ASSISTING LEARNING

The six learning-assistance devices noted in this section are the "old standbys." Most are centuries old in their use. Yet, as visits to students anywhere in the system of higher education will quickly show, they are currently the dominant modes of learning assistance.

The Lecture

Without a doubt, the reigning king in education is The Lecture. The overwhelming majority of a student's learning time in higher education is spent being exposed to this method. Despite any evidence pro or con as to its efficacy, the lecture remains a time-honored, self-perpetuating mainstay of American higher education.

We have been nourished on lectures, we see (hear) lecturing going on all around us, we ourselves keep on lecturing. People call us teachers ("instructors" is often a preferred term), students are used to being lectured to, a change of a procedure might alarm them (Goode, 1971, p. 91).

More than tradition has sustained the lecture, however. Although facts and concepts are delivered much more slowly to the learner's senses than they could be gained through reading, for example, the lecture form has several advantages. The material delivered can be well ordered and condensed by the lecturer. In addition, it can be adjusted to take advantage of new findings in the field or build on class reaction and interest exhibited in a previous lecture. New insights of the lecturer gained either through research or merely through delivering familiar material from a new viewpoint can be added to freshen or make relevant timeworn material.

Moreover, the lecture is personal. The lecturer can get across his views and his enthusiasm for the material. Almost every student remembers one or two lecturers who left their lecture halls spellbound through force of personality, scholarship, or presentation of material in a way that enlivened the senses and the intellect. By use of inflection, emphasis, acting skills, or visual aids of various types, the lecturer can make his material "live" for the student. Moreover, the pace or tempo of the presentation can be adjusted for the audience as the lecturer gains feedback on class acceptance and/or difficulty of the material. This same feedback assists the lecturer in improving his presentation as he adjusts his material to bolster sections that clearly did not get across to previous classes.

The lecture form also has distinct advantages for the lecturer. It is perhaps the simplest way of delivering learning material. The facts, concepts, and interpretations that are to be discussed can be prestructured and carefully supported. Classroom time is merely an exposition of this material. Interaction with the class can be kept at the level that the lecturer desires. Class discussion can be kept well in the bounds of the particular material that the lecturer has prepared for the day. More than in almost any other form of instruction in the classroom setting, the teacher is in absolute control of the class. Finally, the same material can be "warmed over" time after time in succeeding years for delivery with a relative minimum of preparation.

Unfortunately, the lecture form makes two major assumptions that are clearly unreal. First, it assumes that students are homogeneous—that all students in the class need the same material delivered to them to aid their learning process. (The problems brought about by this assumption can be ameliorated *somewhat* by allowing students to question the lecturer.) Second, it assumes that all professors are equally adept at this particular form of delivering learning. Simple observation shows that both these assumptions are false.

So the lecture, like all the other learning methods discussed in this and the previous chapter, has some great strengths and also some weaknesses. In Chapter 6, we shall turn to a more rigid categorization of the strengths and weaknesses of learning-delivery mechanisms.

Textbooks   With the advent of the printed page, teachers were able, for the first time, to write down the material that could previously be delivered only orally. This permitted the development of a second major learning-assistance technique—the printed page. Starting from the days of the early "primer" in the Middle Ages, textbooks rapidly became a heavily used learning aid for most students. At the present time, approximately 100 million textbooks are sold in the United States annually at all levels. More than two-thirds of these are bought by college-level students.

The development of the textbook permitted, for the first time, independence from the teacher's voice, which had dominated learning for two thousand years. Since this development, the textbook has proved to be a necessary but not totally sufficient instrument of instruction. One cannot learn to speak a foreign language from a book. Nor can one totally learn several other skills—such as mechanical ability, which, in general, requires hands-on learning for full comprehension. Yet the textbook is still one of the two most important mechanisms utilized today to assist the learning process. According to Deighton (1971, p. 507), the textbook has the following characteristics:

1 It is a *presenter* of data.

2 It is an *explicator* of relationships among the data. These relationships may be as to time order, cost, likeness and difference, greater or lesser, etc., the basic cognitive structure through which man deals with experience.

3 It is an *illustrator,* providing charts, graphs, drawings, photographs, to demonstrate data or relationships.

4 It is an *exercisor,* providing opportunities for use in practice of data and concepts through study questions, tests, exercises, and the like. These are the means of interaction between reader and content.

Unfortunately, the textbook does not perform all these functions with equal effectiveness. It does, however, have several real strengths. The textbook provides a sequential, orderly introduction to a discipline or subject matter. It provides continuity and contiguity of text and graphic illustration. What is more, it is a *repository* of data as well as being *expository*. This latter characteristic allows students to continually review facts and ideas. And it provides a relatively cheap and stable source of "memory" of data and ideas.

Perhaps most significantly, the textbook is the cheapest known *presenter* of data. At 2 to 4 cents a page, it has no rival on a per word basis, although its price per fact is dependent upon the writer's skill and the density with which he presents information. Since our reading speeds far outweigh our ability to absorb data through any other medium (all of whose presentation costs are significantly more expensive), the textbook wins hands down in terms of cost as a simple presenter of facts.

The textbook is also highly portable. This means it can be used in almost any place at almost any time. In addition, the probability of widespread review of the material before publishing helps to ensure that the data are correct and reasonably well presented.

On the other hand, texts have some weaknesses relative to other learning aids; for example, they suffer from their linearity. The sequence of presentation is the one thought by the author to be most comprehensible to the average student. We know today that there is no such thing as an average student. The clues and lines of reasoning that are of use to one student in the comprehension of material may be of far less use to a student with a different background or different learning skills. Textbooks, as a data or concept source, also suffer from a lack of interaction with the learner. As an *exercisor*, it is clear the textbook is far from optimal.

An increasingly significant disadvantage of texts is becoming evident as the knowledge explosion grows. The lag in time between conception of a textbook and its appearance on the market can easily be two to three years. With the increasing obsolescence of older knowledge through research findings today, this "publishing gap" has rendered many texts out of date even before they hit the market. Rapidly updated new editions have been the traditional publishing attempt to breach this gap.

New "printing" and binding methods may well reduce this disadvantage of texts relative to other learning methods, however. Such developments as phototypesetting and, perhaps most significant, computer-based storing, editing, and typesetting of textual material will significantly reduce the publishing gap (Martinson & Miller, 1971, p. 523). The recent flurry of Xerox-based publishing may or may not make an impact in some areas of higher education where the half-life of data is so short that instructors are forced to use a quickly put-together string of journals as their main text source.

Case Studies The third traditional, technology-free learning method is the case study. Utilized heavily in schools of law and management, for example, the case study and class discussion of various sorts assist the learning process by involving the student in the material to the depth necessary for him to engage in discourse about it.

The case study has several strong points with regard to

learning assistance. Perhaps the most important of these is the high degree of *participation and involvement* that analysis and presentation of the case provide for the learner. Unlike the lecture, which is a heavily passive, receptive mode of learning, the case study is an active, involving mode of learning. Good cases provide a simulated world in which the student can gain experience in decision making without suffering possible consequences.

Many books and articles have been written concerning the pros and cons of the case method (see Fox, 1973). In working through a case, the student learns facts; more importantly, in the hands of a skillful professor, he learns a great deal more about the processes of human cognition, human interaction, and methods of analysis and presentation. In effect, this method is suboptimal for the sheer learning of facts and basic skills and procedures. The learning strengths of case studies are much greater in the areas of analysis, presentation, and group process. With regard to the former, the student is most often plunged into an actual situation with no particular guidelines as to his expected behavior. As a result, he must exert considerable ingenuity and energy in finding "the right question." This problem-finding skill so vital to all types of human decision making can be developed by case studies. In applied fields of any type, no question is more crucial than "What is the *real* problem for which we should be seeking an answer?"

In order to find this problem, the student must develop what might be termed "attentive reading" skills—the ability to carefully read and analyze material presented to him. He must be able to separate facts from assumptions. More importantly, perhaps, he must identify his *own* assumptions—the biases or predispositions to the world that he carries into any given situation. Quite often, he is forced to experiment with different methods of rearranging data to make them analytically meaningful. This active, searching analysis with some of the excitement of the real world, real people, and real situations can lead to discovery of principles and of processes by the student himself—rather than the rote learning of these from textbooks. To many, this is a much more effective type of learning— leading to longer retention of the concepts learned.

Just as a case study provides distinct advantages with regard to analysis, it also can provide insights with regard to group process and presentation—two skills that are important in the later day-to-day life of the student. In many institutions, as students prepare cases, they are forced to interact with each other in a group-preparation mode. As a result they are exposed in a small group, as they will be later exposed in the larger class discussion of the case, to the assumptions, biases, and predispositions of others toward a particular set of facts. A smaller group, without the pressure of an instructor's presence, enhances informal exposition and the "arguing through" of many of these inherent, differing approaches to the world. As a result, the student often gets greater insight into *himself*, as well as into the content of the material.

Finally, the need for the student to present his ideas on the case adds skills to his repertoire. It makes him organize case facts to back up his views and, importantly, provides practice in the presentation and defense of his views against those of his peers.

If the case-study method is strong with regard to analysis and presentation, it is weaker from the viewpoint of rapid assimilation of facts and concepts. It involves students in the learning process. Yet in a classroom case discussion involving thirty to a hundred students, only one or two can be speaking at any given time. Unless in the hands of a skillful case instructor, this method allows much "dead" learning time, as students tune out of the main discussion to ponder case aspects that interest them more—or merely the progress of their favorite baseball team.

Case discussion is, moreover, "high cost" learning. Class size must be kept well under 100 for active learning to take place on the part of each student.

Class discussion of written material

In effect, this is a variation of the case study. Instead of a case drawn from real life, however, the material to be analyzed is drawn from the views of a particular author as set down in an article or some other form. Almost all the advantages noted above with regard to analysis and presentation of cases are possible here. In this method, however, students work with ideas presented by "experts" and must take the stature of the author into account in their analysis. Given a good author, the density of facts and concepts in the article can be quite high. Thus the teacher can trade some of the discovery aspects of the analysis and presentation process in case studies for some of the "sheer information transfer" advantages of the lecture system or the pure textbook mechanism.

Written Assignments The fourth major pedagogic technique is written "self-testing"—which enables the student to work with facts and concepts and to ensure that he understands them well enough to use correctly. This technique has, in general, two phases. First, the student performs a function—utilizing facts and concepts that he has learned. The second phase consists of "feedback" to the learner from the teacher of the correctness of the student's exercise.

Written homework assignments have been the traditional method of letting students exercise the facts and skills that they have learned to ensure that they understand them. In most settings, however, it is unclear whether the primary purpose of written exercises is to assist the *student's* learning or to check (from the *teacher's* view) whether the student has digested certain facts and skills. Whatever the purpose, these assignments are used in several modes—from rote exercises, such as the mechanical application of a given formula, to simple laboratory exercises, such as determining simple unknowns in chemistry lab, to the expression of the interaction of data and/or conceptual understanding in brief written "themes." Feedback to the student on the effectiveness of his efforts is established through a process of marking the papers and handing them back to the student after a lapse in time.

This particular feedback process has several drawbacks. In the first place, papers are often returned well after the student has become interested in something else. As a result of this time lapse his attention has been diverted from the material of the assignment. He has often temporarily forgotten the skills or concepts utilized in the assignment (they are often not "remembered" until the next examination), and as a result he greets the return of his written assignment and the resulting learning assistance with something less than intense curiosity. Second, even if he goes through the effort of resurrecting his skills and attention to focus on that particular assignment, he is often frustrated by the "feedback" he receives. The professor's handwriting is sometimes illegible. If the paper has been marked by a teaching assistant who has "gone by the book," unusual insights—often excellent work—on the part of the student may go unrecognized. At worst, an unmotivated teaching assistant performs an inadequate job of scrutinizing the assignment, and the student becomes frustrated and angry with the marking of the assignment and therefore with the course itself. In this case, the primary feedback the student receives is the implication that the course material is not of enough value to warrant his instructor's involvement in evaluating the student's learning.

"Hands-On" Investigation A close cousin to written self-testing is "hands-on" investigation of phenomena by the student. In both cases the student brings the facts and concepts to which he has been previously exposed to the new learning experience. And in both cases he is most often provided with feedback as to his results.

Hands-on investigation, as we define it, differs from written assignments, however, in a variety of ways. In the first place, the student is forced to become involved with phenomena that may or may not "work out" as he would expect them to. There are no predetermined "right answers" in this mode of learning assistance. Multitudinous variables are often encountered—and the student must apply all his skills to first structure, and then learn from, the situation. Examples of this type of learning-assistance technique are nontrivial laboratory exercises, library-based term papers, and real-world investigation of phenomena.

Laboratory investigations

Laboratory settings allow students to utilize facts and skills they have learned to further embed this knowledge. The laboratory setting can provide what is, in effect, a simulated "real world" that allows the learner to act and to get a reaction that, hopefully, realistically models the reaction that occurs outside the bounds of the training institution. In some cases (e.g., some trivial chemistry experiments) the routines to be followed and the reaction to be expected are exact. This situation would fall in the previous category of self-testing. In many laboratory situations, however, the student deals with a far from prescribed set of variables—although far fewer than are to be found in the real world. It is up to the teacher to ascertain that the variables present in the laboratory provide a realistic enough situation so that learning can actually occur while not overwhelming the student with excess data.

Much learning can be gained from these settings. The most obvious examples of the use of this technique are in the physical sciences, but the "softer" sciences also have their laboratories. Human relations sensitivity training is one such example. Classroom "role playing" is another. In legal training, mock trials are yet another example of this learning mechanism.

Student feedback from this mechanism can be immediate or delayed. The chemical reaction that turns the right or wrong color is an example of immediate feedback—as is instructor intervention in a role-playing situation. On the other hand, laboratory results can be handed in for subsequent marking. In this latter case, all the possibly negative comments concerning feedback noted above under "Written Assignments" apply.

This type of laboratory situation involves more learner senses and more variables than written assignments. Taste, touch, sight, and often smell are all involved. Interaction with other people in several laboratory situations involves the full range of human emotions. At the same time, laboratory training is quite often expensive. It involves instructor time, often expensive materials, physical space for the laboratory, and administrative time and effort for scheduling. In recent years, the recognition of this expense has forced many institutions of higher learning to reduce the amount of laboratory training provided to the student.

Library investigation

The ultimate form of this learning device is the nonexperimental, library-oriented doctoral thesis. In this, and more limited cases such as course papers, the student is urged to use library resources to investigate a particular phenomenon of interest. The search space is somewhat bounded by what others have written—but to the individual student it often appears unbounded.

This type of learning theater is often combined with laboratory—or real-world—investigation. Its strengths and weaknesses are well known and need little elaboration.

Real-world experience

A final learning mechanism is the exposure of the student to the real world. Clearly, real-world experience is a learning mechanism that all human beings experience. Some of the most effective learning—from the viewpoint of strong impact on the consciousness and extended memory—occurs as a by-product of "disastrous" individual experience. Less poignant, less precise, less fully recognized learning takes place on a day-to-day basis in a variety of milder circumstances.

Universities have recognized, and are increasingly recognizing, the learning that takes place in this manner. Recently, more and more institutions are giving credit to older students for job-gained experience. More traditional is the recognition of learning gained through such mechanisms as work-study courses. These are most dramatically exemplified by entire institutions that are organized on a work-study basis—for example, Antioch College in Ohio and Northeastern University in Boston. In addition, many institutions, most especially in engineering or scientific training, have courses with such titles as "Laboratory Training at XYZ Corporation."

It is difficult to measure the effects of this type of learning. The learner's perception of what he has gained may be vastly distorted. He is dealing with an immensely multivariant situation. The influence of exogenous variables on his actions may be considerable and, more importantly, immeasurable. If the learner is testing the results of the application of a particular skill, he is often unable to view some of the results—since many of them are delayed in time—and these may give *opposite* impressions of the immediately observed results. Finally, the learner in the real world most often has as feedback only his *subjective* observations on the results of particular actions taken. It is often very difficult for the "teacher" to comment adequately on the results obtained from any situation. The real world is a rich learning environment—but a very deceptive one.

NON-COMPUTER-BASED LEARNING AIDS It is not only in the area of computers that new tools have been developed to assist the learning process. Column 3 of Figure 3-1 suggests eight other advances that have been made available by new technology or, in two cases, by adaptation of a much older form of technology—the printed page. Just as the traditional methods are competitors to computer learning aids, so are newer methods of learning assistance. When juxtaposed to these traditional methods (Figure 3-1, column 2) and the computer-based methods (column 4), they round out our presentation of a complete set of major alternative forms of learning assistance that can be utilized in the learning process today.

Lecture Substitutes Five alternate, relatively new primary methods of providing oral stimulation to the learning process are discussed in this section. Although they may be substituted for other learning techniques—with some stretching—they are all most closely related to the "listen, watch, and learn" technique most usually represented by the lecture. They are, in the order in which they will be discussed, radio, magnetic tapes and cassettes, films, TV, and videotape. Each of these may be used as a partial aid to, or complete substitute for, a lecture.

Radio

One of the oldest yet least utilized technological aids for the learning process is the radio. The minimal usage of this particular mechanism in the learning process is perhaps best illustrated by the title of a summary work, *The Hidden Medium: Educational Radio* (1966). In recent years television has helped to drive this particular medium, for purposes of higher education, even further into the background.

Radio is far from totally dead, however. There are currently more than 300 educational radio stations in existence, more than two-thirds of them on college and university campuses. Radio can reach its learners (1) by open broadcast on regular AM or FM frequencies, (2) by a "closed" broadcast of special receivers via an FM subchannel, (3) over a wired system using telephone lines or coaxial cables, or (4) by "playback" of programs previously recorded on tape.

For purposes of assisting learning, radio has several favorable attributes. It is a "broadcast" medium that can reach literally hundreds of thousands of listeners concurrently. It has all the virtues of oral presentation. These include the emotional impact that is a particular dimension of lectures. Its audio virtues are unique advantages when it comes to teaching subjects such as music appreciation or language. Radio, with effective background programming of mood—and foreground dramatic skills—can be an active medium that involves use of the listener's mind and imagination.

Furthermore, radio allows decentralized learning with regard to geography—although in contrast to cassettes, decentralization with regard to time (unless option 4, playback, is utilized) is not available. Significantly, radio has been found to be five times cheaper than television (Forsyth, 1971, p. 254). And it is far less demanding than television or the lecture hall in terms of the physical attitudes that learners must take in order to benefit from it. (Eyes can be closed, physical exercise can be taken concurrently, and so on.)

As with educational television, successful efforts have been developed to augment the advantages of radio with the interactive capabilities of ordinary lectures. The University of Wisconsin, in particular, has combined multiplex transmission of lecture materials with telephone question-and-answer periods for continuing education in medicine, law, and veterinary science.

In most cases, however, radio is hampered by a lack of interaction between the source of the material and the learner. Aimed at a mass audience, it cannot be individualized, and the broadcast, as noted above, is usually set in time. In comparison with the live lecture, it is also hampered through a lack of feedback about the value of a particular program—or clues as to how to optimize the impact of a succeeding program. (In some cases this drawback has been lessened through the use of questionnaires, audience testing, etc.) Finally, as with all other audio methods, delivery of facts to the learner is relatively slow through the radio medium.

A further drawback of radio as a learning aid, as with lectures, is the difficulty of scheduling the broadcast to ensure that the target audience is present. As the result of this, educational radio stations have emphasized instructional programs at the elementary school level, rather than at the high school or collegiate level. For the latter audience, they have tended to provide "general enrichment" programming.

There is also little doubt that educational radio has been upstaged by television. "With the advent of educational and instructional television, many broadcasting practitioners and many of the qualified research personnel gravitated to the newer medium; hundreds of ITV facilities were established, hundreds of ITV evaluative studies conducted, and predictably, interest in the instructional uses of radio declined (ibid., p. 256)."

It should be noted, however, that there is no convincing evidence that educational TV dominates educational radio as a learning aid. Chu and Schramm (1971) concluded that the effects of visual images of learning were not uniformly beneficial and depended heavily upon the type of learning involved. They noted that where visual images do not directly facilitate the visualization process, they "may cause distraction and interfere with learning" (p. 182). Heron and Ziebarth (1946) found, in a controlled experiment, that radio was as effective as face-to-face instruction for certain material.

Magnetic tapes and cassettes

Another audio-based method of learning assistance is available through prerecorded voice in the form of either magnetic tapes played through conventional tape recorders or the newer cassette form. It was really the cassette, effectively introduced for the first time in the 1960s, that provided a rebirth of this form of audio instruction. Prior to the cassette, magnetic tape players were relatively expensive and heavy and required somewhat careful handling in threading tapes. Cassette players, on the other hand, are relatively inexpensive ($30 to $50 provides a serviceable unit), light, portable, and easy to use. The prerecorded cassette is slipped into the player in a matter of seconds and the audio begun with the press of a button. With almost all machines, sections of a lecture can be replayed through a simple rewind mechanism.

Tapes to be used for recording purposes are also inexpensive. Raw tape is available in the range of $1 per cassette; prerecorded material is priced in relationship to the "value" of the lecture delivered. Some commercial courses, for example, deliver 20 minutes of prerecorded lecture for a charge of $350. This compares with a gross for a traditional lecture (see page 67) of $2 per hour. Per student cost of this form of audio learning both by itself and in comparison with live lectures clearly depends upon the number of students exposed.

This learning mechanism has most of the advantages of the oral lecture. Inflection, verbal emphasis, and exhortation can all be used by the lecturer in his attempt to get his material across. The visual aspects are, of course, missing. Although audiotape has the disadvantage, noted above, of the lecture form in terms of a slow delivery of facts and concepts to the learner relative to textbooks and other learning mechanisms that are read, it is advantageous for that section of the learning community that "just doesn't like to read." For remedial work, in particular, the human voice can add a certain compelling quality for some students.

Perhaps the most important attribute of recorded audio delivery, however, is its ability to be utilized at the learner's choice of time and place. The potential for a learner to "relax" and hear a brief instructive message is being exploited most in "continuing education." A tape ability to provide a "message" while the learner is doing something else is useful in many situations. It has provided, for example, physicians, managers, engineers, and others who drive automobiles—either while commuting or while driving from one worksite to another on the job—a way of filling in this "dead time" with learning opportunities. Given this particular attribute, there can be little doubt that audio recordings are a new and rising force in the continuing education field.

Display charts, overhead transparencies, and slides
These three media are the traditional "lecturer's aids" that have been-utilized over the last few decades to a greater or lesser extent depending on the subject and the lecturer's proclivities. Recent improvements in the conditions under which transparencies and slides can be used (that is, the ability to leave the lights on in the lecture room made possible by the development of better screens and white blackboards) have made these media more acceptable. These rather familiar items can save the lecturer the need to take class time to write or sketch on the blackboard. Where the material presented is artistic or graphic in nature, the advantages are obvious. Where it is merely script, these media have, in addition to the time savings, provided the lecturer with the added advantage of legibility. In addition, the slides, transparencies, and charts contain cue words or sentences that can be copied to provide the basis of student class notes, thereby saving student time.

Clearly there are certain courses for which this type of aid is necessary. Included among these are art and architecture sessions. In addition to the tangible benefits noted above, however, there are certain intangible benefits for classes in the area of English, history, management, etc. The use of visual aids enforces the discipline of logical development in the lecture. In addition, they document the lecture. Since they are permanent, they can be used time and time again.

Unfortunately, as with other media, these aids have several limitations. Lecturers *and* their lectures tend to change. Thus the investment in a set of slides, transparencies, or charts for one lecture may be inadequate for following sessions of the same course. The investment, therefore, may be partially or totally lost. In addition, the flip side of some of the advantages in the use of these aids are in effect disadvantages. It does take a great deal of care and preparation to develop a good lecture and much more to adequately document it with good graphic material. There is also significant time involved in getting source material converted to media form. (The availability of simple xerography onto transparencies has greatly diminished this latter disadvantage and has certainly increased the use of visual aids in the teaching process.) In addition, the growth of "graphic arts centers" on campuses has tended to make *somewhat* easier the professor's problems of developing good graphic materials quickly and with minimum expenditure of energy. Still, expending the time and energy necessary to develop graphic materials to augment lectures does not *have* to be done by any lecturer. For those not committed to assisting the learning process, the development of graphics takes additional time and effort that might be felt better spent on research community affairs, administrative affairs, or consulting.

Another consideration in the utilization of these media is that they require equipment to be present in the classroom to allow them to be used. Many professors who have had to pick up, transport, and set up their own flipchart holder, slide projector, or transparency projector are well aware of the nuisance this can be in a busy schedule. When bulbs "blow" or outlets are poorly accessible, the lack of ease in utilizing these systems is especially apparent. (Once again, recent developments—especially with regard to portable transparency projectors—have reduced this disadvantage somewhat. The increasingly relatively lower cost of these systems has tended to increase the supply and therefore the accessibility of this equipment to the individual professor.)

Film

Film of one type or another has been utilized in American education for more than six decades. During that time, the standard film gauge has moved from a very clumsy 35mm to 16mm to 8mm to the current standard super 8. The medium has become a better contender as a learning device due to the two major decreases in size, which have led to greater portability, space saving, economy, and ease of operation. The disadvantage of loss in picture quality caused by the decrease in picture size has been for the most part overcome by improvements in emulsions, lenses, cameras, projectors, and screens. Recently, the development of easy-handling cartridges for loading 8mm projectors and improved screens and projection equipment (which eliminate the need for total darkness in the room) have made 8mm film an even more attractive mechanism.

Early studies on the use of motion pictures in classrooms were quite positive. "Under the conditions which were obtained in this experiment, which probably reflect normal school conditions reasonably well, use of the films materially increased the effectiveness of instruction" (Wood & Freeman, 1929, p. 191). With these positive results, the Eastman Kodak Company enthusiastically moved into the educational film market. During the 15 years from 1928 to 1944, Kodak prepared 300 films that were distributed to classrooms across the United States and to 30 foreign countries (Flory, 1971, p. 222). Despite this energy, however, and the many individual efforts throughout the country, film has had a relatively minor role in higher education in the last three decades.

On the surface, one would expect the film medium to be more widely used. It has many advantages relative to other methods of learning assistance. In the first place, it can bring "reality" into the classroom. As one management trainer puts it:

The reality of the films provides a direct challenge to the new supervisors. They can see the action for themselves—how an employee looked, what he said, and his gestures. It's almost impossible to capture these nuances in words; yet, they are important factors for the supervisor to gain insight into the problem being studied (ibid., p. 215).

Another advocate cites several other important attributes of film. These include the ability to telescope time—to present kinetic phenomena in a time-sliced manner so that one can, for example, see plants "grow" or cells divide in a fraction of the time that would be necessary if the real event were to be observed. Through time-lapse photography one can capture the essence of a dynamic event. Moreover, events that cannot be staged in a classroom can be transferred to that classroom through the use of film. Laboratory demonstrations can be viewed in full intensity by larger groups of students. Telescopic or high-speed events that cannot be captured by the eye and brain can be caught. In addition, the film allows the presentation to be reviewed—it can be run and observed as many times as the learner desires.

On the other hand, both from the viewpoint of the professor and that of the student, film does have some disadvantages. In the first place, it is essentially a passive medium—the student merely sits and watches. Second, the film must be skillfully produced. In an age in which students are used to high-quality cinematic production, an amateurish film may be looked upon with distaste no matter how good its content. Production costs of good films are high. For excellent films, costs as high as $120,000 per hour of viewing have been quoted.[1]

Perhaps most discouraging for teachers is the lack of ease of use of films in general. Film is not an easy medium for the average professor to use. He must first review the film in its entirety for content, for even the most reputable catalogs do not tell him just exactly what is in the film and how it fits into his course. He therefore must get the film, review it, and, if it meets his needs, work his lecture around it. He must deal with outsiders to get films—which involves both time and bother. At this point, the professor is faced with the problems of *using* the film. He must arrange for a projector to be available and in working order. The room must be, still usually today, darkened. A screen must be available in the classroom, and electric plugs must be in the right places. When balanced against the ease of drawing a few chalk diagrams on the board, the disadvantages of the film medium often seem overwhelming.

Television, videotape, and cable TV

The newest noncomputer medium on which many hopes are now pinned is television. The medium is flexible. It can be used in either broadcast or cable versions. Television can be either live or infinitely replayable through videotape. Much experimentation is going on with television today in many institutions to spread live lectures to additional classrooms.

A major research thrust, and an operational thrust in many

[1]Personal communication from Professor Eugene Bell, Department of Biology, MIT.

cases, is the use of cable TV for education. Lectures, graphic material, and multimedia access to other materials can be made available through a cable system to students at any place where an output station is available. For privacy, a student can use an acoustical carrel with earphones. Electronically controlled video systems work in a manner similar to the more familiar audio systems that are ubiquitously utilized in language laboratories today. Dialing a program number activates a videotape and the signal is transmitted. With multiple programs available, even where "demand dialing" is not feasible, programs can be scheduled many times during the day so that access to material is much more at the learner's discretion than today.

Cable television is also being used for "interactive lectures." Two-way voice hookups allow interaction while the program is being taped. Subsequent showings include the questions and the lecturer's replies. Cable television will contribute to other forms of educations. As noted in the previous chapter, several experiments with cable television as the conduit for computer signals are now being undertaken.

Politics and the regulation of the cable television industry are one factor limiting the progress now being made toward implementing such systems. The major constraint, however, is economics. The estimated cost of providing switched, two-way color video systems for every house in the United States is on the order of $1 trillion. This compares with the almost $80 billion investment represented by the current telephone network (Carne, 1972, p. 126). It is clear that cable television has potential but that its economics are staggering. Once the investment in cabling is made, however, the incremental costs of providing education in this form—which can be highly attractive—are much less. And cables will most probably be laid with purposes other than education in mind over the next 10 to 20 years.

TV is an interesting medium in that, in its different forms, it shares many of the previously cited advantages and disadvantages of radio and film. Yet there is little doubt about the eventual use of the TV medium in education. TV on a closed-circuit network, or as part of an educational station, is gaining in usage. A closed network, for example, is being used to run educational courses as part of university-based company training programs. The lecturer at the university lectures to the TV camera and has a two-way voice channel linking him to the remote locations in the companies.

One such television network is TAGER (The Association for Graduate Education and Research of North Texas), a nonprofit corporation chartered in 1965 in Austin, Texas, by seven private universities. As of early 1974, eight universities and a dozen major industrial locations take part in the network as shown in Figure 3-2. At more than 50 "classrooms" students see a televised lecture—and also utilize a continuously open audio line to converse with the instructor and students at other receiving locations.

In the studio-classroom the lecturer speaks to a small group of students. Two television cameras are used, both completely remote-controlled from a nearby control room. One camera is mounted on the rear wall of the classroom and provides a picture of the instructor and the classroom. The other camera is mounted over the instructor's head and is aimed at whatever is placed upon his desk. Normally, a specially designed pad is placed on the desk to be used as one would a blackboard. A 10-1 zoom lens provides clarity.

Experience with the open university in the United Kingdom has been widely reported and is an example of public TV being used in conjunction with written materials to reach an audience of people not normally able to avail themselves of further education. This, like the university-business link, breaks down the physical limitations of transferring people to one location to listen to a lecture. At the same time it brings in the benefit of films. It suffers, of course, from the lack of direct human two-way contact and from the lack of the impetus to learning provided by direct contact with a large number of fellow students.

Paper Programmed Instruction (PI) Programmed instruction, although its current fame comes primarily from computerization, is also available in paper form. Several thousand PI texts are available today that present data on a huge variety of subjects to students in true Skinnerian fashion. In this medium, a printed paragraph of information is closely followed by a question to which a student must respond—usually in multiple choice or in fill-in-the-blank. The accuracy of the answer is immediately revealed to the student either on the next line of the text or on the page to which he is "branched" as a result of his answer. Thus the student moves through a body of data in "short steps," with instantaneous feedback on his ability to assimilate the material. Both the act of writing out the answers and learning their correctness are

FIGURE 3-2 *The Tager television network*

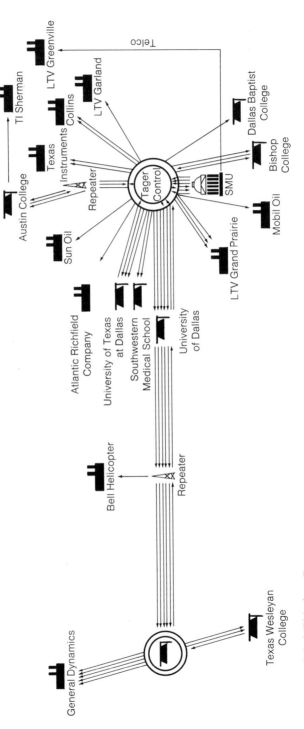

SOURCE: *Talk Back TV* (n.d., p. 5).

viewed as reinforcing. The student is forced to think about the material, and while his rate of data acquisition is slowed in relation to the textbook, retention and understanding of certain types of material have been shown to be improved through this technique.

Paper programmed instruction is very similar to computer programmed instruction. There are differences between these media, though, the paper version being much more limited. The number of branches in the material is limited both by the need to keep down the amount of "flipping the pages" the student must perform and by the limited number of responses that can be made to the possible student answers.

In terms of potential for learning assistance, PI is a poor cousin to computerized tutorial programs, since considerable additional flexibility to respond to answers can be built into computer systems. In addition, once the PI material is "set" and printed, revising it involves a new edition. Computerized programmed instruction can be continually updated on the basis of statistics gathered in the computer system as to the effectiveness of each question. Computerized programmed instruction can be dynamic, with the student being helped by the system itself in its instantaneous analysis of partially correct answers. It is true that very few computerized programmed instruction modules have even a "moronic" ability to respond to the student and his needs by comparison to a human teacher. But PI is at least an order of magnitude less efficacious than computer instruction. In addition, paper programmed instruction suffers from many of the faults of the paper medium itself. Just as do textbooks, it relies on the author's sequence of presentation. Depending on the author, it can be distinctly dull. The "publishing gap" leads to its suitability for only stable, relatively invariant material.

On the other hand, in relation to computerized programmed instruction, PI does have several advantages. The most significant of these (at least for the next few years) is its relative cheapness. Paper programmed instruction texts can also be carried around and used on a decentralized basis. In addition, once a student has filled them out, they provide a permanent record and thus may also be used for reference. As the economics of computers improve, however, and the access of computer terminals increases, the relative advantage now held by paper programmed instruction with regard to cost and ease of use will disappear. But the cost gap does not appear likely to disappear in the seventies.

Independent Study Modules

Yet another paper mechanism developed to assist the learning process is *independent study modules* written to coordinate what is usually multimedia study. These modules are essentially sets of directions that guide the student in his utilization of other learning mechanisms to satisfy certain learning objectives. Virtually unknown several years ago, they are appearing in greater numbers today as a framework around which multimedia courses are coordinated. In general, each module provides the following for the student:

- The objectives of the module.
- An outline of the material to be covered.
- A description of the steps the student is to follow and the order in which they are to be followed. (The student can be told to read a chapter from a book, perform a homework exercise, take a self-test, and so on.)
- In many cases, additional expository material to add to, simplify, or explain more fully the concepts available through the other learning materials that are utilized by the particular module.

In truth, these modules are as different as the various authors who produce them. Their functions are the common core. From the student point of view, study modules have most of the advantages and disadvantages of the other media that they utilize. Although the module itself may be highly portable, if it requires a student to view a film that is only available from a central location, material presented in the modules can hardly be described as "capable of totally decentralized use." Yet part of the material covered by the module, that is, the self-study module write-up itself, clearly can be studied by the student at the decentralized location. The modules themselves present only one-way teacher-student interaction. Yet if the module directs the student to use an interactive drill-and-practice program, the module—seen as a total delivery mechanism and including its material as presented in other media—can be seen as somewhat interactive. The distinction must be clearly made between the paper module "write-up" and the totality of the material itself (which may be presented by several different learning mechanisms). Taken by itself, each module write-up has most of the advantages and disadvantages of a textbook.

Class Response Systems One method of assisting the process of classroom participation now under development and testing is *classroom response hardware*. Response buttons or levers in each seat are electrically or electronically connected to a display panel. Students can indicate one of a series of choices by pressing the applicable button. In this way, a class can vote on a management decision to be taken as the result of a particular set of facts—with the distribution of sentiment visible to all and with each particular person's decision kept private.

Another suggested use for this type of system is to alert lecturers to whether they are moving too quickly or too slowly. Again, individual privacy is maintained. These systems are currently experimental and are very much a product in search of a use in higher education. Yet there are several possible uses— including the two noted.

SUMMARY In Chapter 2 we looked at a model of the learning process. This chapter has summarized a set of 16 types of non-computer-based learning mechanisms that are available to those who plan the learning process in any field. We now turn to computer-based learning mechanisms.

One point is perhaps worth making here. It is clear that previous to the computer it was the very rare course that utilized only one of the available learning mechanisms. Historically, professors have looked at the available "smorgasbord" of devices to assist learning and chosen among them to produce a well-rounded "diet" for each course. We would expect computer-based mechanisms to be worked into courses following this same general principle.

4. The Computer

During the past three decades, computers have become the most talked about, written about, and ubiquitous machines ever to be imposed upon mankind. At their birth, they were different, novel, and exciting. Ten to fifteen years ago, it was felt that by the 1970s they would be replacing many of man's functions—including thinking. Today, with a somewhat more realistic view, they are recognized as an increasingly important tool of mankind—and one that has the potential for great impact upon the education process.

Their impact to date in all fields has been tremendous. By the end of 1972, there was an excess of $30 billion worth of computer hardware installed in the United States alone. Most forecasters were predicting this figure would double by 1977 or 1978—a growth rate in excess of 15 percent a year. Well over a million people were employed designing systems, programming, operating the machines, and providing input data for them alone. According to the American Federation of Information Processing Societies, professionals involved in the data processing field will increase by approximately 150 percent by 1980. Comparative growth rates for accountants, engineers, and physicians are estimated at 40 to 50 percent. Computers are not only clearly here to stay—they are likely to rapidly expand their presence during the next decade if forecasters in the field are even remotely correct.

During the past five years, books and other literature explaining computer systems have proliferated. This chapter does *not* provide a tutorial on computer systems. [For those interested in more detail than this chapter presents, the treatments by Levien (1972), Davis (1974), and Orlicky (1969) are fully recommended.] Rather, we should like to merely isolate for the reader the most significant elements of computer systems so that it will be possible to take a meaningful look at the probable future of computer technology. The treatment is in only enough depth to provide a perspective on (1) the options that are available for utilizing the computer in the learning process and on (2) how changes in computer technology may affect the cost of using the computer in the learning process during the next decade.

HARDWARE COMPONENTS OF THE COMPUTER

As Figure 4-1 suggests, the hardware in a conventional computer system consists of four major components. These are:

- *The processor,* which is programmed to accept data, perform computations, transmit data between the three other components, and, in summary, control the processing performed.
- *Main storage,* which holds the data and instructions used by the processor.
- *Secondary storage,* which also holds data and instructions ultimately used by the processor. Secondary storage costs less than main storage per data item stored, but material stored there must first be transferred to main storage before the processor can utilize it.
- *Input-output equipment,* whose basic function is to communicate between people and the computer system.

Processors

Processors, often called CPUs (central processing units), come in all sizes and shapes. They are characterized by the amount of data that they can "access" (from main storage) at one time, the speed with which each "access" is made, the number of different "instructions" (individual actions that can be performed on

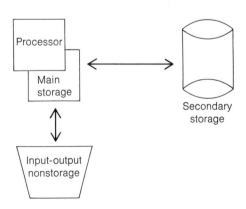

FIGURE 4-1
Hardware components of the computer

each item of data after it is accessed) the processor can execute directly, and numerous other individual features. Two or more CPUs can be linked together to form multisystems capable of working on several jobs concurrently. Processors are today available for approximately $5,000 to several million dollars. Typical processors used by major universities today cost well in excess of a million dollars.

Main storage

The main storage, which is "immediately accessible" (typically in 1/1,000,000 second) by the processor, usually represents about one-third of the computer system's cost. It holds the data and programs currently executed by the CPU. These storage systems were first made up of vacuum tubes, recently have consisted of faster "core" memories, and have now moved into a phase in which they increasingly consist of solid-state semi-conductors. They range from very small memories capable of storing 2,000 or so letters or numbers to larger main storages in the 10- to 20-million-byte size. (A *byte* is a widely utilized unit of storage capable of holding one letter or two numbers.) The larger-memory sizes allow more data and instructions to be *immediately available* to the processor and are therefore found in more powerful machines. Main storages of all sizes are being used in institutions of higher education today.

Secondary storage

This is a catch-all phrase that covers several different types of data storage mediums. Data and programs stored on these devices must first be transferred to main storage to be utilized. One often used device is magnetic tape, upon which data are stored sequentially, and relatively cheaply, but with slow average CPU access time (sometimes measured in seconds for particular items of data). A second and increasingly popular form of secondary storage is rotating devices such as "drums" and "disks," on which data can be accessed more quickly (in thousandths of a second) but at a major increase in cost per item stored. Magnetic strip devices, such as "data cells," which store large amounts of data more expensively than tape but with a faster access time, provide a third major source of secondary storage and represent somewhat of a compromise between the first two device types.

The primary feature of all these devices is the ability to store, hold, and make available great amounts of data. These data can be called for by the processor and read into main storage for manipulation. Most of these devices have the ability to store hundreds of millions of characters of data.

Secondary storage thus differs from main storage in that (1) access to secondary storage by the CPU is slower by several orders of magnitude; (2) secondary storage is vastly cheaper (by a factor of more than 1,000 for "on-line" accessible storage and more than a 1,000,000 to 1 ratio for "off-line" storage, such as a magnetic tape reel that must be loaded onto the computer before use); and (3) due to its relative cheapness, *far* greater amounts of secondary storage are in use. The types and amounts of secondary storage utilized vary from installation to installation and are dictated by needs for particular amounts of data storage, desired speed of access to the storage, and funds available for data storage. All three types of devices (as well as some special secondary-storage devices) are in use in higher education.

Input-output equipment (I/O)

The primary role of this equipment is to convert human-sensible material into a form that can be read by the computer system, to communicate these data to the computer, and then to relay "computed data" back to people. Included in this category of device is such equipment as key punches, key verifiers, key tape and key disk equipment, card punches, printers, and on-line terminals.

Key punches, verifiers, and key tape and key disk equipment are used by operators to translate written material into machine-sensible form. These data are then read in by the card readers or other input devices. Output is ultimately received from the computer system in punched-card form, through card punches, in printed form on printers capable of printing from 100 to over 2,000 lines per minute, or on special-purpose devices such as computer-output microfilm.

The various classes of terminals allows a person to communicate directly with the computer system through a simple typewriter-like device eliminating the "middleman" of punches, readers, etc. Terminals are available in many forms. These include teletype terminals, which are basically slow and mechanical in the input process as well as in the typewritten output of data. More recently, however, the cathode-ray-tube (CRT) terminal, which handles data electronically, has begun to take over this field where printed output is unnecessary. Almost all conceivable categories of input-output equipment are found in use in higher education.

In addition to these four major classes of hardware devices, there are other hardware variations that are of some importance for our immediate story. Included among these are "networks" of computer systems, telecommunications hardware, and other special-purpose devices. Many of these special devices provide ways of effectively linking the various components noted above or of increasing their efficiency. We shall return to this linking function after the section on software.

SOFTWARE In addition to hardware, computers are heavily dependent upon the software they use. The term *software* refers to the programs that run in a computer. Broadly speaking, software can be placed in four categories—operating systems, utility programs, language processors, and application programs. In recent years, *operating systems* have become more and more important as a means of relieving programmers of some of the work of directing the computer. Operating systems are, in effect, programs that have been prewritten for all users to utilize, usually by computer manufacturers. They facilitate effective use of the computer hardware in the execution of user programs. "The term *operating systems* denotes those program modules within a computer system that govern the control of equipment resources such as processors, main storage, secondary storage and I/O devices. . . . These modules resolve conflicts, attempt to optimize performance, and simplify the effective use of the system. They act as an interface between the user's programs and the physical computer hardware" (Madnick & Donovan, 1974, p. 11). As computer hardware has become more complex, so have the operating systems. They now use an ever-increasing amount of main storage—in the largest systems up to several hundred thousand bytes. Yet operating systems today make it possible for computers to perform such functions as running several user programs in parallel by accepting data from remote terminals over telephone lines and automatically selecting, from an input queue of programs that are ready to run, the program that allows the best overall utilization of the computer's capabilities. So important are operating systems today that a computer's capabilities can only be measured by taking into account its hardware features *and* its available software—of which the most important part is the operating system.

The second type of software utilized today can be collectively termed *utility programs* and consists of a set of general-purpose programs that can be accessed by a programmer through the operating system to perform specific functions. Included among these utility programs are programs that automatically print out specified data contained in storage or sort specified data. In effect, utility programs are also prewritten programs that allow users to perform many often repeated computer tasks without the need to "write the program" each time. They are increasingly being supplied by computer manufacturers and independent software houses in more and more efficient versions to accomplish a wide spectrum of tasks.

Language processors are manufacturer-supplied programs that translate a particular set of programmer-written statements into the machine instructions that can be executed by a particular computer. In effect, they translate from "human" languages such as near-English or mathematics into machine-sensible code structures.

Application programs are those written by users to do specific jobs whose procedural steps are unique to the situation. In recent years the high cost of writing these individual user programs has been increasingly acknowledged. As a result, more and more organizations are attempting to utilize prewritten application programs called *packages* that can be changed marginally to fit each user's needs. The cost of program creation is thus spread over multiple organizations. In effect, this is merely a logical extension of the "prewritten program" concept which has been effected in the area of operating systems, utility programs, and language processors. In the early days of computer systems, each user wrote *all* his software. There is a clear trend toward a tomorrow in which the user will create only a minimum of very situation-dependent application programs. The movement toward this has been slow in the application's software area—but programs in many application areas such as payroll, billing, and inventory control are increasingly being "packaged." It is reasonable to expect higher education users to slowly but increasingly accept application packages written elsewhere. Acceptance today is low, however, and the trend will not pick up speed overnight. Yet we believe it will come.

THE TOTAL SYSTEM TODAY
Any computer system in operation today thus consists of three conceptually distinguishable elements. These are the hardware of which it is composed; the heavily prewritten "systems software" (the operating system, the language processors, and the utility programs); and the mostly user-created application programs, which are the actual programs executed to perform the major work of the installation. Typical systems in use today that perform the "backbone" of computing at major institutions of higher learning have a yearly rental cost of from $250,000 up to several million dollars. With all other operating costs—personnel, maintenance, supplies, etc.—added in, total computing costs can easily double these figures. In sum, computers are a major cost item in colleges and universities today. But with our focus on the next decade, two questions need to be answered. First, how is the technology going to change? Second, what difference will this make with regard to the costs of computer systems in higher education?

FUTURE HARDWARE COSTS
We expect hardware costs to diminish rapidly over the next decade. Considering each major component described above, we find the following:

Processors and main memory
Historically the processor and its main memory (or main storage) were thought of as one piece of equipment. As a result, many of the early studies done on the cost of computers treated the two as an entity. More recently, they have been separated both conceptually and in fact as suppliers producing main memory alone have begun to compete with the large manufacturers for the installation of this particular bit of hardware. In one study, F. G. Withington (1972) of Arthur D. Little, Inc., estimated separate cost curves for these devices. As Figure 4-2 shows, the cost of central processors is expected to decrease by an order of about 10 between 1970 and 1980. The effective cost

FIGURE 4-2
Cost of central processors

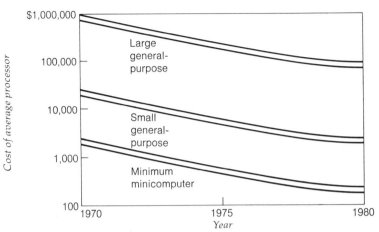

SOURCE: Withington (1972, p. 90).

of main memory (Figure 4-3) will also decrease at about the same rate, with semiconductor memory at 2 cents a bit (one-fifth of current costs) available to deliver cycle times that are approximately twice as fast as today's usual semiconductor memory.

In a recent article, Stuart Madnick (1973) estimates approximately the same *overall* results for the processor and main memory. As Table 4-1 shows, a million bytes of main memory is expected to decrease in cost approximately 50 times between 1970 and the late 1970s. Special memories and processor circuits

FIGURE 4-3
Cost of memory

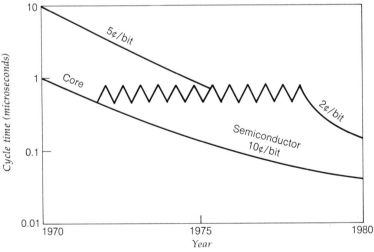

SOURCE: Withington (1972; p. 90).

TABLE 4-1 *Actual and projected costs of the processor and main memory*

System component	In 1970		In the late 1970s	
	Cost	Percentage of total	Cost	Percentage of total
Main memory (1 million bytes)	$120,000		$ 2,400	4
Special memories	40,000	11	2,000	3
Processor logic circuits	50,000	15	2,600	4
Special circuits	20,000	6	8,000	12
Processor subtotal		32		19
Packaging	30,000	9	10,000	15
Power and cooling	30,000	9	15,000	23
Other	50,000	15	25,000	39
Miscellaneous subtotal		33		77
TOTAL	$340,000		$65,000	

SOURCE: Madnick (1973, p. 5).

are expected to decrease to about 5 percent of 1970 costs. These major decreases, however, will be partially offset by smaller decreases in the units used for power, cooling, and packaging of the central processor. As a result, a late-1970s system is predicted to cost about 18 percent of 1970 costs for the processor and main memory.

Clearly these two estimates differ somewhat. However, they agree with most other forecasters, who expect the processor and main storage to approximate 5 to 20 percent of the 1970 costs in 1980. These figures are in reality almost a direct extrapolation of past trends. In an often quoted study, Paul Armer (1965) estimated that the cost per computer operation (processing and storage costs only) had fallen about one order of magnitude every four years, or about 44 percent a year. Later studies by Skattum and Schneidewind found approximately the same figure—50 percent and 48 percent respectively (cited in Sharpe, 1969). The Withington and Madnick estimates are somewhat more conservative than this rate of progress. A 40 percent rate of annual decrease would bring 1980 costs down to approximately 1 percent of the 1971 level. The exact figure at which these units will be available to institutions of higher learning, shrouded by technology and packaging changes and buffered by pricing policies, is unclear. What is reasonably certain is that by 1980 one can expect processors and main storage of equivalent power to be available at a small fraction of their early-1970s cost.

Secondary storage

With regard to secondary storage, the estimates of cost reduction are even greater. Madnick (1973) suggests that by *1975* secondary-storage costs will be on the order of 20 percent of 1971–72 costs. Most of this has already occurred. Withington (see Figure 4-4) believes that the decrease in the per bit cost of mass storage may be as great as 500 times between 1970 and 1980. He expects that the magnetic rotating storage devices (disks)—which currently dominate the secondary-storage scene—will be phased out by one of the many new technologies now under development. Included among these are laser memories, optical memories, magnetic bubble memories, and holographic approaches. With the decrease in cost will also come some increase in access speed to secondary storage.

Input-output equipment

Figure 4-5 shows a set of forecasts for three families of input-output devices. Those in the top group, impact printers and card handlers, are basically mechanical devices. Since these are already quite mature and operating at very high mechanical speeds, they are unlikely to improve very much. Withington

FIGURE 4-4
Cost of mass storage

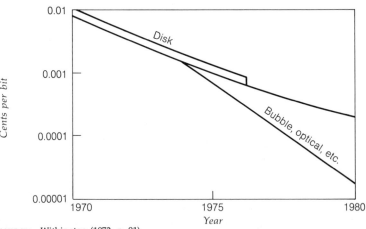

SOURCE: Withington (1972, p. 91).

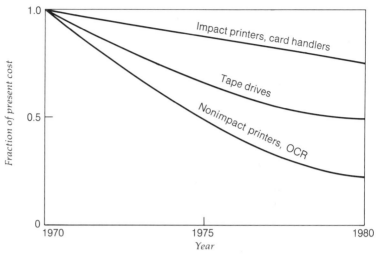

FIGURE 4-5
*Cost of input-
output devices*

SOURCE: Withington (1972, p. 92).

suggests a 20 percent improvement. Tape drives, still essentially mechanical, will also not decrease very much in cost. New packing technologies may improve the performance of tape drives, but a 50 percent decrease in costs is about all that can be expected.

Cost factors for input-output equipment are expected to improve considerably in one area—that of devices essentially electronic rather than mechanical. These include nonimpact printers, cathode-ray-tube terminals, and optical character readers (OCRs). The expected decrease throughout the decade of approximately 75 percent in this area has, for some equipment (notably terminals), already been approached by some of the most recent announcements. It was not very long ago that a cathode-ray-tube terminal could not be leased for less than $125 a month. Inexpensive CRT terminals are now on the market for $40 to $50 a month. This decrease is especially significant since the use of electronically based I/O gear is heavily on the increase.

**FUTURE
SOFTWARE
COSTS** It thus appears that in all the four major hardware categories, costs will decrease rather significantly over the next decade. What then of software? Barring major changes in the economy, the basic software producing unit—the programmer—will continue to escalate in price as inflation continues. Offsetting this trend is an increasing effort to share programs among institu-

tions of higher education[1] and an increase in the acceptance of generalized packages. (The overall use of systems and application packages by computer users is expected to grow by more than 30 percent a year for the next several years according to such sources as Arthur D. Little, Inc., and International Data Corporation.) In addition, more effective programming methods, such as IBM's "lead programmer" technique, and more effective project management should tend to keep software costs within bounds.

On the other hand, as more is learned about the potential of computers, more and more elaborate and "sophisticated" jobs are programmed that demand increasingly more elaborate and expensive programs. Higher education is no exception to this general rule. As Levien puts it, it "appears clear that *instructional software will become the most expensive component of computer instruction systems as hardware-related costs decrease over time*. Indeed, software costs seem likely to be *the* critical cost factors in instructional computer use in the future" (Levien, 1972, p. 487). This statement (the emphasis is Levien's) simply cannot be quarreled with.

THE EFFECTS OF COSTS ON HIGHER EDUCATION

In summary, software costs over the next decade are apt to increase for most institutions of higher education. Inflation and the tendency to put more complex exercises on the computer will tend to force these costs up. The increasing use of packages, the interchange of programs between institutions (although this is minimal today for many reasons), and the development of better programming management techniques will offset this rise somewhat, but not eliminate it. With regard to hardware costs, however, the picture is strikingly different. For equivalent power, computer systems by the end of the decade should drop in cost by a factor of at least 5 and quite possibly 10 or more.

One major effect of these trends on higher education should be the availability at current costs—or less—of vastly more powerful multiterminal, multiprocessor computer systems with greatly expanded storage capacities that will provide more reliable performance and easier access to programs throughout the campus. Additional hardware capabilities will be built into

[1]See, for example, *In North Carolina: Computing Power for Higher Education* (1973, pp. 2–6).

future computer systems. These future systems will undoubtedly have more complex operating systems—which in turn will "chew up" more of the available main memory and computer operating time for their own use. On one hand, these embellishments in both hardware and operating systems will offset part of the reduction in hardware costs. On the other hand, they will have greater ease of operation. Exactly what the trade-off between increased ease of operation and decreased cost per unit will be is uncertain. Whatever the outcome, however, it is relatively clear that computer *costs per program run will decrease,* perhaps greatly, and therefore computers will provide increasingly more cost-effective competition for alternate ways of delivering learning.

The exact decrease in cost per program run will depend on all the hardware and software factors noted above. Perhaps most significant among these factors, along with the decrease in hardware costs, will be the degree of acceptance of "other people's programs" (application packages) by faculty members. As Levien notes, "the cost of computer instruction depends crucially on the development of satisfactory arrangements for the distribution of instructional software" (ibid., p. 489). Utilizing hardware and software extrapolations roughly similar to those presented above, Levien predicts that, given acceptance in this area, the cost of an hour of computer instructional time in the 1980s could be approximately 50 cents—about four times less than a computed faculty contact per hour cost[2] of approximately $2. (Even without widespread program sharing, however, Levien predicts computer instructional costs below this faculty per hour cost.) Moreover, there is no reason to suspect that the continuing decrease in computing cost will end with 1980. There are many who suggest that the 1980s will at least be a repeat of the 1970s in terms of the reduction of computer costs for equivalent power.

CLASSES OF SYSTEMS There are three basic ways that combinations of this increasingly cost-effective hardware (with associated software) can be put together for use by students and faculty. These approaches can be termed *batch* systems, *remote job entry* (RJE) systems,

---

[2]Based on an instructor with a salary of $21,600, spending 50 percent of his time teaching two classes of 30 students for three hours per week for 30 weeks—and ignoring fringe benefits and other costs (Levien, 1972, p. 487).

FIGURE 4-6
Spectrum of computer systems

	Batch	Remote job entry	On-line interactive
In-house	X	X	X
Computer utility	X	X	X

and *on-line interactive* systems. Any of the three approaches can be utilized on an "in-house" basis, where the college operates the system itself, or on a "computer utility," or "out-of-house" basis, where the school rents time and service from an outside supplier. The six-point spectrum is as shown in Figure 4-6. The three systems utilizing the previously mentioned components can be visualized as in Figures 4-7, 4-8, and 4-9 on this and the following page.

In the batch system the student first converts his data and/or programs into machine-readable form—usually cards. He then physically transports this "input" to the computer room, where it is entered into the computer system and the program is run. Output data are produced at the computer and are picked up by the student.

If the university does not have its own computer, an outside "service bureau" computer can also be utilized in this mode. Arrangements must be made for input data to be picked up, run on the computer, and delivered by the service bureau. Time delays—for learning purposes—are, in some cases, greater than desirable.

In effect, the RJE system is the same as the batch system, with one major exception. After converting his data, the student enters them into an input device that is physically remote from

FIGURE 4-7 *Batch system*

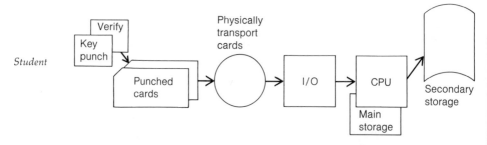

FIGURE 4-8 *Remote job entry system*

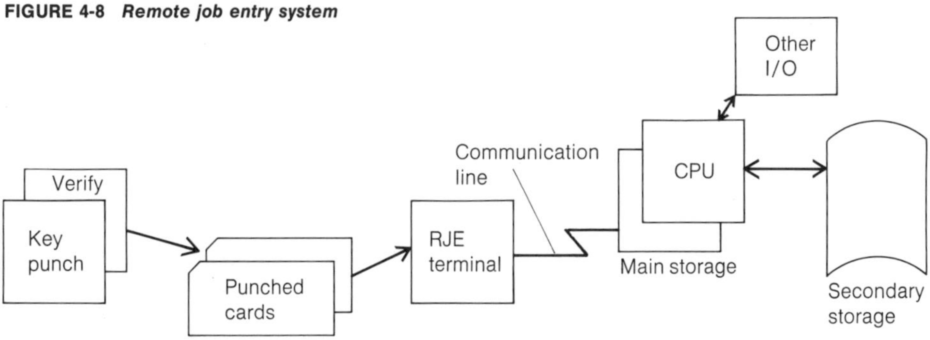

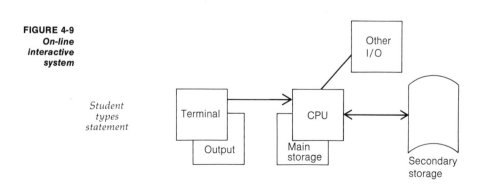

the computer (and hopefully near the student). The data are then carried electronically to the computer, and the programs are run. Output may be received at the RJE terminal site (through a printer), or, if it is voluminous, it may be printed out at the main computer site on a very high-speed printer. This method solves the problem of the student's distance from the CPU.

In the on-line interactive approach, the student communicates directly with the computer. Input is typed on a terminal, and—as in RJE—output can be directly printed out for the learner at the terminal, or, if it is voluminous, it can be printed out at the computer center and ultimately sent to the learner.

Two things, however, differentiate on-line interaction from RJE. The first is the absence of the intermediate form of data input. As noted above, data are typed directly into a direct extension of the computer: the terminal. This facilitates the second and vastly more important attribute: the ability of the

FIGURE 4-9
On-line interactive system

learner and the computer to "talk" to each other. In this mode the learner can get *immediate* feedback on the results of his efforts. Alternatively, he can be guided, prodded, or "helped" by the computer system toward some learning goal. Well-programmed, as we shall note in the following chapter, the computer can thoroughly interact with a student in the "same interactive manner" in which a professor might.

On-line interaction, like the other two modes, can be either wholly owned and operated by the university or utilized on a shared basis by purchasing time from an outside vendor who operates a "computer utility." Today there are in excess of 100 vendors selling on-line power—some 25 having coast-to-coast availability. One alternative to the commercial utilities today is regional computer organizations—such as the New England Regional Computing Co. (NERCOMP) established under National Science Foundation (NSF) funding a few years ago to allow smaller institutions access to major university computer systems.

There is little doubt that "networks"—the ability for one school to link to hardware and software located at another university—are a growing part of the academic computing scene (Greenberger, Aronofsky, McKenney, & Massey, 1974). The ability to not have to "reinvent the wheel" will be, we believe, a significant force in spreading instructional computing. The network concept also decreases significantly the problems of managing the large, rapidly changing technical organization that is built up around computers and software development.

It is clear that institutions like the North Carolina Educational Computing Service (NCECS), the Iowa Regional Computer Network, the Minnesota Computer Time-Sharing Network, and others have made a major difference in allowing easier access to instructional computing. On a smaller scale, organizations like the Babson Consortium and the Massachusetts State College System offer services of a central computer group to a dozen colleges each. Large or small, networks are here to stay—and will have greater impact in the future.

Here, then, are three major approaches. All are in use today. They have a few basic attributes. As one moves from left to right in Figure 4-6 (from batch to on-line), hardware cost increases. Similarly, the size and cost of the software (primarily operating systems) needed to run these systems also increase. Importantly, however, both the number of things that can be done to assist the learning process and the effectiveness of many of these things increase dramatically.

An additional dimension

Recent technological developments have in effect split the available configurations of computing power into three size classes, which might be termed *mini, midi,* and *maxi.* The most recent arrivals, minicomputers, have brought this breakdown into sharp view. Featuring a less complex "stripped-down" CPU and relatively small storage (both main and secondary), the mini—based on the latest technology—appears to be the equivalent of the subcompact car (excellent, serviceable, effective performance) when its limited capabilities fit the user's needs. Importantly, it can be dedicated to a single task and do a highly efficient job of performing that task unencumbered by the many features needed for the "general purpose" uses of large computers.

At the other end of the spectrum are the largest, most complex, most powerful, and most costly maxicomputers. They are capable of running many jobs at one time, of running the most complex jobs most efficiently (due to their large available storage, extensive CPU features, and built-in economies of scale), and of undertaking almost any task desired. They are, of course, expensive, need a large community of users to be efficient, and must be located remotely, therefore, from at least a major share of these users (who are thus restricted at least psychologically by the rules of the central system) as well as by the need to conform to a central authority's decisions as to what software facilities, access methods, pricing structure, and so forth, to provide.

Midis are in-between. They do not offer the local control or the efficiency of a minicomputer, which is dedicated to a specific task. Nor do they offer the large resources, efficient multipurpose abilities, and large-task efficiency of a maxicomputer. They, in effect, represent a compromise, but a useful one for some tasks—and some budgets.

This breakdown enables us to graphically once again partition computing availability as shown in Figure 4-10.

FIGURE 4-10
*A spectrum of
computer choice*

Computer size \ Mode of use	Batch	RJE	On-line
Mini			
Midi	X	X	
Maxi	X	X	

It should be noted that until recent years most schools have concentrated their computing efforts for instructional purposes in the four boxes marked "X." This is now changing. For reasons that will become apparent in the next chapter, the on-line mode is becoming increasingly useful for instruction. And this mode, as well as the batch mode, can be effectively delivered for many types of instruction by small minicomputers dedicated to providing a few simple services.

Tying these "dedicated" minis to the larger maxis may well be a good way to be able to perform all types of jobs today. In effect, the mini becomes an RJE terminal to the maxi—where maxi power is needed—and an efficient low-cost, local processor for smaller jobs. More and more this "distributed processing" mode is being discussed. As G. P. Weeg puts it:

Several of the questions listed in the description of this panel are under experimentation at the University of Iowa today. In particular:

1 How should educational computer use be delivered;
2 Should there be separate computer budgets for departments and courses;
3 Will free-access lead to bankruptcy;
4 Is time-sharing essential?

Iowa's computing center has always been a centralized facility, except for on-line, laboratory-centered computers which are found in some two dozen laboratories. Our facility has been principally batch-oriented, although we have some 80 or 90 interactive terminals located on campus.

To provide for student usage we have in the past couple of years made available our so-called "super-batch" system. This consists of running several special classes which run: SATFIV, PL/C, ASSEMBLER G, SPITBOL (SNOBOL), and WATBOL (COBOL). Every fifteen minutes all jobs of any of these classes are taken in from the job queue and the corresponding in-core compiler run for all jobs of that class. With such a system, our turn-around time for the most popular, SATFIV, is about eight minutes. With handling, the effective turn-around varies from a half-hour to an hour. We run about 600 to 1,000 jobs in the SATFIV class in typical recent days, with peaks up to 1,500 jobs in a day!

Yet with this service we estimate that no more than 20% of our classes make use of the computer for instructional purposes. Is this low percentage due just to the fact that we are batch oriented? Probably not. Believing this, we have mounted a strong educational effort to induce faculty members to see the value of computing as a supplement to instruction.

However, as a result of the study[3] made by Weingarten, Nielsen, Whitely and myself on Regional Computer Networks, I have become more than a little convinced that the mode of computing *does* affect the quantity and perhaps the quality of instructional computing. In particular, our observations at Dartmouth, a university of some 3,500 students, showed that in their peak months some 1,700 students logged on the computer, and that in the total year, just over 3,000 students logged on. Clearly a great number of parameters can cause such a significant involvement of students with the computer, but equally clearly the omnipresence of time-sharing terminals on that campus must be a contributing factor. Moreover, with a broad variety of languages available, BASIC represents 90% of the usage.

At Iowa, then, we are in the process of rethinking our computer delivery system. For the past three years, we have had collegiate computer fund allocations, which in turn were parceled out to departments, and from there to individual courses and instructors. Yet, there has been no convenient way to parcel those funds out to the student, for whom lest we forget, the university exists. The system is fiscally satisfactory, but it in no way contributes to the instructional use of computing.

We have concluded, for a large number of reasons, to back off and start over. Our principal new tenets are:

[3]Weingarten et al. (1973).

1 Instructional computing implies time-sharing conversational computing.

2 Instructional computing should be *free* to the student.

3 A single simple language, BASIC, will handle the bulk of the instructional need.

From our study, mentioned earlier, we are able to conclude that six teletype terminals can serve 250 students who receive one assignment per week requiring the use of the computer. Applying this logic to the University of Iowa with 20,000 students, and aiming for eventual 50% student utilization, it follows that a minimum of 240 terminals are required if we are to stimulate an instructional computer revolution. As a matter of fact, we are prepared to think in terms of an ultimate thousand terminals on campus.

How can such massive computing be provided in these parlous times? We are first of all convinced that if there is a large computer which has the potential of supporting 250 to a thousand terminals that we would have no chance of finding the capital to acquire it. Moreover, after surveying the field, we doubt that such a system exists. But we have observed the mini-computer market and how it grows: faster, more capable, and cheaper as the days go by.

Leaving lots of arguments un-argued, and hosts of meetings undescribed, we at Iowa have decided to attack instructional computing by way of distributed computing. We intend to place on our campus ten, twenty, or more mini-computers, *all* interfaced to our central computer, the IBM 360/65, or whatever we eventually replace it by, to present more conversational programming capability to our students. The bulk of the student time-sharing load will be handled by the mini-system itself. We intend to accompany this with a strong effort to train our faculty in the use of such equipment.

At present we have two HP 2000F mini-computers on campus, and within a few weeks we will have the third one. Since last spring, we will have increased the number of terminals available to our students from zero to 96 in the very near future.

Two details should be mentioned: We are conducting a tightly-controlled experiment on the first installations. Sixteen terminals are in the College of Business Administration; eight each in Education and the Social Sciences. The Business College has an enrollment of about 800, hence, we believe that that college is nearly computer saturated. How this college works out is crucial to continued development. We hope to place 32 terminals in Statistics for use in consolidation of our some two dozen introductory courses in Statistics. And sixteen will go to Dentistry, with sixteen remaining to be assigned.

The physical arrangement is that the mini's are all located in our new computer building in our new computer room. The HP 2000F's are connected to the 360. Our intentions are to use the connections to provide file back up, RJE into our batch system, and access to the time-sharing system of the 360 (Weeg, 1973, pp. 1–4).

This extensive quotation from Weeg points up the continuing evolution of computer technology, an evolution that suggests more options are open to us now. In addition it highlights the importance of the *delivery mechanism,* the kind of computer power, that is used. To be positioned in the wrong cell of the matrix in Figure 4-10 may result in much greater expense, or little usage.

Summary   In this chapter we have very briefly looked at the components and major configurations of computer systems and extrapolated a cost-effectiveness trend into the future. For the reader who is interested in furthering his knowledge of computer systems or his knowledge of probable trends, there are many excellent references (some of which have been cited). Moving onward from the major point *that computers are going to become increasingly cost effective as a mechanism to assist the learning process,* we now turn to a description of the most significant current uses of computer systems in the education process.

5. Computer Technology in Higher Education — Courseware

In Chapter 4 we discussed the state of the art in hardware and the related software. This chapter deals with what has been termed *courseware*—the systems that deal directly with the subject being taught. Courseware has traditionally referred to computer uses in teaching, generally to the combination of computer programs and subject matter content. The use of the computer in education is often termed computer-assisted instruction (CAI). Its counterpart, computer-managed instruction (CMI), refers to the uses of computers to assist in the management of instruction. In this chapter we develop a taxonomy of the uses of computers in education and give some examples of activities in each area.

Technology in education does, of course, go far beyond the use of computers; hence courseware could be interpreted as the combination of any technology with the subject matter. As explained earlier, we are concentrating on computer technology as the most recent and perhaps the most poorly understood technology, but as the one that may well have the most potential.

Even though we do not focus on it in this report, perhaps the most fundamental "technology" that can assist the learning process is not computers, but the method or process by which we identify learning objectives and understand how to structure the material in light of these objectives. The basic reexamination of the subjects being taught and the way to organize their available content to enhance learning and to capitalize on the instructional technology is a poorly understood subject. We have little theory and not much experience from which to build theory.

However, this basic "technology" of breaking the material

down into components and reorganizing it for learning reinforcement has been exploited successfully in a number of cases. For example, the Behavioral Research Labs have had at least one successful application in a school system in California. Their approach has been to go back to the basic learning objectives and the material, and to organize it in small modules that are then presented in an individually programmed, self-study instruction format. There is no hardware technology, such as computers or teaching machines, as the material is presented to the students in paper-and-pencil format. Nonetheless there is a considerable amount of "technology" in preparing the material and organizing it in an appropriate way. A second example of this very important "technology" (or process) of structuring material and learning aids to assist the learning process is one of our own efforts noted in Appendix B.

In the chapters that follow, we discuss the advantages that computer technology provides in an educational setting. It is important to recognize at this time, however, that "technology" can be construed in many ways and that the work of such groups as the Behavioral Research Labs is an example of an application of technology to education.

For our purposes in this chapter the term *courseware* does not include this kind of activity. For the reasons we discussed in Chapter 1 we shall continue to focus on the application of that technology with the highest potential impact on higher education, computer technology. In this context, then, the term *courseware* applies to those instructions and materials that deal with content of the subject being taught.

Within this focus on computer courseware there is a further distinction between instruction *about* the computer and instruction *with* the computer. Instruction about the computer covers the activities in institutions of higher education that focus on teaching the student what a computer is and how he can use it. Instruction with a computer focuses on using computer technology to present materials directly to the student or as support in managing the learning process. Both these topics have a very high potential impact on higher education.

There has been considerable work and discussion on the progress to date in teaching students about the computer. In Chapter 4 we spent some time identifying the conclusions of the most recent major study on this topic (Levien, 1972). This study is both current and thorough, so we make no attempt to reproduce its findings here. Our concern in the following section is with instruction *with computers*. First, the different pedagogic ways that computers can be used are defined, and second, some representative examples showing these pedagogic approaches in action are given.

Although instruction about computers and instruction with computers are both likely to have an impact on the higher educational system, instruction with computers holds the greater promise in terms of impact and increasing effectiveness in the higher educational sphere. The logic behind this argument is developed in Chapters 6 and 7. It should be made clear, however, that the *dominant* instructional use of computers in higher education until very recently has been concerned with instruction about the computer, not instruction with the computer.

TAXONOMY OF COURSEWARE   The basic split in the use of computers in higher education is between teaching about computers and teaching with them. Instruction about computers focuses directly on the computer as a subject of instruction. The courses can be divided into rough categories, those for specialists, that is, people who will go on to design and work with computers directly, and those for individuals who are interested in using the computer as a tool to help them in their own special area of study.

The specialist courses deal directly with the training of computer specialists; this is done either in a department of computer science or in courses in data processing. Particularly in community colleges, courses are offered that train the student in the design and operation of computer systems for standard business applications. The computer science graduates, however, become either hardware designers or specialists in the various kinds of software that must be provided if computers are to be used effectively. The computer science programs, then, provide courses in the theory and practice of computation in both its hardware and software forms.

For those students interested in using computers in their fields of specialty a variety of courses have been developed in computer programming and computer applications. These courses run from simple one-semester courses in FORTRAN or PL1 programming to interrelated sets of courses that teach not only the basics of programming but how to use a variety of special-purpose languages for particular fields. In some universities with a strong engineering and science background, the various departments themselves have taken over the role of the specialist training. It is common in business schools, for example, to teach computer programming to provide background necessary for the business school student to be able to understand the work with computers in business application. Other courses are run by departments of mechanical engineering and political science and, in fact, in almost all fields in an attempt to provide familiarity with the computer.

Instruction with Computer Support

The notion of computer-based *support* for learning is very different from relying primarily on the computer—that is, on the computer as a replacement for the instructor in a given subject area. Any attempt to design an instructional process consisting solely of computer-based instruction is bound to be either inadequate or extraordinarily expensive. All the evidence of usage to date makes this quite clear. Using the computer in a support mode, however, places a premium on thinking through the role of the computer and the type of pedagogy to be used. This "system" planning is fundamental to successful use of computers in all fields; education is no exception.

With this perspective in mind the use of computer support in instruction is illustrated in Figure 5-1. Nothing in this figure is new; all the terms are used in the literature. However, this field is characterized by much terminological confusion, and any evaluation of the field can only take place after careful definition of terms. One widely available early source of information on the use of computers and instruction was the Entelek, Inc., surveys on computer-assisted instruction (see, for example, Hickey & Newton, 1967). In these surveys Entelek adopted the use of four major classes of instructional strategy: tutorial, socratic, game, and learner-controlled. The tutorial classification was further broken down into linear, intrinsic, and adaptive. Carl Zinn (1970) produced one of the most extensive classification projects (Project CLUE), and the categories he used also fit nicely under the major headings used here.

Primary uses in instruction   We focus in this chapter on learning *with* computer support. The other two distinct categories noted

FIGURE 5-1 Taxonomy of computers in instruction

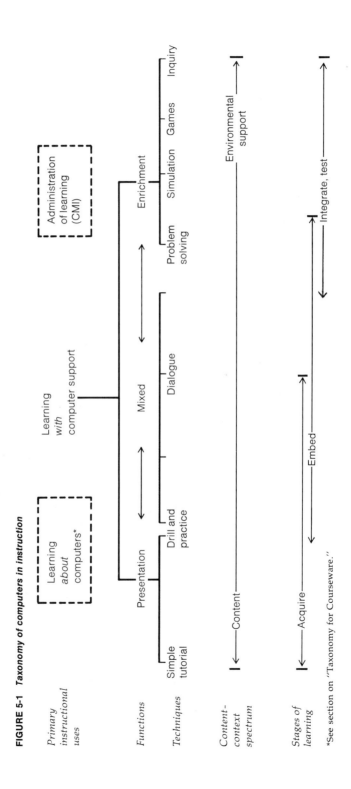

81

at the top of Figure 5-1 are learning *about* computers and the use of computers to help *manage* the instructional process, whether by the students themselves, the faculty, or the administration. Where there are large numbers of students, there has been some feeling that keeping track of the individual student's progress is difficult and that the ability of the computer to act as a record-keeping mechanism should be employed. Similarly, computer systems have been used to provide guidance directly to the student on what he should do next, what is available in the way of courses, and so forth. Although this area may well have potential, it is not of direct concern here in discussing the impact of computers on learning as its effect is clearly secondary. We do not explore it further in this report simply due to our limited focus.

Functions   The taxonomy we have used has a basic emphasis on the extremes of content and context. The distinction between *presentation* and *enrichment* highlights the difference between the use of computers to directly teach the *content* of the materials being studied and the use of computers to support the *environment* in which the student works. This distinction is shown as a continuum, as, for example, when the student uses a computer to work on problems of realistic complexity. It is difficult to classify such use in terms of content or environment. His environment has been enriched because the problem can be realistically complex rather than pedagogically simple, but by the same token the content of what he is learning has been somewhat affected. Nevertheless, this basic distinction— between computers directly affecting the content of what is being taught and their providing a richer environment in which the student can learn—is important. It is important in part because there is much less disagreement and much clearer evidence that the use of the computer in an enriching sense is already a powerful supporting device for the learning process, whereas the evidence on the future use of computers directly in teaching the substantive content of a given field is less clear. While we believe there is potential in the substantive area, it is quite clear that there is *no* overwhelming evidence in favor of the efforts that have been made to date. The middle segment (entitled *Mixed*) fits midway between the poles of *presentation* and *enrichment* and, as will be noted, shares some characteristics, and some techniques, of each. Efforts have been—and will be—made to combine presentation and enrichment, but, in general, work tends to be at one end or the other of this spectrum.

Techniques   Seven techniques (or modes of computer use to aid learning) are discussed in the remainder of this chapter. For each of these, we attempt, in its section, to give the flair of the *pioneering work* that was done—and a historical sense of the technique as well as the *fundamental concepts* involved. We wind up with some *current examples* of the use of each technique—examples that tend to show good, usually "battle-tested" applications of the fundamental concepts involved in the area.

We carry forward six of these techniques to the rest of the book. The seventh, dialogue, although conceptually different, has been not overly utilized in its originally conceived form and has been blended with other forms where used. Therefore it does not appear again after this chapter.

Spectrum   The first of the two rows at the bottom of Figure 5-1 indicates the *content-context spectrum* previously discussed. The second ties the seven techniques of computer-assisted learning to the four *stages of learning* presented in Chapter 2. It should be noticed that some tools can be utilized in more than one stage of the learning cycle.

PRESENTATION   The most basic area of confusion in terminology surrounds the term "computer-aided instruction" (CAI). Often used to mean presentation, it is defined differently throughout the literature. Rather than attempt yet another definition we have avoided the use of the term altogether! Within the presentation category we find *drill and practice* and *tutorial*. There seems to be general agreement in the literature on what these terms cover. Our understanding is:

Tutorial
Presentation of material to the student for the *first time*. Primary focus is on the student's acquisition of new facts and concepts.

Drill and Practice
A reinforcement of previously acquired concepts. Permits practice and allows the user to gain familiarity and competence with the material.

In both cases the level of sophistication can vary enormously. Although the underlying control of either process lies firmly in the (absent) hands of the author, the pace of presentation, type of branching, and level of feedback can vary from primitive to very flexible. Examples of this range are given in the material that follows.

As noted in Chapter 2, the development of presentation-oriented computer tools is based essentially on a Skinnerian learning model. The methods utilized are based on the virtues of repetitive reinforcement, establishing habitual response, and so forth.

Simple Tutorial The tutorial mode is one of the earliest and basic uses of computers in the instructional process. Indeed to many people the term "computer-assisted instruction" is used synonymously with "tutorial." This type of use implies a series of four steps in the teaching of any given concept:

1 Stating the item of knowledge that is to be taught.

2 Clarifying and elaborating the item in a series of sentences.

3 Restating the item to improve understanding. (This step is often done by having the student work out a particular problem or fill in some missing words in a definition to establish that he understands the concept.)

4 Making a transition to the next concept or item to be taught.

This simple four-step model of the learning process can be implemented in a variety of ways. One early method was to use pencil and paper and lay out the material in a series of steps. An early use of the computer was as an automatic page-turning device that merely reproduced what was on the printed page. Over time the computer's strength of logical branching was employed. Thus, for example, the computer could "read" a response to a question, evaluate that response, and branch the student to the appropriate next material. The ability to branch to an appropriate set of material depending upon the student's current state of knowledge is an ability that is uniquely provided by the logical capability of computers and cannot easily be provided another way. However, the technical problems involved in getting computers to understand student responses in an unambiguous way, coupled with lack of knowledge on the part of the researchers and the generally expensive and limited computers that were available, resulted in relatively few systems in the tutorial area that had sophisticated branching methods. For example, to have the computer branch to an appropriate set of materials, the author must have been clever enough to put in sufficient remedial material to cover the large number of alternatives that might arise. Although the technical requirements are now largely met, realistically no author can possibly predict all the kinds of responses that students are likely to make. This limitation restricts the student to the logic of the author.

For any author-controlled pedagogic techniques, there is the basic limitation of prediction. Author-controlled material, then, can only be expected to work when the subject matter is very well understood, well structured, and relatively simple. Under these conditions, it is possible to classify student responses into broad types and therefore to provide in the computer the kinds of materials that the students might find useful. As soon as the material becomes less structured, however, these author-controlled techniques become inappropriate.

The tutorial approach, whether simple or complex, is designed to largely replace the teacher in presenting facts. The point of a computer at this level is to provide a simple, straightforward, and individualized approach. It is intended, at least in part, to relieve the teacher of a considerable burden and at the same time take a substantial step toward providing practice work. Thus it can free a sizable amount of the teacher's time for other types of interaction with students.

Drill and Practice

The second major type of presentation system, also largely author-controlled, is commonly termed *drill and practice*. In drill-and-practice systems the aim is to take over the main responsibility for developing the student's skill in the use of a given concept. This involves leading the student through a series of examples where he can practice the material he has already learned or can have it repeated for him. The assumption with a drill-and-practice system is that the student has already had the concept presented to him, that the material has been seen before, and the purpose now is to gain familiarity and develop some dexterity with the ideas.

As with the tutorial method, the degree of sophistication can be great or little. In addition, drill and practice can reinforce recently presented material (presentation) or allow the learner to selectively recall and review previously presented material. As can be seen in Figure 5-1, it belongs in both the presentation and mixed categories.

These two pedagogic approaches account for almost all the early CAI uses of computers in higher education. Three examples are discussed below. These examples are representative of the work in the use of computers for structured author-control applications. In this report we do not provide an exhaustive listing or a careful detailed description of these various projects. To do so would be to merely duplicate the extensive work done by Zinn (1970) in his Project CLUE document and Levien (1972). The three projects below are representative examples of the work in this field and provide contrast to the material described later. It must be stressed that these projects are representative and are included only to provide some sense of where we stand in the tutorial and drill-and-practice areas. It is interesting to observe the small amount of attention that is paid to the evaluation of the projects. In general, a great many of the studies cited in the bibliography almost completely lack any form of cost-benefit study. Much of the work has been government-funded and has not had to face the test of operational viability. In reading these three examples, it is useful to keep the evaluation question in mind.

Stanford project

A Stanford group, at the Institute for Mathematical Studies in the Social Sciences at Stanford University, has been working on the problem of computer-aided instruction since 1963. Under the direction of Richard Atkinson and Patrick Suppes, the project has been funded at various stages by the Carnegie Foundation, the National Science Foundation, and the U.S. Office of Education. The group has one of the largest and longest-running collections of programs in the CAI field.

The basic goal of the project, originally conceived of as a computer-based laboratory in teaching and learning, has been to carry out a series of experiments in order to find out about processes of concept formation in students, including investigating such things as the optimal block length of items to be learned for any given student. The project is attempting to develop theories of learning that can be used as a base for the development of computer-assisted instruction programs of increasing complexity. The work thus far has concentrated on the drill-and-practice and tutorial modes. Most recently the team has deemphasized the development of operational programs and is concentrating on basic research in areas such as concept formation. The largest percentage of its time and effort has gone into the development of courses at the high school and primary school levels. The project has developed courses in mathematics, logic, algebra, and elementary reading. However, it has also developed a program to teach Russian, which has been used as an introductory part of a two-semester course at Stanford University.

This Russian language program was funded by the United States government for several years at a rate of approximately $100,000 per year. A 1969 evaluation of this program made the following points: "In an audio visual Russian course for college students, CAI students perform significantly better than the control students on final examinations for two of the three academic quarters for the first year course" (Suppes & Morningstar, 1969). During the second quarter the experimental students performed slightly better on the midterm, but their performance was significantly superior on the final. In addition to these "objective" scores on the examinations, the authors also noted the following advantages of using CAI in teaching foreign languages at the university level by this method. "To keep pace with the programmed exercises, the student must concentrate more directly on the language and not return to an internal monologue in English. The concentration required at a computer-based terminal precludes the student's attention from wandering and achieves a degree of efficiency which would be difficult to match in the best organized classroom" (ibid., p. 53).

The report goes on to point out that in many foreign languages—for example, Russian, Japanese, and Chinese—there is a shortage of qualified teachers. Therefore this method not only provides better performance in learning the language but also offers a solution to the problem of the shortage of trained staff. The third benefit the report quotes deals with the motivation of students in the CAI group, which was higher than that in the control group. The drop-out rate in the experimental group was significantly lower, and a number of students voluntarily switched to the CAI group from the control group. About 30 percent of the control group completed the course compared with over 70 percent of the experimental group. This may well be explained by a "Hawthorne effect";[1] nonetheless, there seems to be some motivational impact in using computer-based drill and practice for aspects of certain subjects.

The data that led the authors to these conclusions contain some ambiguities (such as the control group and CAI group receiving different exams on some occasions, and so forth), but the report does indicate that for certain parts of the task of learning a foreign language, the drill-and-practice and tutorial modes of computer-aided instruction can be helpful. The Stanford group did not choose to continue its efforts in this area, however, and there has been little in the way of published results following this 1969 report.

Florida State University

A second well-known, visible case where a great deal of money has been spent in drill-and-practice and tutorial development is at the Florida State University. The CAI Center there received federal funding for a number of years and has developed a wide series of tutorial and drill-and-practice systems on its IBM 1500 computer. The introductory physics and chemistry courses have attracted the most attention, although there are a wide variety of other units in topics such as statistics, educational psychology, engineering design, and so forth.

To provide some perspective on the kind of research and the sort of results that represent the best of current practice of this type in the field, the conclusions and summary of a Florida State University publication describing the physics course are reproduced.[2] This project represents a major effort where substantial sums of money have been spent. The principal investigators have put together a technological package for their physics

[1]"Hawthorne effect" refers to an improvement in a subject's performance that can be attributed to the subject's heightened sense of importance resulting from the care and interest of the experimentor.

[2]The Florida State University Technical Report *Research and Implementation of a Collegiate Instruction of Physics via Computer-Assisted Instruction* (Hansen, Dick, & Lippert, 1968).

course that includes film, audio, and computer-based material. This mix of media is not often found and shows imagination in design that could have interesting implications. However, the data collected do not provide enough evidence to establish the impact, if any, of the computer components. In addition the mix of technological support is expensive, as described in the investigators' annual reports. A further indication of the difficulty of effective drill-and-practice use is the almost complete lack of any new developments of this type at the center. The 1972 annual report indicates no new operation developments under way and a relegation of the physics course material to a "voluntary review status" basis.

The three annual reports quoted here represent a lot of work and present interesting findings. They do suggest, however, that author-controlled material, particularly simple tutorial, has only limited abilities to support the learning process in higher education.

The Florida State University CAI physics course utilized a wide variety of media approaches rather than restricting the informational presentation to the terminal devices (cathode-ray tube, light pen, and keyboard) of the 1500 CAI system. The additional media were: textbooks, audio lectures, and notes, concept film loops, and PSSC films.

The CAI physics course followed the same general outline as the companion course taught by lecture. The CAI students were allowed to schedule their own time at the CAI Center. At the Center, their progress was directed by a computer terminal. Problems and instructions to the student were displayed on the cathode-ray tube (CRT). The student could indicate his response to the computer by typing his answer on the keyboard or by touching a light pen to the appropriate location on the CRT.

A typical lesson in the course began with the student reporting to the computer terminal and taking a short quiz based upon a reading assignment. If the student did not pass the quiz, he was instructed to reread the material and return to take the quiz again. If he was successful, the student was directed to listen to a short audio lecture on the major topic of the lesson. A special cartridge system provided the audio lecture for the student at his terminal. The student was also provided with an outline which included helpful drawings relevant to the lecture. After completing the lecture, the student would be quizzed via the terminal on the audio presentation. The student would then be directed to a single concept film loop or a PSSC film. The single concept film loop presented demonstrations of some of the major concepts included in the lesson. Outlines were also available for the film loops. If the student was directed to view a PSSC film, he would notify a proctor who in turn would operate the film projector. The student then returned to his terminal to take a short quiz on the film. Based upon the lesson content, the student might be directed to other presentations on various media. At the completion of the entire sequence on instruction, the student was given certain review problems via the CRT, and then was given his next textbook assignment.

Special mid-term and final examination reviews were available on another computer system, the IBM 1440. This system consisted of only a typewriter terminal and therefore the student-computer dialogue was typed. This system had the advantage that it provided the student with a print-out of his review. Students from the lecture courses also were allowed to use this computer review. Two sets of paper and pencil practice homework problems were also assigned, one before each examination.

(i) CAI Physics Problem Exercises

When considering the most efficient method of developing an autonomous computer-based course which was to be based upon the structure of an on-going instructional program, the decision was made to first develop those parts of the physics course which could contribute to the understanding of entry performance levels of the student and to the development of appropriate behavioral objectives. The physics problem exercise course involved the development and field evaluation of physics review material, problem exercises, and prototype exam questions to complement the existing lecture series. The review sections represented a parsimonious statement of the central propositions found within the four major content areas of the introductory physics course. In the conventional course, the students are required to identify important definitions and relational statements. The problem sections of the CAI physics problem exercise course were programmed in a form analogous to the problems given as homework assignments. The sample test questions were essentially parallel test items to those found in the hourly and final examinations in the course.

The basic strategy in developing these CAI physics problem exercises was to establish a baseline by which it could be determined whether future curricular developments were really improvements. Consequently, these review and problem sessions provided naturalistic, baseline data by which to judge whether the total course, which includes the complete presentations of all the topics, is equivalent or superior to conventional instruction.

In addition to providing baseline data, the field study of the CAI problem exercises conducted in the fall term, 1966, and the winter term, 1967, established the usefulness of the CAI instructional approach as evidenced by the steadily increasing voluntary participation. Moreover, it provided a set of problem exercises that were revised for inclusion in the full autonomous course, and it helped to identify those particular learning problems that the full course would have to face.

This experience with the FSU students indicated the feasibility of a computer-based course. The merits of approximating a course via this strategy is recommended to other CAI R-and-D projects. Moreover, the positive outcomes suggest the desirability of having this kind of CAI application available for any number of collegiate courses.

(ii) Field Studies

The fall 1967 field study was implemented with 23 students in the autonomous CAI group, a matched group of students taking the conventional physics course and a matched group receiving the conventional lectures plus review questions on the 1440 system.

The learning outcomes as reflected in the final grade assignments for the three groups indicated that the autonomous CAI group was statistically superior to the other two groups, but the differences between the partial CAI and the conventional students were not significant. The high proportion of A grades found in the autonomous CAI group represents one of the few instances in which the upper half of a score distribution shifted under CAI.

The mean length of time required by the CAI students for completion of the course was 10.9 weeks in the 11 week term. However, the mean time required to complete the 29 lessons for the autonomous CAI group was 23.8 hours of instruction. This represents a 17% savings in instructional time.

The CAI lesson material was categorized into three types of instruction (assessment of textbook reading, assessment of film presentations and conceptual assessment via CAI problem presentations). Comparison of performance on various topics in the lesson materials with the prior baseline data previously collected showed that the performance on the textbook assessment and the conceptual problem exercises were markedly constant. However, the conventional course performance was marked by a gradual decrease in achievement as the conceptual complexity of the physics topics is judged to be increasing. In addition, the CAI conceptual problem scores yielded a significantly higher multiple correlation with the examination scores.

In considering the empirical outcomes from this first field test, the substantial, multiple-correlation relationship between the CAI conceptual exercise material and the examination scores that lead to the grade outcomes was most encouraging. A class of linear models is currently under investigation that, hopefully, will provide each student with realistic probability statements about course mastery. If the values become too low, additional practice on a concept will undoubtedly be prescribed. Otherwise, the student will be allowed to self-define his level of course proficiency. The element of student self-commitment may represent a more viable pathway to optimizing the terminal outcomes for an individualized course of instruction.

(iii) Spring Term, 1968

During the winter quarter, 1968, the entire course was reviewed in light of the student performance data, student attitudes about the course, and the logistical problems which had been encountered during the fall 1967 field test of CAI physics. In addition, a battery of cognitive and affective tests were selected to be administered in an attempt to understand the relationship of prior knowledge and entering aptitudes to success in the CAI course.

The performance of the CAI autonomous group (37 subjects) was compared to the performance of the subjects attending only the conventional lectures and to that of subjects attending both the conventional lectures and a four-hour examination review on the 1440 CAI system. Although there was no significant difference in the test performance of the CAI group in comparison to either of the other groups, the CAI did show a learning time savings of approximately 12 percent.

Analysis of student performance on within-course measures indicated stability across and within lessons with the exception of the film quizzes. An anxiety measure was not generally correlated with within-course performance. The multiple R for predicting final grades in course, using the 10 best background and within-course measures, was .86.

The post-course interview data reflected a generally positive attitude on the part of the students. The course organization was highly satisfactory and none of the course concepts were judged to be unduly difficult. About half of the students preferred the 1500 CRT system, 27 percent preferred the 1440 typewriter system, and 23 percent had no preference.

(iv) Fall, 1968

Given the overall success of the CAI physics course as evidenced by the fall 1967 and spring 1968 field studies, this study was concerned with two basic questions: (1) Are particular individuals better suited to a specific media due to their particular interests or personality characteristics? and, (2) What is the effect of augmenting a basic media presentation with student enriched discussions?

Twenty-two student volunteers who participated in a year-long Freshman Learning Experience (FLEX) were used in the study. The FLEX program replaced the standard class meetings with less formal and more flexible arrangement of student-instructor interaction.

The CAI media course used in this study was not the complete autonomous course heretofore described. This project utilized a modified version of the CAI course from which all reading assignments and some film and CAI materials were deleted in order to provide about two-thirds of the normal course load. In this context, the instructional aim of the CAI media program was to enable these students to acquire the basic physics knowledge from the CAI media course in no more than two-thirds of the time that they had available for physics, i.e., using no more than two of the three contact hours per week which were assigned. A classroom meeting used the remaining hour for presentation of additional enrichment material of value to these non-science majors. Therefore, the physics instruction which the FLEX students received was in two major parts:

1 Students received the 29 lessons available on the 1500 CAI/media system which constituted the "basic objectives" of the P107 course.

2 In addition, students received instruction for one hour per week with a physics professor in a recitation session.

In this way, the project provided a means of investigating both the possible student by instructional treatment interaction as well as the CAI/media augmented by recitation sessions.

Comparison of the performance of the CAI FLEX group with the performance of 22 subjects taking the conventional physics course showed *no significant differences*[3] between the groups on final grade achievement or performance on the traditional examination. This outcome is based upon a comparison of a control group with those students in the FLEX group who had finished all 29 lessons of the CAI/media course.

It was found that there were individual characteristics which correlated with academic success that were common to both the traditional and CAI/media modes of instruction in Introductory Physics. However, the more striking results suggest that generally speaking, persons who are slightly less mature in their academic style, who are more sensitive and esthetic, and who are not scientifically oriented, have a higher probability of success if they take their physics instruction via the CAI/media course. On the other hand, persons who are somewhat autonomous, independent thinkers, who have scientific interests and have a mature scientifically-oriented method of inquiry will have a greater chance of success if they take the traditional mode of physics instruction.

In terms of cost-benefit analyses of the CAI physics course, the

[3]Emphasis added.

developmental costs of this CAI R-and-D project absorb approximately 95% of expenditures in comparison with instructional costs. A significant percentage (26%) are required for computer systems programs not furnished by the manufacturer. It is recommended that computer manufacturers extend this software package provided with a CAI system to include a data analysis and management system. As to instructional costs for preparation, it was found that a typical hour of CAI learning materials cost $2,420 to create and cost $5,280 after extensive field testing and revision. The revision process cost for an hour of CAI materials was estimated at $2,860.

Least cost analyses indicated that CAI has both decreasing instructional operating and depreciation cost. It was estimated that within six years CAI will be more economical than conventional instruction although it is currently less advantageous. Cost benefit analyses indicated that the improved learning effectiveness of CAI allows for a two order of magnitude decrease in loss risk as compared with cost comparisons.

This extensive quotation presenting the Florida State University experience is intended to provide a feel for the kind of research results that have been reported. The impact of CAI systems has been hard to measure, and there have been no clear-cut successes of the use of tutorial and drill-and-practice instructional methodologies at the college level. At the time of writing this report, there exist no published results that unambiguously establish a positive impact of drill-and-practice and tutorial modes.

A more recent project at Florida State University is the COMPUCHEM, a program designed to provide computer-assisted instruction in chemistry. Results from this program (see Florida State University CAI Center Annual Progress Report, January 1, 1971–December 31, 1971) differ in detail from the ones reported above for the physics course, but the general tone and conclusions remain the same.

As a final note, the 1972 annual report contains no new work in learning-process support on this campus. That is, the center is engaging in basic research on aspects of the learning process and is not engaged in attempts to deliver or develop new learning systems. As at Stanford, it has turned to focus on some of the basic issues concerning the learning process. Although this is clearly a necessary thing to do, and may well be the direction in which FSU should move, it raises the question of who is tackling the extensive research required to get technology used effectively. This is raised later on in this report, but apart from the University of Illinois and the TICCIT project there seems to be less than the necessary amount of active experimentation under way at this point.

PLATO

The third example involving the extensive use of the tutorial and drill-and-practice modes of instruction is that of the PLATO project at the University of Illinois. The PLATO program began about 1960. One of the basic premises of the program was that the technologies of the sixties were not capable of providing a significant, economically practical contribution to education. "The goals for PLATO have, therefore, been twofold.[4] First, to investigate the potential role of the computer in the instructional process; second, to design an economically and educationally viable system incorporating the most valuable approaches to teaching and learning developed in the investigation" (Zinn, 1970, p. 40). That is, the goals of the project have been both to develop material that demonstrates the role of the computer in the instructional process and to worry about the engineering and technical problems of developing a computer system that can meet the needs of education at a reasonable cost.

There has been extensive work invested in the PLATO system, and the current system, PLATO IV, has evolved over the last 10 or 11 years.

During the past 9 years, three systems (PLATO I, II, III) were designed and built, each embodying improvements indicated by the previous system; a network of four associated demonstration centers was added early in 1969. Exploratory educational efforts with PLATO systems have now involved experiments in at least 20 fields of study and over 100,000 student contact hours at all levels. PLATO I and II stimulated research and development leading to the broader capabilities of PLATO III which was designed for optimum educational versatility without specific concern for costs. PLATO III, in use since 1964, has provided opportunities to develop many powerful new teaching strategies in various diverse fields (ibid.).

[4]For further details, see Alpert & Bitzer (1970).

As of summer 1972, more than 154,000 student contact hours had been logged on the PLATO system (*PLATO*, 1972). PLATO IV went into operation during 1972 featuring a PLATO IV terminal that utilizes an 8½-inch square glass plasma panel.

Thus the major research activity at PLATO is directed toward developing instructional tools, both hardware and software, which meet at least the following two criteria: first, that the operating cost of the tools be less than the nontechnological method they replace, and second, that they be designed for the teaching function they are intended to serve. The basic instructional programming language TUTOR has been developed to be used in a variety of disciplines by the regular university instructors. In addition, the project has developed and built an inexpensive visual display terminal that is projected to cost less than $500 and that will include an audio storage facility, visual information storage, and a plasma display panel with an inherent memory. Prototypes of this terminal have been built and demonstrated.

On the basis of results so far, Alpert & Bitzer (1970) anticipate that it will be possible to expand PLATO to a 4,000-terminal system using a CDC 6600 computer. This would imply a population of well over 20,000 students. They propose a scheme to use a 4.5 Mhz TV channel at $35/month per mile, instead of the individual 3Khz telephone lines at $3.50/month per mile for each console. Each TV channel could handle at least 1,500 terminals on a time-shared basis, each terminal receiving 1,200 bits per second. This means that for a tenfold increase in cost, the channel capacity of the communication line can be increased 1,500 times. As planned, the future system will involve centralizing the location of the computer and running the terminals in clusters at any geographic distance.

Technology has changed sufficiently over the last three years that it is no longer obvious that the PLATO strategy of a large central machine is most effective. Minicomputers provide a cheaper alternative under *some* conditions, and they seem likely to appeal to the decentralization tendencies of a university (see, for example, Weeg, 1973).

The project has been careful to maintain an attitude of openness and flexibility toward the kinds of instructional methodology it will support. In practice so far the vast majority of the programs that run on the PLATO system have been pro-grammed in the language called TUTOR. A lesson in TUTOR consists of textual information, associated visual displays and diagrams, and questions and answers. Most of the answers to the questions are prestored, and the student's response is matched with the stored answer or answers. TUTOR allows the teacher to write commands that can accommodate misspelled answers and permit branching in the case of wrong answers. The student is allowed to seek additional help by punching in the appropriate command, and if the teacher has provided for such a request, the system will respond appropriately. Assigned operations allow the student to be branched selec-tively depending on his last response.

TUTOR commands are available to allow the teacher to gather data and perform statistical analysis. This means that he can edit the course material and update it on the basis of student performance. The teacher uses the same terminal as the student to enter course material and encode or alter information stored.

Use of the TUTOR language is easy, but the resulting pro-gram is quite often relatively unsophisticated drill and practice or tutorial with elementary branching permitted.

Evaluating educational effectiveness is still difficult, since the data sample is limited. Despite the very large number of hours in which the system has been used, the data for a typical course have been limited to only several hundred hours of student instruction. Thus although improved performance of CAI stu-dents over control groups has been reported, there are not enough data points to draw solid conclusions. However, the results so far have led those involved in the project to the following two conclusions:

1 That computer-based education is a plausible approach to improved individualized instruction in a very wide array of courses or subject material areas.

2 That the nature of educational testing and evaluation requires, and will be radically affected by, the availability of large, computer-based educational systems; a valid measure of effectiveness calls for a large sample of data and a longer period of comparison than has heretofore been available (Zinn, 1970, p. 41).

It is probably fair to say that the attention of the principal investigators in the system has so far been focused on developing low-cost, viable hardware and software. There has not been a major focus on validating the educational effectiveness of the individual courses. Nonetheless, the number of student hours spent on terminals is larger by far than that of any other project in the country, and progress has been impressive.

TICCET project

A second major project in addition to PLATO is the TICCET project.[5] This is also a massively funded long-term project which grew, in part at least, from developments in minicomputers and experience at the elementary school level. Much of the initial effort has gone into developing new robust hardware, designed to reduce costs by a factor of 10 over previous computer delivery systems.

These hardware reductions are accomplished by using a normal television set with a special keyboard as the basic terminal and having a 64,000-word minicomputer with some 100 million characters of disk storage. The computer also generates audio messages. By use of the new solid-state circuitry, both physical size and cost are kept low.

The educational goals for the project are described by the project team as follows:

The primary educational goals of MITRE'S TICCET program are humanization, relevance, and individualization. In using these emotion-laden words, we have simple, specific meanings in mind.

By humanization, we mean enormously more one-to-one conversation between student and teacher. In elementary school, this is accomplished by the teacher walking around the classroom and pausing to converse with individual students. In the college environment, I would expect this might be compressed into private appointments with the instructor—say, one-half hour every three weeks.

By relevance, we have in mind not only hand-tailoring of the curriculum to the individual student, but also the result of greatly increased two-way communication with the instructor, i.e., feedback on designing overall goals of the curriculum. In my opinion, this is sorely missing from the college environment.

By individualization, we mean that each and every student pro-

[5]Much of the material for this description is drawn from Stetten (1972).

gresses in his own style, learning mode, and rate in *all* subjects during the whole day—*whether or not* he is on the computer terminal. (It is our expectation that he is not on the computer during most of the day.) The essential characteristics of individualized instruction are:

- The student learns to teach himself.

- The educational materials become learner-centered.

- The student progresses at his own rate and in his own style.

- The instructor becomes a manager and a diagnostician instead of a lecturer or a dispenser of information.

- The instructor spends most of his time in *one-to-one conversation with students rather than always standing in front of the whole class.* The students are free to move about and to talk to each other about their activities (the college-level equivalent is the virtual abolishment of scheduled lecture periods) and they spend most of their time working by themselves (Stetten, 1970, p. 36).

The costs described by the MITRE staff to accomplish these goals are:

For a school population of 1,200 students, 120 TICCET terminals would provide one hour of terminal service per day per student in a 10-hour day. Purchase price and installation of the TICCET system, amortized over an 8-year period, would be about $25,000 per year. The cost of maintenance and other incidentals, including curriculum royalties, add another $20,000 per year. Thus, the total cost for the TICCET system would be $45,000 per year, or about $40 per student per year or 20 cents per terminal hour (ibid., p. 40).

The functions that TICCET aims to provide are:

1 Administering tests.

2 Analyzing test results.

3 Prescribing remedial instruction or identifying the next step in instruction.

4 Identifying most effective paths and modes of instruction for individual students.

5 Identifying weaknesses in instructional content material and modes of instruction for feedback and course improvement.

6 Scheduling student use of instructional equipment and facilities to minimize student delay and maximize efficiency of plant utilization.

7 Maintaining student progress records in a form to optimize interface of instructors and students.

8 Presenting visual instructional frames with multiple paths to accommodate individual differences.

9 Providing speed and ease of operation, programming, and maintenance.

10 Providing student flexibility in choice of instructional material and mode within limits prescribed by the author.

11 Providing motivational aspects such as quick response, clear image, relative silence, comfortable use features, high reliability, and accessibility on demand.

12 Providing programs (instructional and machine) designed to encourage maximum student effort.

13 Providing alarm to the instructor when the computer identifies student problems (exception reporting).

Comparing TICCET to large, dedicated CAI systems, we find that the mini-computer can provide to its 100 or so users essentially the same service that the large machine provides to its thousands of users. Our experience, based on a simulation model and mathematical analysis of the small computer system, shows that TICCET can provide each of 120 students with 60,000 instructions per minute of algorithmic service, and further, that all 120 students can be working on a different lesson. From the user's standpoint, the decentralized approach also allows a simpler management implementation of the system onto the campus (ibid., p. 41).

From these quotations it is clear that TICCET should shed some light on the ability of a new hardware approach to deliver tutorial and drill-and-practice support for instruction. At the end of 1973 the project status was:

Contracts have been signed between the MITRE Corporation and two community colleges on the TICCET project. Phoenix Community College and Northern Virginia Community College have been selected and have agreed upon the contractual details for participating in the TICCET demonstration from 1974 through 1976. These two community colleges have leadership potential within the junior college movement and are cooperatively developing a detailed implementation plan with BYU and the MITRE Corporation for the test of the two 128-terminal TICCET systems. The Educational Testing Service is also cooperating in the implementation of this plan by measuring the costs and benefits of the TICCET courseware being developed in ICUE for mathematics and English composition.

Progress on all fronts, hardware, software, and courseware, has been significant in the TICCET project. The one-terminal demonstration system, which was installed in December, was replaced by a five-terminal processor, electronics package developed by MITRE. The software enables our packagers to begin inputting authored lesson material. Authors may play it back as a student would, using the primary instruction control buttons that allow the student to select his own learning tactics (Bunderson, 1974, p. 22).

The test material for the initial project is in mathematics and English and will use students from these two junior colleges. Large-scale testing has not yet begun, and it may be some time before results from this large project are visible.

The size of these projects (PLATO and TICCET) is large, and it is important to keep them in context. Professor Alfred Bork, who has been involved in the computer-assisted education field from its inception, has made a comment with which we are in entire agreement:

The two large-scale projects now using the computer for learning, with massive government support, are PLATO at the University of Illinois, and the MITRE Corporation project with courseware centered at Brigham Young University. Both are very interesting projects. To regard them as exhausting all the possibilities, however, is quite wrong. Many interesting teaching materials that exist today could *not* be run on either of these systems. I think it would be unfortunate if the success or failure of these two large projects dictated all further educational use of the computer (Bork, 1973, p. 4).

Recent illustrations

The recent literature has not been overfull with examples of successful, ongoing use of the *tutorial* mode in higher education. Suppes has noted the overwhelming tendency of commercial companies, which flocked to the business of producing tutorial materials in the late 1960s, to *get out* of the business recently (Hoffman, 1973, p. 21). The tutorial mode is being used effectively at some institutions for remedial work with slower, disadvantaged students or those who are simply behind their classmates and need to catch up (ibid., p. 22). In its remedial-learning use, it is effective. It is attention-getting, provides prodding and pacing of the student, and works well where basic facts or concepts are necessary—as in the basic English curriculum that runs at several schools, such as Baruch College of the City University of New York (CUNY).

The tutorial mode is also being used effectively in situations where rote learning is necessary. An example of this is the medical terminology course taught at Ohio State Medical School ("Colleges Plug In . . .," 1973, p. 63). But applications like this are relatively rarely implemented in higher education today if the literature and our conversations and site visits are a guide.

With regard to *drill and practice*, exactly the opposite appears to be true. Professors are increasingly utilizing the power of the computer to help embed concepts acquired through another technique. A major illustration of current use appears to be in the accounting area—where students initially learn from professors and textbooks, but then must practice the techniques in order to embed them.

Our own use of the CLOSE program (see Appendix B) is one example of current use of the drill-and-practice method. Far more widely utilized are Wilbur Pillsbury's *Computer Augmented Accounting* workbooks. They present a series of accounting-practice exercises for which the student enters "original data on keypunch cards. The computer is used to make the tedious, routine computations that usually produce little, if any, learning experience for the student" (Pillsbury, 1970, p. i). The programs journalize, post, and prepare trial balances.

At this early introduction, to minimize the details of IBM card format and keypunching, a free-form subroutine has been written for the programs. In the keypunching process the student need only leave a space between account numbers and/or amounts; the details of specific columnar punching are avoided, permitting the logic of accounting principles and procedures to be stressed (Pillsbury, 1973, Introduction).

No knowledge of computer language is necessary. Other examples of drill and practice applied to accounting abound.

The drill-and-practice area, for embedding purposes, is one

of the fastest-growing areas for computer instructional use. In mathematics, formulas and problems that formerly had to be worked through tediously by hand are being worked with at the computer by students with many of the same benefits cited by Pillsbury. In statistics, students can work with data files and actually try out the techniques they have just been taught on large data-bases—thus observing the techniques in action and ensuring that they know the factors involved in their use. In behaviorally oriented statistics courses, the SPSS system is much utilized in this regard today (Nie, Brent, & Hull, 1970).

Summary of Presentation Modes

One of the dominant characteristics of the drill-and-practice and tutorial modes as they have been implemented is the very strong degree of author control they exhibit. That is, the patterns of interaction are governed by the author when he builds the program. The student is asked to make simple responses, fill in the blanks, choose among a restricted set of alternatives, or supply a missing word or phrase. A series of alternatives will cause the program to present additional material based on the student's response. The program is very much in control, however, and the student has little or no flexibility. In the projects quoted above it is apparent that such systems can be effective on the structured, repetitive, routine kinds of material. Attempts in these and other projects to use these instructional modes for more complex judgmental material have generally been unsuccessful.

As was mentioned above, the tutorial and drill-and-practice modes of computer-based instruction are by far the most common. Practically all the money that has been spent by the government and foundations in supporting the use of computers for instruction has been spent in these two areas. According to the RAND study (see Table 5-1), 66 percent of the programs in their sample fall in these two modes. Our experience has been that although this may accurately represent the *number* of programs, the *dollar* effort that has gone into these two categories is substantially above 95 percent. There have been very few efforts, and those few have been minimally funded, in the other areas of instructional technology. These observations are substantiated by Project CLUE, perhaps the largest study of efforts in the use of computers and instruction.

TABLE 5-1
Distribution of instructional programs by instructional logic

Logic group	Programs	Percentage
Tutorial	411	46.2
Drill and practice	176	19.8
Inquiry	53	6.0
Socratic or dialogue	35	3.9
Gaming	29	3.3
Simulation	27	3.0
Problem solving	2	0.2
Testing	20	2.2
Other	49	5.5
Not stated	88	9.9

SOURCE: Levien (1972, p. 354).

In summary, the results in the drill-and-practice and tutorial modes of instruction are ambiguous at the university level. It does appear that there is evidence to support their use for structured, repetitive kinds of material, although there has yet to be a demonstrable cost-effectiveness finding that would support their use in replacing instructors at the college level. Possible misapplication of the technique vis-à-vis substantive course material, plus the general failure to do research on the impact of such systems, has resulted in a feeling of disenchantment. Little new work except in remedial learning is reported with regard to initial *presentation* of material, and no supportive evidence is available in the literature.

MIXED SYSTEMS   The second major category of computer support for the learning process is systems that have characteristics of both presentation and enrichment. In the presentation category just discussed the focus was on initial presentation and on gaining familiarity with the material through drill and practice. The essence of the systems in the mixed category is the degree to which the learner (as opposed to the author) is in control. Certain implementations of drill and practice have left a good deal of control in the users' (learners') hands, although there is an inherent limitation on flexibility, as the author has to have thought precisely of the question and content about which the learner will ask. This instructional mode implies that the teacher and developer of the instructional programs develops a set of questions and a dictionary of the most likely anticipated student answers and stores them in the system using one of several author languages based on conventional programmed instruction methods. In the interaction the system checks the student's answer in each instance and branches in a preset fashion. The obvious limitation of this method is that it depends mainly on the instructor's ability to anticipate all possible answers, interpret them in a suitable fashion, and plan the branching accordingly. Thus the appropriateness of any response from the computer system depends directly on the availability of prestored material. Even if the considerable logistics of preprogramming for all possible answers were overcome, it is unlikely that the selective methods of choice would ever allow completely adaptive conversation with the system.

With increased understanding of the technology it is becoming possible to provide more user control, letting him decide where he would like to work, which material is to be looked at, and how to proceed. This increase in learner control we have labeled *dialogue,* and although it has potential, it is purely experimental at this stage. The goal, however, is to provide disciplined review of material with the learner in command.

Apart from drill and practice and dialogue, the problem-solving mode is also part of the mixed category. Such systems provide access to problem-solving tools, and the student uses these to attack some problem and in so doing reviews the concepts and skills he has acquired. This style of operation is reviewed carefully later in this chapter.

To provide a sense of how the dialogue systems could develop, we discuss below two representative examples of work in this area. Each of these projects is indicative of the degree to which learner control can enhance the review process. Neither project is subject to continuing intensive review, IBM having largely withdrawn from the field and Professor Joseph Weizenbaum of MIT having changed his interests. Nonetheless the ideas they originally explored are being gradually assimilated in other projects and do indicate the potential that exists.

A more elaborate example of learner control, set in a practical teaching context, is provided in Appendix B. Here a variety of learning techniques are packaged to provide the mix necessary to support an entire course. In this chapter, however, we restrict ourselves to examples of work in the field to illustrate the taxonomy we are using.

Dialogue Systems

The experimental dialogue systems are intended to function like a human tutor, rather than as fact disseminators or concept reinforcers. To develop such a computer-based system, it is necessary to begin with some model of the human tutor. The tutor can be thought of as existing in a closed-loop interactive process with the student and as having a number of functions. The functions can be described by following the entry of the student and his progress through the process as follows:

Let us suppose entry is effected by means of a question directed at the student. The student perceives the question, acquires its meaning, and fits it into the context of his previous experience so that it can be processed. Ultimately he responds. The tutor receives this response and must now process it. This, in turn, leads to the tutor's selection of an appropriate response, and the process continues.

It is the tutor's generation of output, questions, and other responses that any computer-based system must duplicate. The material that follows discusses two projects of this general type. Very little work has been done with these kinds of systems, and what has taken place has been purely experimental. Little money has been spent and little experimentation conducted with students in a real teaching situation. Nonetheless these systems use the strength of the computer to achieve real intellectual stimulus for students. If computer assistance for the instructional process moves beyond supporting the very routine, well-structured material, this particular type of instructional pedagogy is likely to have a major payoff—although not in the near future.

Learner-control course in statistics

This project was carried out at the IBM educational research department in San Jose, California, under the direction of Dr. Ralph Grubb. It was one of the first attempts to provide a responsive system. The main purpose was to test the efficacy of a course in which the student has explicit control of the content and direction. As described in Dr. Grubb's report the main objectives were as follows:

1   To present instruction in such a way that the student can chart his own course through the subject matter

2   To test whether it is more effective if learners control the way instruction is presented to them than if the way of presentation is entirely controlled by the instructors

3   To investigate the "trials" through the subject matter followed by each student as the students explore the subject matter by a process of trial and error

The facility offered by this program was such that

When the student registers for the course the first display he encounters is a map of the statistics course with appropriate directions for its use. The maps consist of series of boxes connected in various ways, inscribed with topics or concepts that the student can access in order to route his way through the course. The student points his light pen at the area of the map that interests him. Immediately his screen is erased and he is confronted with a more detailed map of the subsection of the course. As he makes successive choices with the light pen he proceeds deeper into the successive levels of the course. At the lower levels of the structure he may enter on the keyboard constructed responses to questions or problems posed through the computer. If he chooses he can also point his light pen at any time to one of several target areas to the side of the screen that will return him to the previous map or main map or take him to the glossary (Grubb, 1968, p. 40).

In addition there were usually other target functions represented on the screen that would transfer the student laterally to a number of related topics in the course. Thus students could, as it were, zoom down to different parts of the map and investigate its features in detail.

General impact

This approach to instruction is unique and is certainly at a more sophisticated level than presenting the programmed instruction frames sequentially. The student had the opportunity of seeing the course as a whole, obtaining an overview at any time, and exploring the subject from different vantage points at any level. These facilities do not exist in more programmed instruction texts or corresponding CAI programs. The method is also a natural use of the information-retrieval properties of the computer. If the student wished simply to learn from the course that which was sufficient and important for his purposes, he could do so conveniently with this form of instruction.

Grubb's approach to the learning process is based on the assumption that motivation and learning efficiency are increased when the student is allowed to control his own learning. He has tried to validate this, and his results are discussed below. Figure 5-2 shows the regression of posttest scores obtained by different groups of students plotted against the students' pretest scores. Grubb states that "the results so far reveal that complete learner control (LC) within the study

FIGURE 5-2 *Regression of posttest score on pretest score for five experimental conditions*

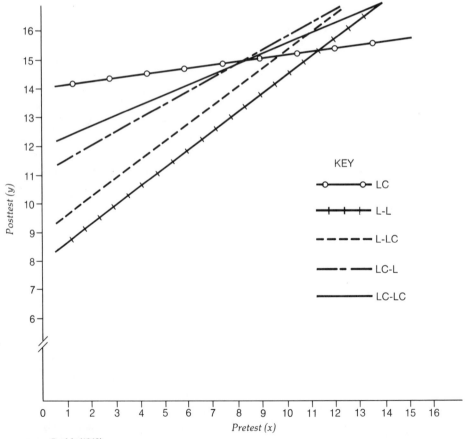

SOURCE: Grubb (1968).

parameters, on the average produced uniformly high performance over the entire range of pretest performance. Learning acquired under conditions of anything less than learner control for the study produced a posttest performance that was more heavily dependent on pretest performance" (ibid., p. 40).

The graphs imply that the best students (high pretest) did equally well in either of the two situations—learner control (LC) or non-learner control (LL). Those students in the learner-control situation with a range of lower pretest scores, however, had uniformly high posttest scores; these scores were of the same order of magnitude as the posttest scores of the best students. This was not the case for non-learner-control instructional strategies.

The ELIZA system

The ELIZA system was designed primarily to determine if a computer could be programmed to "understand" typed student sentences. The system was developed by Professor Weizenbaum at MIT and has been used in a variety of experimental settings to test the limits of the dialogue possible and the effect on the students using it. An example of the system in use is given below in a script written by Dr. Edwin Taylor of the Education Research Center at MIT. In this conversation[6] one can see the ability of a computer to "understand" what the student is saying and to reply in a seemingly intelligent manner. Notice that the student is allowed to ask ELIZA questions, provided they are within the appropriate context. In this conversation, all computer dialogue is in uppercase letters, all student dialogue in lowercase.

PLEASE CONSIDER HOW WE MIGHT SYNCHRONIZE TWO CLOCKS TO READ THE "SAME TIME." ONE OF THESE CLOCKS IS IN SAN FRANCISCO, THE OTHER IS IN NEW YORK. AS YOU THINK ABOUT THE PROBLEM, ASK ME ANY QUESTIONS THAT OCCUR TO YOU. WHEN YOU ARE READY TO PROPOSE A SYNCHRONIZATION METHOD, TYPE "READY." THEN I WILL QUIZ YOU ABOUT YOUR PROPOSED METHOD
how far is it from new york to san francisco

THE DISTANCE FROM NEW YORK TO SAN FRANCISCO IS APPROXIMATELY 3000 MILES OR 5000 KILOMETERS

[6]This dialogue is taken in its entirety from Weizenbaum (1966, pp. 36–45).

what about different time zones

TIME ZONES AND DAYLIGHT SAVINGS TIME ARE MATTERS OF HUMAN CONVENIENCE AND NOT PHYSICAL PRINCIPLE. ASSUME THAT IF OUR METHOD OF SYNCHRONIZATION WERE EXTENDED OVER ALL THE EARTH ALL INHABITANTS WOULD OPERATE ON A SINGLE TIME STANDARD
may I use light signals

CERTAINLY, FEEL FREE TO USE LIGHT
may I use moving clocks

WELL, GIVE IT A TRY AND SEE WHAT HAPPENS
now I am ready

IF YOU ARE READY, TYPE THE SINGLE WORD "READY." OTHERWISE PLEASE DO NOT USE THE WORD
ready

NOW I WILL QUIZ YOU ON YOUR SYNCHRONIZATION METHOD. DOES YOUR METHOD OF SYNCHRONIZATION INVOLVE THE PROPA- GATION OF SOME SIGNAL—OR MATERIAL OBJECT—FROM ONE PLACE TO ANOTHER
of course

WHAT KIND OF PROPAGATING SIGNAL OR TRAVELING OBJECT DO YOU PROPOSE TO USE
a light signal

WELL, OF COURSE THE LIGHT SIGNAL WILL NOT FOLLOW THE CURVATURE OF THE EARTH. SO LET US ASSUME THAT SOME SYS- TEM OF RELAY TOWERS IS USED. NOW LET ME ASK WILL THE LIGHT SIGNAL TRAVEL TO OR FROM SOME INTERMEDIATE POINT OR WILL THE LIGHT SIGNAL TRAVEL DIRECTLY BETWEEN NEW YORK AND SAN FRANCISCO
I will bounce it off the intermediate point the moon

IS YOUR INTERMEDIATE POINT EQUIDISTANT FROM NEW YORK AND SAN FRANCISCO
not necessarily

PLEASE ANSWER "YES" OR "NO"
no

A SYNCHRONIZATION PROCEDURE CAN CERTAINLY BE CARRIED OUT USING A POINT THAT IS NOT EQUIDISTANT FROM NEW YORK AND SAN FRANCISCO. HOWEVER, THIS CASE IS COMPLICATED TO ANALYZE. ARE YOU WILLING TO USE INSTEAD A POINT EQUIDIS- TANT FROM NEW YORK AND SAN FRANCISCO
yes

THANK YOU. TO SUMMARIZE, THEN, MY UNDERSTANDING IS THAT YOU EXPECT TO USE TWO SIGNALS AND THAT THESE SIGNALS WILL EITHER CONVERGE ON OR BE SENT OUT FROM A POINT EQUIDISTANT FROM NEW YORK AND SAN FRANCISCO. IS MY UNDERSTANDING ON THIS POINT CORRECT
no it is not

WILL YOU USE ONE SIGNAL OR TWO
one signal

IF YOU ARE USING ONE SIGNAL, THEN THIS SIGNAL TRAVELS BETWEEN NEW YORK AND SAN FRANCISCO BY WAY OF THIS INTERMEDIATE POINT. NO MATTER WHETHER THE PATH IS DIRECT OR INDIRECT, SOME TIME IS REQUIRED FOR THE SYNCHRONIZATION SIGNAL TO TRAVERSE THIS PATH. HAVE YOU CONSIDERED HOW THIS TRAVEL TIME WILL AFFECT YOUR SYNCHRONIZATION PROCEDURE
certainly

HOW CAN YOU POSSIBLY MEASURE THE TRAVEL TIME OF THE LIGHT SIGNAL BETWEEN NEW YORK AND SAN FRANCISCO WITHOUT ALREADY HAVING SYNCHRONIZED THE CLOCKS IN THE TWO PLACES
I don't know

HERE IS A HINT. COULD ALLOW A TEST SIGNAL TO TRAVEL BY A PATH CONNECTING NEW YORK WITH SAN FRANCISCO SUCH THAT A SINGLE CLOCK COULD MEASURE THE SPEED OF THIS TEST SIGNAL. NOW LET ME ASK AGAIN. HOW CAN YOU POSSIBLY MEASURE THE TRAVEL TIME OF THE LIGHT SIGNAL BETWEEN NEW YORK AND SAN FRANCISCO WITHOUT ALREADY HAVING SYNCHRONIZED THE CLOCKS IN THE TWO PLACES
I can use a round trip signal and measure this time on a single clock

VERY GOOD. THE TIME FOR A ROUND TRIP SIGNAL CAN BE MEASURED ON A SINGLE CLOCK. HOWEVER, A DIRECT SYNCHRONIZATION SIGNAL TRAVELS ONLY ONE WAY. WHAT ASSUMPTION ARE YOU MAKING ABOUT THE ONE-WAY TRAVEL TIME OF THE SYNCHRONIZATION SIGNAL
that it is half of the round trip travel time

EXACTLY. YOU HAVE PROVIDED A WAY TO ALLOW FOR THE TRAVEL TIME OF THE SYNCHRONIZATION SIGNAL. I AM SATISFIED THAT YOU KNOW HOW TO SYNCHRONIZE THE TWO CLOCKS. I RETURN YOU NOW TO THE CTSS SYSTEM

Within this fairly rigid structure, notice that ELIZA functions rather well. It answers the student's questions ("may I use light signals," "CERTAINLY, FEEL FREE TO USE LIGHT") and modifies its questions according to the student's answers ("WHAT . . . OBJECT DO YOU PROPOSE TO USE," "a light signal," "WELL, OF COURSE THE LIGHT SIGNAL WILL . . ."). There have also been some relatively successful applications of the ELIZA system in which the student is, at least to a degree, allowed to ask questions within a more general framework. Further, the ELIZA system was found to be flexible enough that the student could pay attention to the subject matter rather than the necessary machine input format—the student could write ordinary English statements that the system could then analyze for key words.

Although this system offers a good deal of flexibility, it merely responds to student questions and does not have any overall control or pattern that would allow it to be used for teaching in an effective fashion. It was not, of course, designed for teaching in the first place, but rather to show that a computer was capable of maintaining a dialogue with a human subject. As an experimental system, it more than fulfilled its author's intentions and provides us with further evidence as to the potential of intelligent use of computers in the instructional process.

Conclusions: Mixed Systems   The two systems that are discussed above have both provided a slightly different perspective on the kind of power and potential that could exist in computer-based systems. These experiments represented some of the best of current practice at the time this project was started. As a result of our initial survey at the start of this project for the Carnegie Commission, we classified the systems that were in existence in the United States into the three categories we are using in this chapter, namely *presentation systems* (author-controlled), *mixed systems* (learner-controlled), and *enrichment systems*. Given the learning process and the characteristic strengths of the computer, we felt that the mixed category held much the greatest potential in the longer run. As can be seen from the projects discussed in this section, however, there is not much evidence on which to base such an assertion. As a result of the potential that was seen in the three projects we have just discussed, it was decided to undertake some further basic research to establish whether the idea of the responsive (mixed) system was indeed as powerful as it seemed. A major effort was launched to experiment with a system—an effort that resulted in the Associative Learning Project. The system that was built and the results that were obtained with it are discussed separately in Appendix A. From the experimental work that was conducted with the Associative Learning Project it is clear that the potential of the mixed system still exists—but the kind of breakthrough and effort it entails suggest that the payoff will not come in the near term.

Current applications

Dialogue as we have described it is not a widely used or clearly differentiable technique today. Learner-controlled tutorial CAI appears to have merged back into efforts to upgrade the author-controlled tutorial and drill-and-practice modes. ELIZA-type discourse is now found to some degree in drill and practice, but also in simulation and other enrichment tools.

Perhaps the closest approximation to dialogue-based learning assistance is now employed in medical schools. Particular patient cases are stored in the computer, and the student interacts with the system as he would in dealing with a real patient. The situation changes dynamically as various questions are asked by the students, tests are made, and treatments are suggested. At Massachusetts General Hospital (a Harvard teaching hospital) 22 teaching programs in clinical subjects have been prepared, and many of these are the type of clinical encounters just described (Hoffer, Barnet, & Farquhar, 1973; Hoffer, 1973). Ohio State and other medical schools are also utilizing this technique. In reality, these clinical encounters are "simulations"—and should be placed in this category today. But they owe some of their heritage to the concept of dialogue-type learning assistance.

SYSTEMS THAT PROVIDE ENRICHMENT We have termed the third major category of instructional use of computers *enrichment*. Within this category we identify four major classes of systems: problem solving, simulation, games, and inquiry. The *problem-solving* category includes those systems that make general-purpose languages, and packages of analytical tools available to the student so he can use them to solve problems. The *simulation* category includes cases as well as the standard type of simulation models which can be used to create an environment appropriate for the topic at hand. These simulations range from those such as the one used by the Apollo astronauts in practicing moon landings to providing business school students with a marketplace that represents what a company might actually face in practice. *Games* are merely simulations arranged so that players may compete against each other. The final category is *inquiry*, the kind of enrichment that is provided when a student is able to ask questions of a data-base that represents phenomena he would find in the real world. Examples of such data-bases are the Standard & Poor stock market tapes and computer-based histories of legal cases. Systems that provide enrichment do not necessarily provide any particular instructional methodology, but rather aim at improving the quality of the environment in which the student is learning. The evidence in the Massachusetts survey and in publications such as *SIGCUE*[7] suggests that the major use of computers in higher education at this point is in the area of enrichment. Access to computer power for solving problems of realistic complexity, or to remove the mundane clerical work involved in processing numbers, has a major impact on what is taught at universities and how much can be absorbed. We argue later in this report that it is this area, together with drill and practice, that has the most impact now and is likely to have the most impact over the next several years.

Once again it should be stressed that the examples given here are illustrative only; they do not represent a sample that covers the full range of types of use.

Enrichment through Problem Solving

Dartmouth College

Providing an environment that increases the student's problem-solving abilities has been accomplished in two ways. The first of these is to provide the student with a general-purpose language, and the second is to provide him with a preprogrammed package, typically involving an analytical tool. Advocates of this approach[8] claim that the use of these resources helps the student to think in a rigorous and consistent manner and teaches him how to structure problems and arrive at solutions.

[7] Association for Computing Machinery (ACM), Special Interest Group on Computer Uses in Education, 1133 Avenue of the Americas, New York, N.Y. 10036.

[8] One of the ablest of these is Professor Arthur Luehrmann of Dartmouth College.

A good example of this is the system developed by the faculty at Dartmouth College in New Hampshire. This has proved to be an excellent and widely available system with a view to providing easy flexible access to the computer for the students and faculty. The Dartmouth College Regional Computer Center is now under the direction of Professor Thomas E. Kurtz. The services it offers reach about 35 schools and 15 colleges that cover a large section of New England stretching from the University of Vermont in the north to the city of Boston in the south. The system can support considerably more than 100 terminals simultaneously, and a typical day during the school year will see a total of some 1,000 terminal hours recorded in about 10,000 "jobs" run (see Zinn, 1970).

The basic goal of the Dartmouth system has been to provide unlimited access to a powerful time-sharing computer system for students of all ages. The purpose of this access is to extend the range of problems which students are able to attempt within any given discipline and in general to enrich their course work. Dartmouth College also started this project in 1964 in part because it was convinced that all university-educated students should be able to handle the computer and understand both what it meant and how to use it in their education.

To make this objective feasible, Dartmouth developed a language that is relatively easy to use and requires no peculiar scientific or mathematical skills. The BASIC "conversational" language is now available commercially on most time-sharing systems. The BASIC language can be thought of at two levels. At one level it is a rich language that allows easy and efficient description of a wide range of problems involving both the manipulation of textual material and the manipulation of numbers. At another level it can be used as a simple but nevertheless powerful language for the usual kind of arithmetic processing. Due to this combination of simplicity and power and an ability to handle both numbers and text, it is much the most commonly used conversational computer language in use today. It includes enough of the logical and conceptual aspects of all the major programming languages and yet requires a minimum amount of both attention to detail and effort to learn.

Students new to programming can learn enough from the "teach" language on the system to be able to write simple programs within minutes of sitting at the terminal. Within 15 hours they can be programming adequately on quite difficult problems. In an evaluation conducted by Dartmouth College it was found that a typical student would spend three-quarters of an hour per week during the 10-week academic term on the teletype and an equal amount of time in planning his programs. The entire computer training occupied 15 hours of the student's time. This was sufficient for the students in the freshman class to be able to use the computer fairly extensively in their courses.

John G. Kemeny, now president of Dartmouth College, was responsible for much of this development. He states:

No other academic program yields as high a dividend for time invested as a freshman computer program. A significant minority of the students avail themselves of the time sharing system in connection with more advanced courses. Assignment of problems requiring computer solutions is a matter of routine in any course that has math as a prerequisite. In particular, engineering and business schools in Dartmouth have made the most imaginative use of time sharing in a variety of courses. The biggest users in Dartmouth are the Tuck Business School (Kemeny, 1967, p. 65).

Kemeny describes the system as being similar to an "open stack" library of subroutines. Programs and algorithms developed by any student are available to the student body as a whole. This encourages sharing of knowledge and techniques and eliminates redundancy of effort.

One of the most striking features of the Dartmouth approach is the motivation experienced by the students, who display a great deal of excitement in using the terminal and developing solutions to their problems. One of the central impacts that the faculty at Dartmouth have identified is the discipline imposed on the student by having to program a problem and make it work. They argue (persuasively) that this encourages logical thinking and in-depth understanding of any given problem. At the same time creativity is encouraged because of the access to a variety of analytical packages to apply to the problem. Unique and constructive ways of approaching problems are invented by the students themselves. In many disciplines at Dartmouth, courses have been considerably reformed and enriched by the availability of the computational power. Students can attempt what would be otherwise impossible problems, where the mathematical complexity can now be resolved by the computer. Hence the problems within some of the courses resemble real-life situations, for example, planning a trip to the moon and working out the trajectories. Kemeny predicts the use of the computer will go a long way in closing the gap between the abstractness of modern mathematics and the practical applications. He hopes the basic goal of mathematics and education—"teaching fundamental principles"—will be extended to the point where the student can translate powerful mathematical algorithms into computer programs and use them to do sophisticated work and even fundamental research. In other words, the process of designing the computer program provides an understanding of a body of knowledge itself.

To encourage and develop this approach to enriching the university education, Dartmouth has founded the Computer Educational Materials Development Center (CEMDEC). This group provides the crucial summer support and technical-editing assistance necessary to bring the materials to a usable level of quality in a number of universities. Dartmouth has provided its students with an enriched environment that is actively used. Computer terminals and the BASIC language have opened up an enormous range of possibilities.

APL language

BASIC is a useful language that works in a robust way for a large class of "ordinary" problems. If the problem to be tackled involves mathematical complexity, however, the BASIC approach is cumbersome. Several attempts have been made to open up more complex problems to students in a way that would not cause effort to be spent on programming details.

The most successful approach to providing students with an environment that allows them to have support in solving complex problems has been the development of APL. Unlike the Dartmouth system this has not been developed at a university, nor did it have the large-scale efforts that had been provided in the Dartmouth setting. The language was developed by Dr. Kenneth Iverson in his work with the IBM Corporation.[9] This language is substantially more sophisticated than BASIC and

[9]See, for example, the use of APL in teaching IBM publication G320-0996-0, IBM, New York, 1969.

provides an ability to easily implement complex logical and mathematical forms. An example of the kinds of uses that are being made of APL is given in the following material:

APL, standing for A Programming Language, derives from the title of the book by the same name, written by K. W. Iverson and published by Wiley in 1962. That volume, modest in size but not in scope, was the formalization of an algorithmic notation which K. Iverson first began to set down in the late 1950's while at Harvard (Foster, 1971, p. 174).

Professor E. M. Edwards of the University of Alberta recounts his experiences with APL in electrical engineering education as follows:

The information explosion presents a serious challenge to today's educators. One is caught between the fire of teaching too many topics too poorly and the frying pan of overspecialization. One effective approach is to teach general principles using specific examples. Properly done, this technique will leave a student with an ability to cope with today's technology and the background to understand tomorrow's. The teaching of servos, for example, requires either highly idealized examples of a great deal of calculation (often many iterations with different values of parameters). In the first approach the whole concept of the "engineering compromise" is missed. Engineering compromise is the analytic or intuitive selection of an optimal operating point or region within the multidimensional region of the system space in which system operation is possible.

One of the main differences between the experienced professional and the fresh graduate is that the experienced man has acquired the intuitive ability to arrive at a workable engineering compromise. It is impossible (at the present) to teach intuition, so we must therefore convert the process to an analytic one if we are to close the gap. The "laborious calculation" approach loses the student among the trees of calculation to the extent that the forest goes unseen. Enter the computer. The student can now manually work an idealized example to acquire the concept being taught. With the aid of the computer he is then able to examine the possible solutions of real problems and thus acquire a better understanding of real system design. Few would disagree, therefore, that it is vital to expose our students to some aspects of computing science. The problem is: what aspects of this large subject can we most beneficially treat in the short time available in an already overcrowded curriculum? It is my intention to show that teaching the APL language and some example of applications of computer techniques in the particular specialty of interest will provide the most effective use of the available time (Edwards, 1971, p. 179).

Donald A. Rudberg is with the department of electrical engineering, Montana State University, Bozeman, Montana. At one point in his writing he comments:

With the previous discussion of APL in terms of its power and compactness, it seems inconsistent when someone claims that it is also the best language with which to begin interactive programming. But it is. This is a result of its having an immediate execution mode and global variables. Neophytes can use APL in adding-machine fashion and get instant results. I claim a green programmer can get results from APL within five seconds of signing on. Furthermore, notions of identifiers, value assignments, computation sequence, and the primitive operator set can be learned without defining a program. Every person with a background in algebra already knows how to do simple operations and needs only a terminal. Our experience with freshman electrical engineers at Montana State is that they take to APL readily. We give an 8 hour introduction essentially covering the APL/360 Primer. After that the student is on his own.

In this connection, it is worth observing that APL is a language in which the user can acquire the level of proficiency he desires and be perfectly at home with it. If he has an interest only in simple problems he can deal with only a small operator set. If he is an ardent programmer (i.e., a nut), I really do not know the bounds of what he can do. APL has no basic kit of tools or program structuring rules that must be acquired to make it useful. As McCracken says, "What he doesn't know won't hurt him. . . ."

As the student progresses through undergraduate work, problems and concepts couched in array notation become prevalent. During the sophomore year, circuit analysis introduces arrays and demands solutions. Array notions are extended in the junior and senior years. Laboratory courses require reduction of experimental data; control and communication theory express many of their concepts in arrays. Since the object of computation at this stage is insight, not numbers, the array handling and thought translation properties of APL make it a natural undergraduate choice. I think we have all found that the more the student is freed from computational mechanics, the more insight he gains into the problem.

In graduate education and research, I consider that there are essentially two languages to be used: Fortran for batch jobs and APL for interactive work. Fortran's power and capability as a batch language are so well known that I will discuss APL only.

It is at the graduate level of usage that one begins to perceive and employ the richness of APL. Its host of primitive operators and compactness of syntax are those very elements so appreciated by experienced users and its thought translation qualities are even more valuable than before. I must admit to a feeling of restriction and growing frustration when using other languages, so habituated have I become to APL's ease of thought translation (Rudberg, 1971, pp. 184–185).

Both BASIC and APL provide significant problem-solving support to the student. This is one form of enrichment that can substantially alter the environment in which the student is working. For certain types of subjects and for certain levels of students the BASIC language is an example of an appropriate kind of tool. For more sophisticated applications, particularly those with an engineering bias, the APL language is more appropriate. A spectrum of languages exists, of which we have seen two, that can be used to provide a viable and powerful supporting medium for the student in his pursuit of knowledge in certain kinds of fields.

Although they are in widespread use, and with a large and enthusiastic following, the use of computer languages as a supporting device in the educational environment is one that has been overlooked by much research. In thinking about the use of computers in higher education, a lot of attention and research effort has gone in the area of computer-aided instruction and not much has been spent in the enrichment area. As a measure of its success and usefulness it is interesting to note that despite this lack of funding, the access by students to problem-solving languages has been steadily on the increase over the last few years. There is every reason to believe that this will continue.

Current applications

Dartmouth remains, in 1974, an excellent example of institutional use of computer-based problem-solving capabilities. Through NERCOMP and other methods, it has made these facilities widely available in the New England area, and they are widely utilized (Greenberger et al., 1974). The use of BASIC and APL, as noted above, has spread and is very wide (Chapter

7). The ability to provide students with a computational language and computational power is perhaps the simplest and cheapest way for an institution to get involved in computer-based learning assistance. It appears to be increasingly the method chosen.

Simulation and Analytical Tools

The second major way in which enrichment can be provided to the student is through the use of analytical tools. There is a somewhat arbitrary distinction between the provision of useful problem-solving language and the provision of analytical tools. Nevertheless the distinction is useful as the provision of analytical tools gives the student access to a prepackaged supporting mechanism to use as part of his problem-solving activities. There is, of course, the further possibility that the provision of such analytical packages will become widespread in business and government, and it is therefore useful to learn how to use such packages early.

In the current context, however, the principal use of these analytical tools is to provide the student with a means of gaining insight into the experimental data or real-world phenomena that he is faced with. An example of one of these comprehensive packages is the TROLL system, which is representative of the best of the current systems. The introduction to the TROLL manual is quoted below:

TROLL (Time-shared Reactive On-Line Laboratory) is an interactive computer system which provides a comprehensive environment for quantitative research in such fields as econometrics, management science, and political science. TROLL was originally designed to bring interactive programming capabilities to applied econometrics. However, the system has a broad range of capabilities which make it a useful tool in many scientific fields where the primary data are time series or cross-sectional data vectors. A time series in TROLL is defined as a vector of observations in which a constant interval of time is assumed between observations.

TROLL's principal research capabilities are:

- Simulation of time-dependent systems. Such a system is represented in TROLL as a model consisting of simultaneous nonlinear equations (the traditional form of econometric model). TROLL can simulate models of up to 1,000 equations.

- Regression analysis, for estimating parameters of equations using a wide range of standard and advanced techniques, e.g., ordinary least squares, nonlinear estimation, two- and three-stage least squares, polynomial distributed lags, and auto-regressive corrections.

- Data analysis and transformation, e.g., seasonal adjustment, smoothing, extrapolation, removal of outliers, interpolation for missing data, other screening facilities, and standard statistical tests.

- Access to the National Bureau of Economic Research Data Bank of over 1,500 annual, quarterly, and monthly macroeconomic time series.

TROLL is designed in such a way that the above capabilities can be used together (in any combination) or independently, at the researcher's convenience. In a typical econometric simulation project, for example, *all* of the system's major capabilities could be used in the following sequence of operations:

- Access time-series data from the NBER Data Bank.

- Transform selected time series (e.g., from annual to quarterly) to satisfy special requirements of the model.

- Enter equations of model and perform initial regression analysis.

- Respecify equations based on initial regression results; check new equations by using regression capability again. Repeat cycle until equations reach satisfactory form.

- Simulate the model, using coefficients produced in last application of regression capability. Repeat simulation using revised simulation criteria.

- Plot simulation output.

Regardless of the application for which the researcher uses TROLL, the system provides a special type of flexibility which directly reflects its interactive nature. The researcher receives immediate feedback at each step of his project. Thus, interim results can be used to revise initial theories and assumptions, and this can be done with an ease and rapidity which are unthinkable with conventional "batch" computer systems. In short, TROLL facilitates *experimentation*. . . .

TROLL has been designed to be "friendly"—i.e., to make input, processing, and display of information easy and flexible. TROLL has its own "file system," which enables the user to create, update, and process a large time-series data base. (The size of a data base is virtually irrelevant and has little effect on system efficiency.) The file system is used to store not only data but also models and the output of regression and simulation experiments. Thus, one can interrupt and resume processing without expensive restart procedures. . . .

Finally, the file system makes it possible for users to share not only one author's data and models (with appropriate permission) but also public libraries such as the NBER Data Bank. We hope that the sharing facility will encourage TROLL users to develop and maintain public libraries of both data and models.

Work on TROLL began in the fall of 1966 as part of the Econometrics Project of the Department of Economics at the Massachusetts Institute of Technology under the direction of Professor Edwin Kuh. . . .

By June of 1968 TROLL/0, a prototype system, was running on M.I.T.'s Compatible Time-Sharing System. For over two years TROLL/0 was used at M.I.T. for thesis research, faculty research, and classroom support.

In the fall of 1968 work began on a completely redesigned and expanded version of the system. This new version, known as TROLL/1, is now programmed and operates on the IBM-360/67. TROLL/1 was released to the general public in late 1971 after an intensive period of testing and documentation.

Since September 1971, the TROLL operating system has been used as the basic support system for software development and research at the Computer Research Center for Economics and Management Science of the National Bureau of Economic Research (Eisner, 1971, pp. 1–5).

From this quotation it is possible to get the flavor of the kind of support delivered to a student as part of his education (to say nothing of the support for research). This kind of enrichment is not deliverable by any mechanism other than a computer.

TROLL is one of the largest projects of its type. In other areas similar, although often simpler, work is going on. Ready access to statistical packages for other kinds of data analysis would be an example. Simulation languages such as IBM1, GPSS, and SIMSCRIPT are abundant today, allowing multiple means of simulating processes for teaching-learning purposes.

Current applications

The use of simulation and associated analytical tools is growing—although the investment involved by schools is greater in this area than in the problem-solving area. As a result, the use of this tool—a very powerful one—is not nearly at the level today as we expect it will be in the future.

Any one of multiple examples might be chosen to illustrate current use. Two or three will suffice:

At North Carolina State University, for example, Dr. Samuel Tove, professor of biochemistry, uses the facilities of TUCC to simulate biological experiments. "Simulated experiments enable students to study enzymes by examining the chemical reactions they catalyze," he explains. "Developing that kind of data through actual laboratory experiments is just too expensive at the undergraduate level. The equipment alone would cost half a million dollars. And a lot of students aren't ready for the complicated experimentation involved, or they haven't the time."

Rather than letting the students learn only from working on standard textbook problems, as was the practice in the past, Dr. Tove gives each student a simulated experiment produced by the computer. "The student has his own data and can analyze it to find his own answers," he says. "Most important, the data contains the same kinds of errors that the student would encounter if he conducted an experiment in a laboratory. When he plots the data, he finds that all the dots don't fall on the line—which is just what would happen if he took his data from a real experiment instead of from a textbook."

Dr. Tove emphasizes that the computer is not meant to replace real laboratory experience, especially for students who plan to do advanced work. "But at the undergraduate level," he maintains, "they can study enzymes just as well through simulation—and at a much lower cost" (*In North Carolina.* . ., 1973, pp. 3–4).

North Carolina also has, in physics, programs that simulate experimental equipment that is not available to undergraduates, such as mass spectrometers and particle accelerators. Again data can be analyzed as if from a live experiment—and the curriculum is enriched. Today psychologists are also simulating experiments, and social system simulation—such as those behind *The Limits to Growth* (Meadows, Meadows, Randers, & Behrens, 1972)—is also being increasingly utilized for teaching purposes as well as research. The ability to show the dynamic interaction of many variables is a powerful teaching tool.

Games Simulation and analytical tools allow the student to build models and test data. There also exist prebuilt simulation models ready to be exercised by the student. The difference between a simulation model and a game is simply that a game is a simulation model constructed to allow teams to manipulate an environment (which is simulated) competitively. At the end of the game one team has provided the simulation with the "best" decisions with regard to action in the simulated environment and "wins." Effectively done, a game can provide participation, involvement, and emotion on the parts of the players. The game can tie together many concepts and illustrate their interaction. Business games are one example of this. A great many business schools have games that provide a decision-making laboratory for the student, a laboratory where he can practice and test some of the skills he has acquired in other courses. In some graduate business schools[10] this laboratory experience forms the focus of several courses.

Current applications

Games, although not abundant, are an increasing factor in learning assistance today. As noted above, they are an especially useful integrative mechanism. Management games, an early leader in the field, continue to be improved. For example, IBM, which has utilized a management game in its training courses for almost two decades now, is continually developing improved games—the latest programmed in APL (*Computing Newsletter,* 1973, p. 4). The New York University management game is installed in five other schools in the United States and at Tel Aviv University in Israel. Most recently, a version has been played in Hungary ("Karl Marx U. . . .," 1972).

Other uses of games are increasing. Economics as a field has several games that illustrate differing types of levels of competition. The social sciences—with emphasis on public policy and environmental impact—are developing and utilizing games that allow players to get involved with the motivations and viewpoints and possible actions of differing interest groups in society.

Inquiry The last major category of enrichment is the inquiry capability provided when the student is given access to a large data bank. Because of the difficulty in building such a base, these systems are not widely available. The legal profession provides an example of what is possible. Students in Pennsylvania, among other states, are able to retrieve statute law through terminals

[10]For example, Carnegie-Mellon University, Pittsburgh, Pa.

by using key words or concepts. Thus in researching a question the student saves considerable time that might otherwise go to searching through books and at the same time can be more certain that what he is retrieving is relatively complete. As we build more and more computer-based data files, this process of flexible retrieval can become an integral part of many courses. As suggested in the discussion of TROLL in the previous section, it is now available in an economics data bank. The Standard & Poor data tapes on the daily stock market transactions are another example. However, this area of inquiry has to be classified as a very minor segment of the enrichment area and is included here purely for the sake of completeness.

In the long run, of course, it opens up the questions of the automated library, automatic bibliographic retrieval, and the like. These are areas of staggering potential, and areas that are being actively pursued by the library profession.[11] The enormous size of the problem makes useful progress slow, and since the problem is complex, no attempt is made in this study to assess the current state of affairs or the timing of useful computer-based access to library material. It does not appear to be imminent.

Current applications

We have suggested above some current applications in this area. One additional data-base inquiry system currently receiving attention is Dartmouth's Project IMPRESS.

The goal of Project IMPRESS is to give the undergraduate student ready access to the wealth of existing social science data, so that he will be able to examine them with considerable freedom. He is given a range of data bases, a convenient language for describing the information he wants, and interactive access via the computer. He is able with relative ease to deal with a large mass of data, such as returns of a presidential election or even several independent collections—perhaps surveys on the same question at two or more different times. Access to such information allows him to make analyses and investigate relationships; he might ask, for instance, for the distribution of political party preference in a given survey by race or by age (Mosmann, 1973, p. 109).

[11]See, for example, Project Intrex, Massachusetts Institute of Technology, Cambridge, Mass.

In like manner, students today are being given access to financial data, such as the COMSTAT tapes, in the finance area—and, we expect, will be given access to an increasing number of similar data in the future.

CONCLUSIONS   A taxonomy of the current status of the courseware area has been presented. It is designed to show the major points of activity and to permit easy discussion of where the action has been and where it is going.

The field is full of confusing terminology; many of the same words mean different things to different people. An attempt has been made here to be reasonably precise, and it is hoped that the combination of definition and example has created a fairly clear picture of what is meant by each of the terms.

The effort spent until recently has been in the areas of tutorial and drill and practice. It has been suggested by our comments that tutorial usage except in the experimental setting has never been large in higher education and is diminishing. The enrichment area appears to be growing rapidly, and although still a relatively small percentage of the entire computer budget in a university, it has the unique feature of being used for student learning without government subsidy. A factor that suggests it really is useful! This shift toward enrichment is a shift toward greater "learner control" and less "author control," a characteristic that seems to be critical to the *process* of learning. It also, as we shall consider more fully in the next chapter, allows greater university-based assistance to students in the last two stages of the learning process—integration and testing.

The experimental dialogue systems are underresearched but hold out some possibility of adding some learner control to otherwise fairly structured techniques.

At a more philosophical level, there is an overwhelming sense, in all the material quoted in this chapter, of a *one right way*. That is, each author working at any one point in the spectrum in Figure 5-1 is deeply committed to his "new" approach, and almost always argues for his point of view. This narrow focus and this enthusiasm often generate real progress and are the hallmark of a charismatic innovator. In looking back over the last 10 years, however, it seems that there has not yet been enough enthusiastic support for a mixed strategy. As we argued at the end of Chapter 4 and shall continue to argue, enough progress has been made on the individual points on the spectrum to allow for the construction of a smorgasbord of instructional technologies. It seems entirely reasonable that each point on the continuum is eminently suited for a particular stage of learning and a particular body of material to be taught. We argue later for such an approach, but it is worth noting at this point that any support for learning, if it is to handle the diversity of a university setting, will almost certainly have to have a smorgasbord flavor to be successful.

6. Matching Technology to Learning

In this chapter we present a model to assist in the choice of learning mechanisms for various educational processes. The model is a simple start and can be refined as we increase our understanding of the factors involved. However, we are attempting in this chapter to synthesize our existing knowledge into a model that is workable and can be used to guide developments and decisions today.

In Chapter 2 we developed the learning matrix to illustrate the stages of the learning process and the various types of materials to be learned. In this chapter we will describe each of the learning mechanisms discussed in Chapters 3, 4, and 5 in terms of a set of attributes that can then be matched with the type of learning (represented by a cell in the learning matrix) whose characteristics it best fits. The resulting map permits both an assessment of the impact of technology thus far and an evaluation of the degree of impact that can reasonably be expected in the future.

ATTRIBUTES OF LEARNING MECHANISMS All objects can be described in terms of a significant set of properties (which we shall call *attributes*). If the attributes are well chosen, the description of a particular object will be robust and will allow the object to be well defined and clearly differentiated from its nearest neighbors. This chapter presents 16 such attributes that we believe describe most learning mechanisms. Since any attribute can be possessed by a learning mechanism to a greater or lesser degree, each mechanism can be ranked (on a scale) according to its relative possession of each attribute.

The attributes that we have chosen to describe each learning mechanism have been grouped into four major categories. The major categories are self-explanatory. These are aspects of the mechanism that affect:

- The *content* of what can be taught
- The *user*
- The kind of *communication* between user and mechanism
- The *economics* implied by the mechanism

Content Related

1. *Ability to telescope time*
Some processes can be comprehended more fully by a learner if the natural phenomena are speeded up or time-sliced so that a "total" picture can emerge within a reasonable amount of learning time. Time-lapse photography provides this ability. Computer-based simulation also does. This attribute thus allows the learner to fully grasp the implications of a long-extended process in much less time than nature would allow.

2. *Ability to present structure*
Some learning mechanisms have the ability to clearly present the student with the overall structure of the material that is to be learned. Others, because of limits in the human language or some limitation in the presentation medium, are able to present only the basic skeleton behind a set of material. This attribute measures a learning mechanism's relative ability to present the forest with enough clarity that the learner can visualize the place of each of the individual trees and thus grasp the inherent organization of a concept or a series of concepts. Some learning mechanisms present structure through graphic, visual illustration. Other mechanisms, such as some computer models, allow the student to iterate through enough data points quickly so that the essential structure of a concept or a methodology becomes apparent. At the low end of this scale is the real-world environment as a learning device. The complexity of the real world makes it very difficult to derive structure from this experience.

3. *Provision of a rich environment*
There are times in the learning process when it is desirable to keep the material and the data available to the student well structured. There are other times, however, when the learning task is clearly and significantly furthered if the student is able to

work in a rich, multivariate, data-plentiful environment. If the student is merely learning definitions in the principles of accounting, for example, it is of little use for him to have a rich data-base. On the other hand, if he is attempting to understand the dynamics of the growth of the Russian economy, it can be very useful for him to have many economic series at his beck and call. For some learning tasks, the availability of multiple types and quantities of data and the methods of processing these data are very favorable. Learning mechanisms that rank high on this attribute are of value in these tasks.

4. *Ability to provide ill-structured material*
Some learning mechanisms do an excellent job of merely presenting fact. Among these mechanisms are, for example, programmed instruction texts. Other mechanisms are more suitable for providing the student insights into material that has many facets, that can be considered from many points of view, and for which a "correct solution" depends upon several contingencies. This type of material is quite imprecise, and the student must recognize that a "true" perception is subject to the impact of varying value judgments or differing points of view. One excellent mechanism to present this "ill-structured" material is the case study. As noted in Chapter 3, cases involve the student in assessing not only his own basic assumptions but the assumptions and values of others as the class determines the most preferred solution from a range of alternatives.

5. *Flexibility for adding new material quickly*
New concepts, facts, and ideas are constantly being evolved. Some learning mechanisms can provide these new factors to students almost immediately after they become known. These mechanisms are highly adaptable and can be easily adjusted by the addition or deletion of material. The lecturer, for example, can integrate new material into his course and present it to students very quickly. At the other end of the spectrum, movies, like textbooks, generally have a definite production lead time.

6. *Support for the learners' structured, clerical tasks*
In every homework exercise or experimental situation from which one learns, some amount of rote calculation, careful structuring of data, and the like are demanded of the student.

These learning overhead factors take time, thought, and care; yet many of them are *not* a major part of the learning exercise. Rather, they are the clerical burdens that the student must necessarily lift in order to get at the significant learning tasks in a particular exercise. Certain learning mechanisms, for the most part computers, have the ability to take most of this clerical work away from the student by prestored rules of calculation, formating, and available computation routines.

7. *Support for unstructured data manipulation*

The previous attribute measures the ability of particular learning mechanisms to provide a set of task-specific tools that make work on a particular learning project simpler. This attribute measures the learning mechanisms' ability to provide a wide range of tools to allow the student to better structure the learning environment and to manipulate the learning variables within that environment for purposes of greater comprehension. A learning mechanism for a maximal rating on this attribute would provide for the student a complete set of mathematical models, simulation tools, editing facilities, dictionaries, and—in general—a complete, instantly available, general-purpose set of those tools that are utilized by scholars and students in the process of obtaining, verifying, embedding, and creating knowledge.

User Related   ### 8. *Degree of learner control*

This attribute is concerned with the ability of the learner to adjust the pace, speed, and direction and the amount of feedback in the learning process so that he is, in fact, in control of his learning experience. At best, this attribute allows the learner to be involved in his own education and to be active and creative in molding the learning experience to his needs and his abilities. If a mechanism possesses this attribute, the learner must be heavily active (on the active-passive dimension) with regard to the learning process.

9. *Ability to adjust to individual learner needs*

Most learning mechanisms are geared for the average student. This attribute suggests that the learning mechanism should also be ranked on its ability to be adjusted to individual learner needs. The usual textbook, which is written from a single point of view and which follows a progression aimed at the average student, ranks low on this attribute. An on-line storage bank of multiple types of data and models to process data ranks considerably higher.

10. *Ease of use*

Some learning mechanisms are simple to operate both for the learner and for the teacher. Others are much more difficult to utilize either intrinsically or because they require an initial period to understand their basic method of operation, because they require coordination with other people to gain access to them, and so forth. In these cases a conscious extra effort is required to use them. In this sense, a book, because of our culture and our habits, is a relatively simple learning mechanism to use. Movie projectors, which involve multiple difficulties in obtaining the camera or obtaining the movie from a distant library, are more difficult to utilize. Computer programs, which require at least initially a nonproductive learning period in order to utilize them at all, are likewise somewhat less favorable than the textbook on this dimension.

Communications Related

11. *Amount of sensory impact*

This attribute is possessed by a learning mechanism that affects one or more of the senses. A mechanism may have visual impact or audio impact or both, for example. It is known that we retain only a certain percentage of what we hear, and a higher percentage of what we both see and hear, and a still larger percentage of things we experience through more than two senses. This is the expressed reasoning behind the use of audiovisual methods of presentation by teachers, salesmen, and so on.

The more senses a learning mechanism appeals to—thus the greater the impact on the learner's ability to retain what has been presented to him—the higher its rating on this attribute.

12. *Amount of emotional impact*

This attribute is possessed by learning mechanisms that appeal not only to the cognitive aspects of man but also to the affective impulses that play a part in motivating the learning process. A lecturer who makes his subject alive and exciting for the student possesses this attribute to a high degree. Motion pictures, through use of color, sound, and drama, can also rank high on this dimension.

13. *Degree of learner feedback*

A primary attribute of some learning mechanisms is their ability to allow the learner to know early whether he has understood the meaning of a fact, internalized a skill, or grasped a concept and, if not, to assist him in minimizing his learning difficulty. The traditional prime method of learner feedback has been graded written assignments, but in general this is a *slow* feedback process (due to time lags in the handing in, marking, and returning of the assignments), and deserves fairly low marks on this criterion. Some devices that provide more timely feedback are paper programmed instruction texts, computer programmed instruction, and computer drill-and-practice programs—all of which provide almost instant feedback to the learner. The latter two methods dominate paper programmed instruction on this attribute, since they can provide relatively complex feedback based not only on a student's answers to a current question but also on his past responses. In addition, stored data concerning a student's particular background knowledge can be used as well as instructor knowledge of typical student errors.

14. *Ability to access data or concepts previously learned*

In certain aspects of the learning process, it is helpful to be able to review or recall to mind concepts or facts that have been learned in the past. The lack of a necessary formula or a particular definition can stall, sometimes to a very great degree, the flow of learning. On-line computer inquiry to a dictionary or textbook index provides vastly different recall speeds than do lecture notes, for example.

Economics   ### 15. *Low cost per data item or concept*

This attribute measures each mechanism on the sheer economics of presenting data to a learner. It ranks a mechanism with regard to the maximum speed at which learners can be exposed to facts and concepts—through any sensory mechanism. This attribute makes no allowance for the quality of the presentation; it is based merely on the possible rate of data input by the learner and the cost per bit of data. For example, a learner can read, on the average, 300 words per minute. A page in a book costs approximately 2 cents. At 350 words per page, the cost per word is 0.00007 cents. Alternatively, during the same time it takes to read a page, the learner could hear 150 words uttered by a lecturer. Assuming the cost of the lecturer for that period of time in a class of 100 students is $1.50 per student, the cost of obtaining a lectured word is 0.0002 cents. On the basis of sheer economics, the printed page surpasses the lecturer as an original data input mechanism.

16. *Decentralized availability*

Some learning mechanisms, such as books, may be used in any place at any time. Others, such as heavy laboratory equipment, can be utilized only in a specific place and, if limited availability necessitates scheduling, only at particular times. Most mechanisms fit somewhere between these two points of the spectrum. It is clear that a learning mechanism that is available ubiquitously to the student is far preferable to one that can be utilized only after a period of travel and/or in particular periods.

A RANKING OF EACH LEARNING MECHANISM As noted above, each learning mechanism can be rated with regard to the degree to which it possesses the favorable aspects of each of the 16 attributes. Table 6-1 summarizes these attributes, and Table 6-2 presents an estimate on a 1-to-10 scale of their rankings. In Table 6-2, a 1 signifies that a learning mechanism scores very high on an attribute, whereas a 10 shows that a learning mechanism has a very low ranking.

These rankings represent a combined estimate; partly they are based on a number of years of experience we have had in teaching in universities, and in working on the in-depth study of technology required for this report. In addition, however, we asked a cross section of MIT faculty and staff for their rankings. The results presented in Table 6-2 represent the average of the faculty sample, which agreed for the most part with our own, prior, subjective ratings.

The matrix permits focus on either a particular attribute or a particular learning mechanism. For example, attribute 12 (the ability to provide emotional impact) is possessed in great degree by radio, film, videotape, and cable TV. The emotional impact, however, of such things as programmed instruction—whether it be paper or computerized—is almost nil.

Focusing on the mechanism, the ubiquitous textbook scores very well on the attributes of cost, decentralized availability,

TABLE 6-1
Summary of
attributes of
learning-delivery
mechanisms
(tools)

A. *Content related*

    1. Ability to telescope time

    2. Ability to present structure

    3. Provision of a rich environment

    4. Ability to provide ill-structured material

    5. Flexibility for adding new material quickly

    6. Support for the learners' structured, clerical tasks

    7. Support for unstructured data manipulation

B. *User related*

    8. Degree of learner control

    9. Ability to adjust to individual learner needs

    10. Ease of use

C. *Communications related*

    11. Amount of sensory impact

    12. Amount of emotional impact

    13. Degree of learner feedback

    14. Ability to access data or concepts previously learned

D. *Economics*

    15. Low cost per data item or concept

    16. Decentralized availability

and ease of use either by faculty or by students. On the other hand, it ranks very low with regard to individualized instruction, the ability to provide new material, learner feedback, and several other dimensions.

The purpose of ranking each mechanism with respect to a set of attributes is to allow a mapping of the mechanisms onto the learning process. Each mechanism or tool is designed to support learning, but each does so in a different fashion. In order to understand the potential impact of various technologies, it is important to understand where they fit in this process. The next stage in the analysis, then, is to look at the attributes necessary for any given cell of the learning model.

TABLE 6-2 *Ranking of learning mechanisms*

Mechanism	Attribute															
	Content							User			Communication				Economics	
	1	2	3	4	5	6	7	8	9	10	11	12	13	14	15	16
Audio																
Lecture	5	3	8	1	1	10	10	8	1	5	5	3	8	10	3	8
Case study	5	10	3	3	5	10	10	8	5	5	5	5	8	10	5	10
Class discussion	5	10	3	3	1	10	10	8	8	5	5	5	3	10	5	10
Tape	5	5	8	5	3	10	10	5	10	5	5	5	10	5	5	3
Radio	5	5	8	5	3	10	10	10	10	3	5	5	10	10	5	3
Visual																
Visual aids	5	3	10	10	1	8	10	10	8	5	3	5	10	8	5	10
Film	1	3	5	1	10	8	10	8	10	8	1	1	10	8	8	5
Videotape	1	3	5	1	5	8	10	8	8	8	1	1	10	8	8	5
Cable TV	1	3	5	1	5	8	3	10	10	5	1	1	10	10	8	3
Written																
Textbooks	5	3	8	3	10	10	10	10	10	1	8	8	10	5	1	1
PI	10	5	10	10	8	10	10	10	8	1	8	10	3	8	3	1
Study modules	10	3	10	5	8	8	10	8	8	3	8	8	5	8	3	1
Written assignments	10	5	10	10	5	10	3	8	8	1	8	8	3	8	10	1
Computer																
Tutorial	10	5	8	10	8	10	10	5	5	5	8	10	3	5	5	3
Drill and practice	3	5	8	8	8	3	5	3	5	5	8	8	1	5	5	3
Problem solving	1	5	5	8	8	3	1	3	3	5	8	8	1	3	8	3
Inquiry	8	8	1	1	8	5	8	1	3	5	5	8	5	1	10	3
Simulation	1	5	1	1	8	1	1	1	3	5	3	5	3	3	10	3
Games	1	5	3	1	8	1	3	3	3	5	3	3	5	5	10	3
Others																
Laboratory experiments	5	5	1	10	8	10	10	3	10	8	5	8	1	10	10	10
Real-world experience	10	10	1	10	5	10	10	3	5	10	3	3	5	10	10	8

**THE ATTRIBUTE
NEEDS OF EACH
CELL OF THE
LEARNING
MODEL**

The learning model presented in Chapter 2 has 16 separate cells, suggesting that the learner goes through a differentiable type of learning experience from cell to cell. If this is so, it is reasonable to conclude that the learning mechanisms available to the learner should vary from cell to cell in a manner that best supports the differential learning process.

Figure 6-1 shows each cell of the learning model from Chapter 2 annotated with the attributes of the learning mechanisms that are most significant in supporting the learning process in that particular cell. These are called *primary* attributes and are shown at the top of each cell. Also shown for each cell are attributes of learning mechanisms that are especially desirable in *some* types of learning tasks that occur in that cell but that are not as ubiquitously necessary as are the primary attributes. The numbers shown in each case refer to the attributes note in Table 6-1.

Cell 1-1: The acquisition of facts

The acquisition of facts is usually a high-volume process that requires the learner to be provided with learning mechanisms that are cheap, easy to use, and available whenever the learner desires to turn to the process of an initial acquaintance with a new body of knowledge. Thus, attributes of cost (15), decentralized availability (16), and ease of use (10) are shown as primary

FIGURE 6-1 *The learning process and attributes of learning mechanisms*

	Acquire	*Embed*	*Integrate*	*Test*
Facts	10,15,16 ——— 1,2,11,12	13 ——— 2,6,8,9,10,15,16	2,8,9,14 ——— 7	13,14 ———
Skills	15 ——— 10,16	8,13 ——— 2,6,9,10,15.16	2,6,8,9,13 ——— 7	3,6,13,14 ———
Established concepts	2,4 ——— 10.15.16	2,6,13 ——— 8.9	2,6,8,9,13,14 ——— 4,7	1,3,6,7,8,9,14 ———
Frontier concepts	2,4,5,9 ———	2,6,7,8,9,13,14 ——— 3,4	3,7,8,9 ——— 1,4,6,14	1.3,4,6,7,8,9,14 ——— 5

factors in cell 1-1. For some initial acquisition of facts, the attributes of sensory (11) and emotional (12) impact as well as the ability to telescope time (1) and present structure (2) are important.

For example, if a large body of boring facts has to be absorbed by the learner in a short period of time, the learning process is more effective if sensory and emotional forces can be employed to motivate the learner. This learning situation is not all that frequent, and as a result, these factors are shown as being secondary for this cell.

Cell 1-2: The acquisition of skills and procedures

Learning attributes applicable to this cell are somewhat similar to those of cell 1-1. However, they differ in emphasis. The prime attribute necessary for the initial acquisition of skills and procedures is, we feel, low cost (15). There are many thousands of skills and procedures that must be initially communicated to learners. It is necessary, therefore, to keep cost low in this cell. For the same reasons as were just noted, it would be desirable to have mechanisms in this cell available on a decentralized basis and easy to use. However, some of the procedures and many of the skills that are to be learned require access to essentially immobile, sometimes difficult-to-operate equipment. Chemistry or biology laboratory equipment is a prime example of this. As another example, much computer-operator training requires the availability of an actual console. Therefore, cost is deemed a primary factor in this cell, while decentralized availability (16) and ease of use (10) are relegated to secondary importance.

Cell 1-3: The initial acquisition of established concepts

Concepts are perhaps the meat of education. Unlike facts, they are sometimes not intuitively obvious or simple to grasp. They can be seen as part of a relatively complex structure or as having a rich structure of their own. The student must understand this structure and, in many cases, the overall structural context (no matter how "messy" it is) in which a particular concept exists if he is to effectively grasp the concept itself. As a result, the two attributes dealing with presentation of structure (2) and provision of ill-structured material (4) are felt to be primary with regard to the initial acquisition of established concepts. Attributes of secondary importance include most of the other attributes noted above in previous cells concerning the acquisition of facts and skills—particularly ease of use (10), low cost (15), and decentralized availability (16). These attributes are of importance, yet they are not the primary keys to learning within this particular cell.

Cell 1-4: The acquisition of frontier concepts
As noted in Chapter 2, frontier concepts are those that have recently been added to the repertoire of significant concepts in the field or are in the process of being added. Learning them is primarily based on the two primary attributes noted in the cell above, namely the ability to present structure (2) and to handle ill-structured material (4). There are two significant additions, however. Since many of these frontier concepts are based on the findings of recent research, the learning mechanisms which are involved in this sector of the learning process must be able to provide new and timely material to the student (attribute 5). And since nonintuitive or complex concepts must often be integrated to the individual student along lines *he* understands, attribute 9, the ability to adjust to individual learner needs and background, is often necessary here.

One might suggest that the secondary attributes noted above in cell 1-3 are also of secondary importance to the acquisition of frontier concepts. However, since there are relatively few frontier concepts at any particular time to be communicated to learners, the cost per fact (within normal limits) is of relatively little importance in this area of learning. Likewise, the minimal number of these concepts suggests that the availability of learning mechanisms on a decentralized basis or of those that are easy to use is also of relatively low importance in the learning of frontier concepts. A case could, perhaps, be made for the importance of telescoping time to present some frontier concepts. We have chosen, however, not to classify this attribute as a secondary need of this cell, since the number of cases in which it would be needed is relatively small.

Cell 2-1: The embedding of facts
For most learners, the process of salting away facts that they have come in contact with is performed either by a method of self-testing (in which the student sits down and tries to think

through his new knowledge) or, more commonly, by a set of class assignments for which the answers are to be determined and handed in. In this process feedback is provided to the learner, both through his own perception as to whether he has understood the material and through graders' notations on an exercise he has handed in. This feedback is perhaps the critical ingredient in the embedding process.

Through feedback-oriented exercises the learner is forced to attempt to recall, manipulate, and put in a small, relevant focus those facts he has "learned." Various methods of feedback allow him to recognize whether he has or has not embedded the facts in his consciousness. Thus attribute 13, feedback, is a primary attribute with regard to the process of embedding facts.

Seven other attributes are shown as secondarily desirable in this cell. The new attributes introduced at this point in the learning process are 8, degree of learner control, and 6, clerical support. In embedding new material, it is important for the learner to be able to control the pace and direction of his movement. Mechanisms that allow this flexibility enhance this aspect of the learning process. The remainder of the attributes noted as secondary attributes in this cell are also desirable. Embedding can take place more easily if the structure is clear (2) and if the mechanism is matched to the user (9). Because of the high volume of facts, the attributes of cost (15) and decentralized availability of the mechanism (16) are always important, as is ease of use (10). However, the critical factor in the embedding process is the ability of the learner to receive enough feedback to ensure that he does understand and has carefully filed for future reference the facts he was to have learned.

Cell 2-2: The embedding of skills and procedures
The arguments noted for the cell above hold for this cell too. There is perhaps a greater need for learner control (8), but the rest of the attributes are similar.

Cell 2-3: The embedding of established concepts
Since concepts are more complex than facts, skills, and procedures, it is (as noted in the section on acquisition) important to be able to understand the structure of the basic concept and, quite often, the place of this particular concept within a larger

conceptual structure in order for the particular concept to be meaningful. This, we argue, holds true not only for the initial acquisition of the concept but also for the embedding of the concept. Therefore, attribute 2 (ability to present structural relationships) joins the feedback attribute (13) as a primary attribute within this cell. In addition, the clerical work (6) required to understand a concept can often be tedious and get in the way of the learning process. An example is doing the addition or subtraction involved in the process of "closing the books" in financial accounting. This tedious process, if done manually, can take hours and comprises a set of facts that clouds the conceptual accounting issue. If the learner could call for assistance in the arithmetic, he would be much aided in embedding this new concept.

The importance of understanding concepts in relation to facts, skills, and procedures makes cost, decentralized availability, and ease of use of the learning mechanism less important than other factors. As a result, in the embedding of concepts these three attributes are dropped from the secondary list and the secondary emphasis is placed on learner control (8) and individualization of instruction (9). The reasoning behind this is simple. Students can pass through most courses without understanding all the facts or procedures that are taught. On the other hand, they can (or should) not leave a particular course without understanding the basic established concepts of that course. As a result, factors such as cost and decentralized availability of learning assistance are of vastly lower priority in this cell than attributes such as the ability of the learning mechanism to assist the learner with his individual needs.

Cell 2-4: The embedding of frontier concepts

The embedding of frontier concepts is not a simple proposition. It requires all the factors just noted plus, we believe, the ability for the student to prove the validity of these concepts to himself.

Frontier concepts involve many ideas that the student has previously been exposed to but also many that may appear counterintuitive given the student's previous conceptual base. The learner will have to approach his understanding and engraining of these concepts from a very individual base—(8), (9). He may have to probe the available data—(6), (7)—and his existing knowledge in many ways (14). In many cases, he will also need the ability to discuss his findings in relation to the existing theory—(2), (13).

Cell 3-1: The integration of facts

Integration, whether it be a new fact or a new frontier concept, into a student's own internal conceptual structure is a very poorly understood process. It is certainly particular to the individual, and any learning aid must facilitate this (9). To perform the task of integration of any part of knowledge into the broader conceptual scheme, a student must attack the problem in his own way (8), for his own conceptual background heavily determines how and in what way the new material is integrated. Furthermore, he must have access to his previous conceptual framework, its structure, and many of its details—(2), (14). In some cases, he must have the ability to manipulate parts of the structure (7) to see how they are affected by the new fact, procedure, or concept that has been offered. In a sense, he adjusts his world view for the new data, and when he has fully integrated the data, he assesses the impact this change has on his world view.

Cell 3-2: The integration of skills and procedures

Beyond the need to perceive structure (2), other support is required to link a new skill to those previously learned. To provide practice in this, the learner requires clerical support (6) so that he can move quickly and easily from one linkage attempt to the next. Once again the flexibility (9) of the mechanism to be adjusted to the user and the ability of the learner to control (8) his attempts to "put it all together" are aspects that should be present if support is to be given the linkage process.

For example, suppose the skill involved is the process of differentiation in calculus. The learning mechanism for this cell, where we are concerned with linking differentiation to integration, should have three primary attributes: structure (2), the ability to show the relationship between the two; support (6), the ability to manipulate terms and call for automatic integrations; and feedback (13), the ability to give fast response to the student on the quality of his attempt. Having the learner in charge of the pace and direction (8) of his efforts, while the degree of difficulty (9) of the problems he works on is easily adjustable, is also necessary. Often, data manipulation ability (7) can be helpful.

Cell 3-3: The integration of established concepts

The ability to present structure (2) and the support for clerical tasks (6) and for the individual to control the process—(8), (9)—remain important. Of equal importance, however, is the ability to access concepts previously learned (14). Flexible access to a data-base of concepts is a necessary ingredient in the integration process. These concepts can be in textbooks, notes, or other written material. In this form the user has to remember where and how to access them. Slightly more flexible can be computer-based retrieval that can recall families of concepts by association. In either case the ability to access is important.

Less often significant, but nonetheless useful, is the ability to provide ill-structured material (4) for the learner. It is often necessary to see how established concepts link to the less well understood material that surrounds them. A mechanism that can help one to do this well is particularly effective here. Similarly, in linking established concepts, it can sometimes be useful to employ data from one concept in another—the ability to handle data (7) then becomes important. The concept of depreciation and the concept of a balance sheet, for example, might well be integrated by taking a set of numbers on a hypothetical company and seeing the effect of depreciation on the balance sheet. Finally, if the integration is to be complete, then feedback (13) to the learner becomes important as he checks his understanding of the position in which the concept is placed.

Cell 3-4: The integration of frontier concepts

The dominant attributes here are the ability to let the learner work in a rich environment (3) that permits him to link up other concepts with the one in question and allows him to control the process—(8), (9). Class discussion with an experienced professor is one example of how this might occur. This can be further enhanced by access to data manipulation (7) facilities that permit the concept to be seen "in motion" as, for example, occurs with certain kinds of laboratory equipment. Previous concepts (14) are important in integration but perhaps less so with unstructured concepts than with structured; hence this is left as a secondary attribute. In like manner, in dealing with frontier concepts, the student may want once again to have access to ill-structured material not previously learned (4), to be able to telescope time (1), or to have clerical assistance (6) in working with his concepts.

Cell 4-1: The testing of facts

This stage in the learning process involves testing the accuracy of one's knowledge of facts and pushing on these to see whether they remain constant in all situations. This use and evaluation of facts is straightforward but does require feedback (13) and an ability to access previously learned facts or other data (14). Thus, for example, the fact that "water seeks its own level," once known by the learner, may cause him to ask the question "Why?" or "Will this happen in a vacuum?" and so forth. To answer these questions, he needs either to rely on other facts previously learned, to look at new data, or to acquire new facts, and so the learning cycle repeats itself.

Cell 4-2: The testing of skills and procedures

To test skills and procedures requires a learning mechanism that is robust and one that provides an environment (3) in which the skills can be tested. For example, to use a computer to test computer-programming skills would allow the learner to practice in a real environment, thus testing his skills. Access to the commands of a particular programming language (14), coupled with feedback (13) and some support to allow the testing to occur easily (6), provides the minimum necessary support for learning in this cell.

Cell 4-3: The testing of established concepts

For a student to try out a new concept (whether it be established or frontier) in an environment dissimilar to the one in which he learned the concept, several factors are significant. First, this most difficult learning task is, once again, a highly individual matter (9). As with facts and skills, the environment in which concepts are tried can be dictated by the teacher, but since concepts are the root of learning, it is *more desirable* for the student to pick for himself the site at which to test this knowledge. It is clearly desirable for him to have some control over the learning process (8) so that he can play with several possible adaptations of the concept to new situations. In a sense he must have a very individual set of wide-ranging tools, and he must also have access to an environment that is rich in data (3) to allow him to assess the consequences of the concept in situations with vastly differing configurations and contingencies. Since the matter of probing for model-fit is difficult, the student set on this path should have as much clerical assistance (6) and as many configurations of data and data processing tools (7) as possible to assist him in his endeavors. Therefore there is a need for data and data manipulation if a student is really to test out his understanding of a concept. The ability to telescope time (1) can also provide powerful support in testing. Access to data and model (14) is also clearly necessary in this complex task. Computer simulations of the flow of traffic are an example where data manipulation and collapsing time are put to good use in testing the concept of "queueing theory" in an actual situation. The testing of concepts in a thorough way is an important piece of learning because it can provide much of the motivation to learn more, as, for example, when the test turns up some unexpected results and the learner must seek a reason why.

Cell 4-4: The testing of frontier concepts
The differences here are of degree rather than kind; all the remarks for cell 4-3 hold equally well for this cell. There is the addition of the requirement to be able to perhaps internally view some additional poorly structured material (4). To the extent that the mechanism can handle such material, the learner has an easier time grasping what has to be tested. The learning aid must sometimes also have the ability to capture and retain new data quickly (5), since it is from these new data that frontier concepts spring—and on new sets of similar types of data that they can be tested.

A CONCEPT OF ATTRIBUTE GROUPINGS　It is clear through examination of Figure 6-1 that many attributes are found in several cells consistently grouped with certain other attributes. An analysis of these groupings leads to the definition of seven major sets of *attribute groupings*, shown in Figure 6-2.

The groupings in Figure 6-2 are of more than just casual interest. As noted in Figure 6-3, they transpose Figure 6-1 into a

FIGURE 6-2   *Attribute groupings*

Cost effectiveness (C-E)

10   Ease of use
15   Cost
16   Decentralized availability

Real-world emulation (EMUL)

1   Telescope time
3   Rich environment

Acquisition enhancement (ENH)

1   Ability to telescope time
2   Ability to present structure
11   Sensory impact
12   Emotional impact

Data recall and manipulation (MANIP)

7   Data manipulation ability
14   Fast access to data, models, etc.

Adaptation (ADAPT)

2   Present structure
4   Deal with ill-structured material
5   Present new material
9   Individualization

Learner control and assistance (L/CTL)

2   Structure clearly presented
6   Clerical assistance
8   Learner control
9   Individualization

Feedback (FDBK)

13   Feedback

FIGURE 6-3 *Relative importance of attribute groupings in cells of the learning matrix*

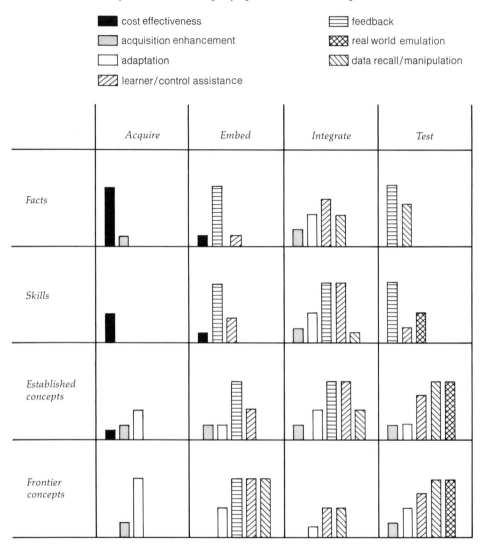

more compact form in which attribute groups dominate. It is perhaps of most interest, however, to note the patterns into which these groupings fall, shown in Figure 6-4. This figure overlays five major *areas of influence* (we shall use the shorthand term *area* henceforth) onto the 16-cell learning model. The first area (I) is that of the acquisition of facts, skills, and some established concepts, which is heavily dominated by cost-effective grouping (C-E). The second major area (II) emphasizes the

FIGURE 6-4 *Attribute groupings by stages in the learning process*

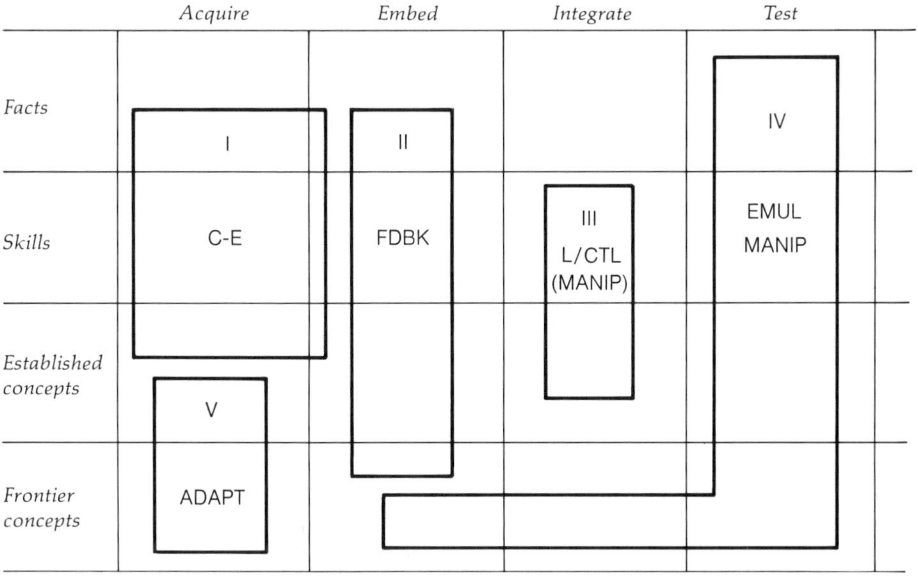

NOTE: Feedback is an essential ingredient in learner control manipulation. Enrichment is at a secondary level in almost all areas.

importance of feedback to the embedding process. The third area (III) emphasizes the importance of the attribute of learner control, and sometimes manipulation, to some parts of the integration stage of the learning model. The fourth overlay area (IV) emphasizes the importance of a rich environment and data manipulation to the student who is attempting to try out new concepts in a new situation or is struggling to integrate some concepts into his current knowledge. Finally, overlay area V suggests that in the acquisition of frontier concepts and established concepts the learning aid must be highly adaptable. It must be able to present new material and extrapolate therefrom in a way that is meaningful for the individual learner.

Figures 6-1, 6-3, and 6-4 suggest that the support needed for the learner grows more complex as we move from the upper left-hand corner toward the bottom and right. The number of attributes grows, and the expensiveness of the attribute as translated into learning mechanisms in terms of manpower and dollars also increases. This is a partial explanation of why most formal education has remained to the top and left side of the matrix.

Figure 6-4 can be translated into its implications for the use of technology in the learning process by ranking each learning mechanism on its merits with respect to meeting the demands of the dominant group in each cell of the matrix. To do so, we return to the attribute ranking shown in Table 6-2 and select the mechanism that ranks highest in each *area* of Figure 6-4. The first of the groups shown in Figure 6-4 is the cost-effective group.

I. *Cost-effectiveness attributes*

These are determined with regard to the acquisition of facts, skills, and simple established concepts—cells 1-1, 1-2, and 1-3.

The attributes that dominate the learning process in the area of acquisition of facts, skills, and established concepts (area I) are those bearing on cost effectiveness. A large percentage of all students' time is spent in this activity, and it is critical to be able to handle large volumes of both facts and students. The attributes of cost, decentralized availability, and ease of use are the ones of central concern. The mechanisms that come out best are as shown in Table 6-3. The textbook clearly dominates, closely followed by paper programmed instruction. Even the cost of computer technology, which is certainly decreasing, will not, we believe, affect the decentralized availability or ease-of-use attributes possessed by the paper-based mechanisms in the next decade. There is no innovation presently visible in the communications or computer technology fields that will bring any of the other mechanisms up to the rough levels of these three attributes.

For these three cells in the learning process, then, it can be argued that the five mechanisms listed have the greatest poten-

TABLE 6-3 **Learning** **mechanisms with** **high cost-** **effectiveness** **attributes**	*Low-cost* *data (15)*	*Decentralized* *availability (16)*	*Ease of* *use (10)*
Texts	1	1	1
Radio	5	3	3
Cable TV	8	3	5
PI	3	1	1
Study modules	3	1	3

tial and are the ones on which the most developmental effort should be spent. It can also be argued that computer technology is *not* likely to prove to be a serious contender in the next few years. Unfortunately a great deal of money has already been spent (see Molnar, 1971) on attempting to use computers in exactly this role; such efforts are currently unrewarding for this aspect of learning because the textbook will remain more effective for at least the foreseeable future. Since funds for computer assistance to higher learning are limited, it appears best to *not* spend them in this area at this time.

Technology will certainly affect the textbook, however; with microfiche readers it already has. These optical replacements have lower cost and considerably reduced storage requirements. For a library system they are most attractive, but for an individual student they are less satisfactory. The lack of hard copy for later referral, clumsy optical readers, and similar disadvantages of microfiche are likely to leave the textbook as we know it as an active leader in the acquisition stages of learning for a long time to come.

As was pointed out earlier, Table 6-2 is a very simplistic view of learning mechanisms and their attributes. However, it is explicit and incorporates our best estimate. For those who feel strongly about modifications, these can easily be made and the analysis repeated with different attributes and different weights. For the initial acquisition of facts, skills, etc., we expect, in general, that textbooks and other paper forms will continue to dominate in the near future. For special audiences radio and TV are a secondary choice—but a less adequate one. In addition, there will be special cases where other mechanisms are helpful. The "attention-drawing" and sense-stimulating aspects of such mechanisms as computer tutorial programs can, for example, be specially utilized in remedial learning with disadvantaged groups, poor learners, etc.

II. *Feedback attributes*

Embedding of facts, skills, and established concepts—cells 2-1, 2-2, and 2-3.

In contrast to acquisition, the embedding of skills is dominated by laboratory exercises, computer drill and practice, and computerized problem solving (see Table 6-4). In the laboratory, the student can try an experiment and "immediately" see

TABLE 6-4
Learning
mechanisms with
a high feedback
(13) attribute

	Learner feedback
Tutorial	3
Drill and practice	1
Problem solving	1
Paper programmed instruction	3
Class discussion	3
Laboratory	1
Simulation	3
Written assignments	3

his results. He is involved physically and mentally in a quality process of education, according to most educators. This is often expensive education, however.

As stated in Chapter 5, computerized drill and practice is excellent for providing immediate feedback to students as well as helping in the learning process. The feedback is fast and direct. Although costly today (1974), we expect this to become a dominant method of learner feedback in years to come. Computerized problem solving, as is evident from earlier discussion, is important in providing feedback for skills, procedures, and concepts rather than facts per se. One can expect this area to grow also, as the computer handles clerical chores and lets the student concentrate on the intellectual parts of problems— diagnosis, setting up solutions, and so on. Once again a very large number of students spend a considerable portion of their time in this stage of learning, and any improvement in effectiveness will have a massive impact on the educational system.

As today's dominant mode of feedback is written assignments and laboratory exercises, we earlier scored the former somewhat lower than alternative methods since it generally has a time delay of some dimension. Because of their expense, some laboratories are being phased out of the educational process today. We expect that computer-based support will move in to supply the feedback required by learners (in many cases allowing them to simulate lab experiments), although cost and availability still remain bottlenecks today. In the future we can expect these bottlenecks to decrease on the cost side as shown in Chapter 4—and this alone will impact availability. However, the marginal gain of shifting to computer terminals to handle this stage of the learning process may not be perceived as worth the cost by many faculty. In any event the widespread availability and ease-of-use attributes will prevent massive shifts to high-technology embedding in the immediate future, although computers appear to be a reasonable bet in the next 5 to 10 years in the embedding process.

III. *Learner-control attributes*

Integration of skills and established concepts—cells 3-2 and 3-3.

Integration is basically a personal thing. There is a need for the learner to work by himself to "put things together." This requires learning mechanisms that assist structuring and allow the learner to be proactive—to explore his own paths.

The mechanisms that lend themselves to support of the integration of skills and established concepts are given in Table 6-5. These fall into two categories, those devices with strong, direct, learner-control attributes on the one hand and those with an ability to present structure on the other. With the possible exception of computer-based drill and practice, simulation, and problem solving, there is little overlap in strengths.

These three computer-based mechanisms have the potential to be strongly under user control, although this potential is not always realized in practice. For example, drill and practice can

TABLE 6-5 *Learning mechanisms with high learner-control attributes*

	Learner control (8)	Present structure (2)	Clerical support (6)	Individuali- zation (9)
Drill and practice	3	5	3	5
Inquiry	1	8	5	3
Simulation	1	5	1	3
Problem solving	3	5	3	3
Film	8	3	8	10
Videotape	8	3	8	8
Study modules	8	3	8	8

be implemented on a computer with virtually no user control. When the computer puts out a request, the system is often programmed to expect a response in a standard format. Little structure is presented to allow a student to link one fact or concept to another. The student cannot manipulate data or test new connections. However, the basic technology does lend itself to control by the user, as the software can be written to accept user control and to incorporate extensive enough data to allow integration with previously presented concepts, facts, etc.

With the inquiry, simulation, and problem-solving mechanisms learner control can be implicit. These types of devices can be manipulated by the user to provide linkages with other material as he sees fit. With some of these systems (see Appendix A) this modification and manipulation occurs on-line as the user proceeds through his learning effort. Laboratory experiments have some of the same attributes of learner control but typically with a much higher expense. Given the expense of most laboratory facilities and the difficulty in using them for unstructured integration purposes, this mechanism has not been considered here.

Although these four mechanisms (drill and practice, inquiry, simulation, and problem solving) rank high on learner control, they are weaker on their ability to present the overall structure of a given set of skills or concepts. The second group (film, videotape, etc.) is weak on learner control but strong on structure. The ability of these visual mechanisms—through graphs, time collapsing, and other presentation techniques—to give a viewer a sense of structure is very strong. But since a film or presentation is made previous to the time of use, user control is limited to selecting a package, one that may or may not contain the right mix of content for the student. It is hard to see any technology that will change these aspects of visual presentation—certainly no new approach is visible now. It is reasonable to assume that for something like the next few years this aspect of learning is unlikely to change.

This analysis suggests that to effect integration of new skills and established concepts into an individual's existing knowledge base requires a mix of learning mechanisms. Moreover, the mechanisms suggested do not include any of the traditional ones. Some of the newer ones that have a computer technology base appear most effective for this stage in the learning process.

This aspect of learning and the fourth stage of the learning process (testing) have long been neglected as points of focus in education. Integration in particular has been neatly side-stepped with such phrases as "We leave it up to the student to put this in context." Since integration is a very personal issue—each student has his own way of learning and his own unique set of experiences—it is not possible to prescribe to the student a set of activities that will efficiently accomplish integration. In some real sense it must be left up to the student.

In the past, some integration was accomplished with adequate lectures, and, with more power available through technology, it is now becoming possible to do a better job. Whether the technology is being actively deployed for this is a moot point. Films seem to be used more often for emotional and sensory impact than for presenting an overview or structure. Similarly, many more dollars for development and student hours of use have been spent on using computers for fact or skill acquisition than they have on integration. Nonetheless, the potential is there. (See Appendix A, for example.) This use of technology may not have occurred to any great extent yet, but it will inevitably increase as we begin to see the benefit that results. The increasing use of the manipulative capacity of the computer, under the control of the learner, is an example of this increase.

IV. *Emulation and manipulation attributes*

Testing of facts, skills, and concepts and embedding and integration of frontier concepts—cells 2-4, 3-4, 4-1, 4-2, 4-3, and 4-4.

The mechanisms that lend themselves to support of area IV, which includes some segments of the integration and testing phases of learning from our taxonomy, are the four given in Table 6-6. As in the previous two areas, computer-based mechanisms have the greatest ability to support this stage of the learning process. A student support system that provides computerized access to simulation ability dominates, followed closely by problem-solving capabilities, games, and inquiry systems. Of the more conventional "tools," laboratory support scores fairly highly. Other traditional mechanisms, such as class discussion and written assignments or tests, have some strengths but are not nearly as strong.

TABLE 6-6 *Learning mechanisms with high emulation and manipulation attributes*

	Rich environment (3)	Telescope time (1)	Data manipulation (7)	Fast access to previous data (14)
Simulation	1	1	3	1
Inquiry	1	8	1	8
Laboratory	1	5	10	10
Written assignments	10	10	8	3
Class discussion	3	5	10	10
Case discussion	3	5	10	10
Real world	1	10	10	10
Games	3	1	3	5
Problem solving	5	1	1	3

The attributes that comprise the two major groups of real-world emulation and data manipulation are of interest in this area. Other aspects of the process of integration and testing are clearly relevant, but we argue that these are the dominant ones. In most instances today mechanisms with these attributes are relatively unavailable to students, and as a result the testing phase, particularly of concepts, is left up to the student and often takes place after he has left the university.

To provide a simulated real-world experience in which to test concepts and skills is not easy. If we rely solely on traditional mechanisms, it is time-consuming and expensive as well. Field trips or elaborate laboratories can be extended only to a few students and are enormously time-consuming. Case studies, which are widely used in some fields, such as business and law, are more effective; as is clear from Table 6-6, however, they do not allow much in the way of access to previous data or to manipulative capability.

The emulation and manipulation notions are self-evident in the sciences and engineering. To test one's concepts of bridge design in a laboratory by building toy bridges and loading them to see where they fail is an obviously powerful method of testing. This slow, expensive, mechanical means of testing is now being replaced by conceptual testing whereby the student draws a bridge on a computer-driven visual display and simulates the collapse. This sharply reduces the setup time and busywork (building the bridge) that the student must employ and is thus much more cost effective. It may be, however, that the time saved by such teaching changes just offsets the amount of time the student must spend in learning new material if he is to keep up with our expanding knowledge base.

In other fields, such as English, the written assignment is the manipulative mechanism. The student may create a short story, poem, or other work. Even in these cases, however, fast access to data—automated retrieval by content or theme of previous authors, for example—could provide powerful support for learning. In this field technology has barely begun to take hold. Although the basic technology for, say, a computer-compatible library either already exists (mass storage) or is close (laser-based storage), we are a long way from moving from today's technology into this new technology. We can store a book, for example, on a computer disk file or, more recently, a laser-based computer storage device. However, to convert all our existing books, with today's technology, to such a system is out of the question. Further, if we were to do that, we would then have to expend further effort to codify the content of the books in such a way as to make them usefully accessible for comparison or idea-testing exercises. Neither of these steps is close to being a reality.

A middle ground, however, has emerged. The gap between the toy-bridge laboratory and the experimental English essay is too large for any form of technology to span. But subjects in-between—for example, mathematics and many aspects of the social sciences—do lend themselves to conceptual, if not physical, models. Here a student can now access a previously constructed model or build one himself. Or it may be possible to access supporting concepts, such as differentiation in calculus, and use *computer*-based differentiation skills in solving the problem in physics that one is using as a test of a recent learning experience. The built-in manipulation ability gives the student access to a richer, more realistic setting than he would otherwise have.

In a similar way, the ability to emulate the real world and manipulate data can provide the critical extra dimension required to embed or integrate frontier concepts. By their very nature such concepts are imprecise and hard to deal with.

Discussion with colleagues is the time-honored method for embedding and integrating these concepts. As discussed above, however, more technologically based solutions are possible; in the sciences and engineering, technological support is probably necessary—as such it has an enormous influence. In this frontier area, though, we are not in a position of encouraging its use; the demands of the concepts themselves force its adoption. We believe this will continue to occur slowly over time.

V. *Adaptation attributes*

Acquisition of complex established concepts and frontier concepts, cells 1-3 and 1-4.

The mechanisms that support the adaptation required to help the learner acquire frontier concepts and complex established concepts are given in Table 6-7. These are dominated, in this analysis, by the lecture. In terms of the adjustability of the mechanism, there can be no doubt that most lecturers are able to adjust their material, to their audience or to the availability of new facts, with considerable ease. Indeed the adjustment to the audience goes on during a lecture. All the remaining mechanisms suffer from a major limitation on one of the four attribute

TABLE 6-7   *Learning mechanisms with high adaptation attributes*

	Ability to adjust to individual learner needs (9)	*Ability to present ill-structured material (4)*	*Flexibility for adding new material (5)*	*Ability to present structure (2)*
Lecture	1	1	1	3
Inquiry	3	1	8	8
Simulation	3	1	8	5
Film	10	1	10	3
Videotape	8	1	5	3
TV	10	1	5	3
Class discussion	5	3	1	5
Tape	10	5	3	5
Radio	10	5	3	5

dimensions. Class discussion, with intelligent professor guidance, can also be useful here.

The computer-based technologies tend to be modestly flexible in their ability to be tailored to each user; they can learn from the user's responses and modify themselves accordingly. For example, if the student answers all questions correctly in computer-based tutorial instruction, the system, sensing this, can be built in such a way as to provide bigger conceptual jumps between frames. In the inquiry and simulation areas, of course, the system is built to be used by the student in any way he pleases and thus is infinitely adjustable, given what is there. These mechanisms are not as powerful as a human lecturer because there is difficulty and sometimes extensive lead time necessary to adjust to what is there. Inquiry and simulation are still not simple when it comes to adding new material and are not particularly useful for initially presenting new structures to students.

The visually based mechanisms do well on the structure dimension—they can present well-structured concepts effectively, thus making their acquisition easier. They also possess the flexibility to portray ill-structured material. It seems unlikely, however, that we shall be able to develop technology in the near future that will make a material difference in the ability of these mechanisms to adjust to one student or a group of students at any moment in time. The basic nature of the medium prevents this. Technological advances in production of videotape will eventually cause this medium to be substantially improved in adding new material. The overall impact on the higher education system, however, is likely to be small, as the number of students and concepts where videotape is employed is not great.

The audio-based mechanisms are almost as flexible as the lecturer but suffer heavily from lack of easy adjustability. Once again the basic nature of the mechanism prevents any major advances here.

CONCLUSIONS This analysis of the mechanisms available to higher education and their likely impact on the learning process suggests strongly that the emphasis must be placed on maintaining an adequate smorgasbord. To emphasize one mechanism, to invest in one, fashionable technique, is necessarily going to be unsuccessful. A great deal of what many computer enthusiasts have seen as stubbornness, if not downright stupidity, on the part of their colleagues at not leaping to utilize a particular technological innovation might more reasonably be termed common sense. Advocacy of any one of these mechanisms to the exclusion of the remainder is foolish.

The analysis has shown that the different stages of learning require different types of mechanisms to put the material across in an effective way. We are able, in some cases, to do an adequate job using only one mechanism, particularly if it is one as versatile as a good lecturer. Such a single-minded approach is not effective, however. Different technologies support different aspects of learning.

In a similar fashion different learning mechanisms should match the differing kinds of material that need to be taught. The teaching of facts poses different problems than does the teaching of frontier concepts. At this point in building this model we have not chosen to distinguish between the material in different fields. This might be a useful analysis to make. It seems to us, however, that in all fields of learning our four categories exist, and that the generalizations one can make about the impact of technology are more likely to hold true for these basic categories than they are for a particular subject area.

Where do computers fit? One of the questions asked in Chapter 1 was, "Where should the money be invested in computers to assist the learning process?" The analysis in this chapter presents, on the basis of one learning model and a particular ranking of learning-mechanism attributes, a clear answer to this question.

From this model it is clear that the traditional learning mechanisms will continue to be used, and in some aspects of the learning process are unlikely to be replaced. We believe that dollars should not be spent "computerizing" these areas except in special circumstances. As this chapter notes, areas I and V (cost effectiveness and adaptability) in the learning model demand attributes of learning mechanisms that are possessed today, and probably for the next several years, most plentifully by traditional mechanisms. In area I the textbook dominates (see Table 6-3), followed most closely by paper programmed instruction texts. In area V the professor, utilizing the learning mechanisms of the lecture and classroom discussions, appears best fitted. Computers do not appear likely to be able to assist the learner as well as the professor for the next several years—except for special cases, such as remedial learning in area I.

There are major areas where computers and other forms of technology can have a highly useful impact, however. Where feedback, the need for learner control of the learning environment, and access to and manipulation of data dominate the learning process (areas II, III, and IV), we expect to see sharply increasing technological components. In these three areas, as we have noted, the attributes demanded of mechanisms to assist the learning process present a close fit with those attributes possessed by one or more of the six major adaptations of the computer to assist the learning process. In area II, learning requirements match most clearly with computerized drill and practice and problem solving—although traditional paper written assignments will undoubtedly dominate this area for awhile yet. At least on a normative basis, however, the case for computer-aided drill and practice in area II is a very reasonable one. We would expect the decrease in computer costs over the next several years to allow computerized drill and practice to make major inroads into this area—to the benefit of student learning.

Areas III and IV involve segments of the learning process which, to a very great extent, have been left to the student alone because most traditional learning mechanisms are relatively inadequate. Here we expect that mechanisms such as computerized simulation, games, inquiry, and problem solving, which dominate in their ability to assist the learning process, should and will receive significant application and ultimately dominate educational efforts in these areas.

This model suggests where higher education dollars can best be spent with regard to computer assistance to the learning process. However, it is only a *general* model. Material for each course must be examined as to its *particular* attributes, and the most appropriate learning aids must be selected for the material in that course. An example of this particular exercise, as carried out by one of us, is described in Appendix B.

As we review this model and its implications, we find exceptions in every instance. Computer-based tutorial instruction for remedial-learning purposes is one such exception in area I. Audiocassettes appear to be helpful in some drill-and-practice sessions in area II. And so it goes. Education and the learning process are too complex and too varied to be captured in one relatively simple model. Yet we need a simplified model of reality on which to base decisions. This one is useful to us. We hope the model and/or the method is also useful to others. It is hoped that deans, department heads, and course managers will find it helpful in examining the material they teach—and in picking the places to allocate resources when they contemplate spending additional capital in the area of learning technology, most especially computers.

The limiting factor in adapting computers and other technology to aid learning, at the present time, is our ability to understand the learning process, not our ability to develop technology. Indeed we already have far more technology than we have applied well. The individual professor's understanding of the teaching process, and which mechanism should be used for which material and which stage, is poor. Work is required in the area of understanding the adult learning process. This basic research, at the heart of the education business, is not proceeding rapidly. We are impressed with what is not known and convinced that we and many other faculty have devoted too little time to understanding the process of learning. Without such understanding it is hard to believe one is doing the most cost-effective, let alone effective, job of delivering knowledge to one's students.

7. Massachusetts Survey: 1974

Chapter 6 presents a model of what we believe professors *should* be doing with regard to computers in the learning process. After writing it, we became intrigued with the question of exactly what it was they *were* doing. Existing descriptive studies on the use of computers to assist learning were outdated. As a result, we undertook a study of computer utilization in all educational institutions offering a bachelor's degree or higher in the state of Massachusetts in early 1974.

For the survey, 73 institutions offering a bachelor's degree or higher and representing a student population of over 260,000 were identified. The survey was conducted during April and May 1974. Initial personal contact with each school was made by telephone. In some cases, particularly with small schools having relatively homogeneous student populations, this initial telephone interview was adequate to obtain the necessary information. In other cases, particularly with larger universities, personal interviews were conducted with faculty, administrators, and computer-center staff who were knowledgeable about activities in the various parts of the university. Eight man (and woman) weeks were spent in the face-to-face interviewing process.

An effort was made to collect data in a form compatible with that of previous surveys. Two basic types of information were collected: (1) the level and the type of computer activity of the school as a whole, including information on overall expenditures, hardware configurations, computer science activity, and general directions of the school, and (2) courses being taught that made use of the computer in some manner, including class size, specific nature of computer use, level of course offering, and the date computer use was initiated.

It was possible to contact all 73 schools. People willingly provided all information requested within the limits of its availability on campus. Of 61 schools using the computer—where detailed information was sought—58 schools were able to provide us with accurate and complete data that can be considered fully representative of the facts for those schools in the spring of 1974.

It should be noted that the schools in Massachusetts do not provide a random sample of the nation as a whole. As in Comstock's survey of California institutions (Comstock, 1972a), our data will reflect the presence of several large institutions well known for the quality of their academic programs and for their unusually high budgets for research. There may be a bias in Massachusetts vis-à-vis other states due to the relative magnitudes of different academic fields. We have no reason to believe that such a bias exists. Tables 7-1A and 7-1B attempt to identify another bias by comparing the distribution of schools by degree level and enrollment in the 1974 Massachusetts survey with the schools identified nationally by the Southern Regional Education Board (SREB) in its 1967 survey. It is apparent that Massachusetts has some bias toward institutions offering master's and doctorate degrees; 70 percent of the Massachusetts sample were institutions granting these degrees. The comparable national percent is 57 percent (two-year institutions or those offering associate degrees excluded). It is unlikely, however, that this bias will greatly limit the usefulness of comparisons. Comparisons at the disaggregated level will of course not be affected.

The discussion that follows comprises (1) a discussion of aggregate data and the identification of major institutional trends, (2) a discussion of instructional uses that focuses on variations in use by discipline, and (3) a discussion of the nature of the computer use within all disciplines.

AGGREGATE DISCUSSION: SOME INSTITUTIONAL TRENDS

Of the 73 colleges and universities in Massachusetts offering a bachelor's degree or higher, 61 schools, or 84 percent of the total, were actively using the computer in some way. For this use, we found that they are currently spending over $23 million or about $89 for every student currently enrolled. Of the 61 schools using the computer, only 52 (71 percent of the total) make any use of the computer in instruction, at a cost of about

TABLE 7-1A *Institutions of higher education included in the Massachusetts and SREB national surveys*

| Level and enrollment | Massachusetts survey, 1973–74 | | SREB national survey, 1966–67 | | |
	Number of schools	Percentage of schools	Number of schools	Percentage of schools (including associate)	Percentage of schools (excluding associate)
Associate					
Below 500	0	0	287	11.6	
500–2,499	0	0	343	13.8	
2,500–9,999	0	0	120	4.8	
10,000–19,999	0	0	23	0.9	
20,000 and above	0	0	0		
Bachelor's					
Below 500	9	12.3	257	10.4	15.1
500–2,499	10	13.7.	526	21.2	30.9
2,500–9,999	2	2.7	46	1.9	2.7
10,000–19,999	0	0	2		0.1
20,000 and above	0	0	0		0
Master's					
Below 500	6	8.2	101	4.1	5.9
500–2,499	21	28.8	196	7.9	11.5
2,500–9,999	10	13.7	191	7.7	11.2
10,000–19,999	0	0	10	0.4	0.6
20,000 and above	0	0	10	0.4	0.6
Doctorate					
Below 500	1	1.4	70	2.8	4.1
500–2,499	2	3.7	101	4.1	5.9
2,500–9,999	7	9.6	94	3.8	5.5
10,000–19,999	1	1.4	70	2.8	4.1
20,000 and above	4	5.5	30	1.2	1.8
TOTAL	73	100.0	2,477	100.0	100.0

TABLE 7-1B
Distribution of
enrollments of
institutions
included in the
Massachusetts
and SREB
national surveys
(in percentages)

Level and enrollment	Massachusetts survey, 1973–74	SREB national survey, 1966–67	
		Including associate	Excluding associate
Associate		24.4	
Below 500	0	1.2	0
500–2,499	0	7.4	0
2,500–9,999	0	10.5	0
10,000–19,999	0	5.3	0
20,000 and above	0	0	0
Bachelor's	7.6	14.6	19.4
Below 500	1.4	0.9	1.2
500–2,499	3.8	9.7	12.9
2,500–9,999	2.4	3.6	4.8
10,000–19,999	0	0.4	0.5
20,000 and above	0	0	0
Master's	33.6	24.2	33.8
Below 500	1.5	0.5	0.5
500–2,499	11.9	2.3	4.9
2,500–9,999	20.2	15.7	20.8
10,000–19,999	0	2.2	2.9
20,000 and above	0	3.5	4.7
Doctorate	58.9	35.4	46.7
Below 500	0.2	0.3	0.4
500–2,499	1.2	2.1	2.7
2,500–9,999	12.1	7.5	9.9
10,000–19,999	4.3	15.3	20.2
20,000 and above	41.1	10.2	13.5
TOTAL	100.0	100.0	100.0

$4.5 million per year (about $17 per student). Over 1,200 courses were identified in these 52 schools that make some use of the computer. We found that research expenditures in a relatively few schools consume a much larger portion of the total computer expenditures of the state than does any instructional or student use.

Type of Activity Figures 7-1a and 7-1b show a comparison of resources allocated to administrative, research, instructional, and "other" uses of the computer. Instructional use in this instance includes instruction about the computer as well as instruction with the computer. Figure 7-1a shows the breakdown from a national survey of the SREB for the operating year ending in 1967 (Comstock, 1972*b*). Total dollar amounts are estimated figures for the entire population of 2,477 colleges, extrapolated from returns of the SREB's questionnaire mailed to 1,965 institutions. We have deleted schools granting associate degrees for the sake of comparison with the 1974 Massachusetts survey. Figure 7-1b shows comparable data from the Massachusetts survey of 73 colleges for the operating year 1973–74. These data are also presented in Table 7-2.

Table 7-3 provides a more detailed comparison, showing the percentages allocated to each type of activity for schools of certain sizes and at different degree levels.

The data in Figures 7-1a and 7-1b show a striking decrease in the portion of computer expenditures being allocated to instruction. Table 7-3 further illustrates that institutions at every degree level—bachelor's, master's, and doctorate—experienced a decrease in the instructional portion of their computer expenditures. Two possible sample biases were explored: the presence of large research institutions in Massachusetts, and the predominance of doctoral institutions that may spend smaller portions of computer budgets for instruction. In the first instance, Table 7-3 illustrates that this portion of the budget has declined for institutions granting degrees at all levels. In the second matter, the SREB survey reported 81 percent of total expenditures coming from doctoral institutions; the corresponding figure in Massachusetts was 82 percent. The data thus suggest that this decline reflects the dramatic decrease in the availability of foundation and federal funding for research and instruction, as well as, most probably, an increase in need for administrative effort as financial control became increasingly important during the period 1967 to 1974. Clearly, much greater portions of total institutional budgets, at all degree levels, are being allocated to administrative applications.

It should be noted the Rosser report of the National Academy of Sciences found that about 20 percent of the total computer

FIGURE 7-1a
Allocation of expenditures by type of use, SREB national survey, 1966–67

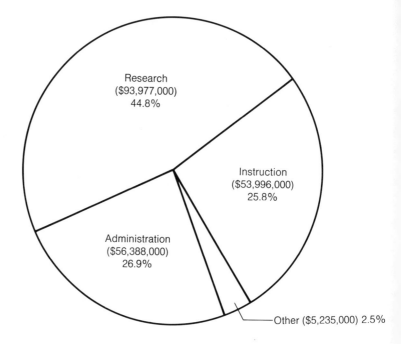

NOTE: Figures exclude expenditures by associate degree colleges.
SOURCE: Adapted from Comstock (1972*b*, pp. 150–153).

FIGURE 7-1b
Allocation of expenditures by type of use, Massachusetts survey, 1973–74

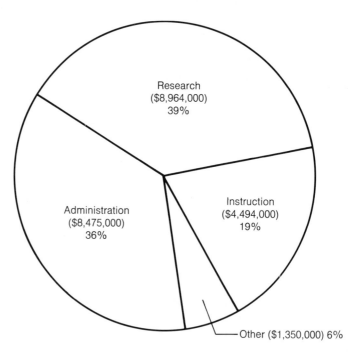

168

TABLE 7-2 Allocation of expenditures on computers, by type of activity

	Massachusetts survey, 1973–74		SREB national survey, 1966–67			
	Thousands of dollars	Percentage	Thousands of dollars	Percentage including associate	Thousands of dollars	Percentage excluding associate
Research	8,964	38.5	94,785	40.4	93,977	44.8
Administration	8,475	36.4	64,524	27.5	56,388	26.9
Instruction	4,494	19.3	69,413	29.6	53,996	25.8
Other	1,350	5.8	5,800	2.5	5,235	2.5
TOTAL	23,283	100.0	234,676	100.0	209,560	100.0

SOURCE: Data for 1966–67 derived from Comstock (1972b, table 11, p. 155).

TABLE 7-3 Allocation of expenditures on computers, by type of activity (in percentages)

Level and enrollment	Massachusetts survey, 1973–74				SREB national survey, 1966–67			
	R	A	I	O	R	A	I	O
Bachelor's	0.7	61.4	36.8	1.1	13.0	36.5	46.2	4.3
Below 500	0	39.2	60.8	0	30.7	38.0	20.3	0
500–2,499	0.8	63.2	36.0	0	11.3	33.1	52.4	3.1
2,500–9,999	0.8	67.9	28.5	2.9	13.4	41.2	38.8	6.6
10,000–19,999					20.0	20.0	60.0	0
20,000 and above								
Master's	4.0	61.2	33.8	1.1	17.0	41.2	38.6	3.2
Below 500	7.5	86.2	6.3	0	40.0	50.0	10.0	0
500–2,499	3.3	69.7	26.1	0.9	16.3	40.2	38.3	5.2
2,500–9,999	5.1	42.3	51.0	1.9	14.4	42.5	40.2	2.9
10,000–19,999					17.0	34.5	45.4	3.1
20,000 and above					19.7	32.9	43.4	3.9
Doctorate	43.0	33.1	17.3	6.5	51.8	23.7	22.2	2.3
Below 500	0	0	0	0	64.5	21.9	13.6	0
500–2,499	18.2	24.3	57.5	0	53.4	23.3	22.6	0.7
2,500–9,999	60.0	21.2	10.6	8.3	47.4	24.1	24.2	4.3
10,000–19,999	20.0	30.0	50.0	0	47.4	27.6	22.9	2.1
20,000 and above	28.9	45.6	20.1	5.4	61.2	18.4	19.3	1.2
Total	38.5	36.4	19.3	5.8	40.4	27.5	29.6	2.5

NOTE: R = research; A = administration; I = instruction; O = other.

SOURCE: Data for 1966–67 calculated from Comstock (1972*b*, table 11, p. 155).

expenditures were being allocated to instruction in 1965 (National Academy of Sciences, 1966), and predicted that this portion would decrease. Comstock's survey of California indicated that instruction comprised 27 percent of institutional budgets in 1968–69 (Comstock, 1972*a*, p. 229). The Massachusetts level of 19 percent is a clear reduction.

The extraordinary growth in *all* types of computer expenditure in higher education must be considered if a proper perspective on these changes is to be maintained. In 1969, Comstock (1972*b*, p. 134) extrapolated a predicted compound annual growth rate of about 22 percent until 1972, which would bring total expenditures in higher education to $688 million. A rough estimate can be made from our small sample of what this figure for national expenditure stands at today. The SREB study identified about 7 million students enrolled in 2,477 institutions in the country in 1967. Of these figures, the 1974 survey covered roughly 4 percent of the students (261,000) and roughly 3 percent of the schools, with the 1967 basis for extrapolation.[1] If we also assume that the average student in Massachusetts consumes about the same amount of computer resources as in other states, we can conservatively estimate that the total expenditure on computer usage in higher education nationally is now above $575 million, an increase from 1967 of almost 250 percent. This represents a compound growth rate from 1967 to 1974 of about 16 percent.

Although this growth seems large, it appears to have been somewhat smaller than the 22 percent predicted (until 1972) by Comstock, which would have projected about a $1,031 million figure for 1974. The comparison of these figures is shown in Figure 7-2. We expect that this decrease in the growth rate has been gradual since 1967, and that the actual growth rate today is at somewhat less than 16 percent. Interpreting this change in dollar growth is difficult due both to the dramatic changes in computer costs and to the inflation the United States has experienced in recent years. As suggested in Chapter 4, computer capacity per dollar today far exceeds that available in 1968–69. Even considering inflation, the equivalent computing capacity

[1]In fact, total enrollment figures now approximate 8.9 million in 2,606 institutions nationally. Thus the above extrapolation will yield conservative figures. (See U.S. Office of Education, 1973, table 110, p. 93.)

FIGURE 7-2 *Instructional computer activities by institutions of higher education*

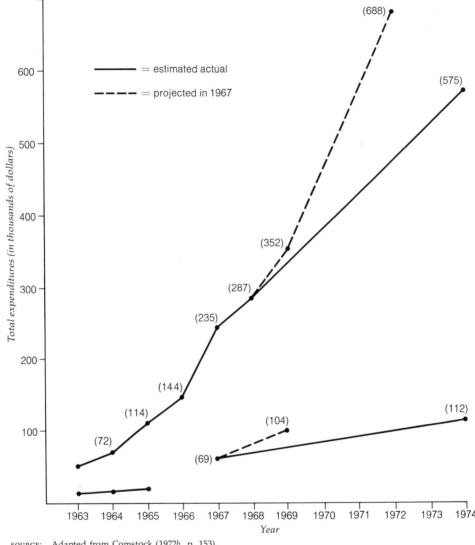

SOURCE: Adapted from Comstock (1972*b*, p. 153).

of today's hardware far exceeds the computing capacity implied by a $1 billion expenditure in 1967. With regard to the area with which we are especially concerned—instruction—the dollars spent appear to have doubled, and actual computer power delivered has therefore greatly increased.

Computer Use by Institutions As shown in Table 7-4, which compares data from Comstock's survey of California institutions in 1969 with our present data,

TABLE 7-4 Computer use in higher education, by type of institution

Type of institution	Massachusetts survey, 1973–74			California survey, 1968–69		
	Total institutions	Number using computer	Percent using computer	Total institutions	Number using computer	Percent using computer
General institutions						
Doctorate	13	13	100	15	15	100
Master's	28	27	96	42	33	79
Bachelor's	13	11	85	16	5	31
TOTAL	54	51	94	73	53	73
Other						
Medical	0			8	8	100
Specialized professional and technical	8	8	100	12	7	58
Music/art	6	2	33	6	2	33
Theology/religion	5	0	0	15	0	0
TOTAL	73	61	84	114	70	61

SOURCE: Data for 1968–69 derived from Comstock (1972a, table 40, p. 196).

TABLE 7-5 *Average total expenditures per school using computer*

Type of institution	Massachusetts survey, 1973–74			SREB national survey, 1966–67		
	Dollars	*Number using computer*	*Average*	*Dollars*	*Number using computer*	*Average*
Bachelor's	503,502	17	29,618	19,169,000	189	53,804
Master's	2,448,701	30	81,623	30,418,000	272	111,831
Doctorate	20,544,035	14	1,467,431	169,009,000	266	635,372
TOTAL	23,496,238	61	385,184	209,596,000	727	288,303

source: Data from 1966–67 derived from Comstock (1972b, tables 4 and 11, pp. 143, 155).

we found very few general institutions that were not making some use of the computer. The difference between today and 1969 is primarily that the smaller general institutions offering a master's degree or less have caught up to the larger institutions in terms of access. In addition to the increase in the use of smaller and cheaper minicomputers, the availability of large-scale computers to smaller groups of users through time-sharing networks and other administrative arrangements has been effective in making this widespread availability possible. Since 1967, when the SREB study revealed that only 39 percent of the institutions of higher education in the country were making any use of the computer (Comstock, 1972*b*, p. 143), the number of institutions using the computer has grown steadily. Judging from our results, it is clear that further growth cannot take place by introducing computers into institutions formerly having no computer. Instead, growth will come from new applications and new equipment for institutions already familiar with the technology.

There is evidence that this kind of growth has already begun, but only in institutions offering a doctorate degree. Table 7-5 indicates that for the institutions for which there was relatively little access to computers in 1967 and 1969—the institutions offering bachelor's or master's degrees—average total expenditures per school have gone down markedly. This suggests that the major source of growth within these classes has come from more use of computers by institutions that had never used them before. For doctoral institutions, just the opposite is true. Growth occurred through new applications in institutions already familiar with the technology.

INSTRUCTIONAL USES OF THE COMPUTER: AN OVERVIEW

In discussing the use of computer instruction in higher education, it is useful to distinguish between two distinct types of application. The first—instruction "about" the computer—involves a particular part of the curriculum at a university that attempts to convey to the student various aspects of computer technology itself. The most common use of the computer in courses about the computer is student practice in learning to program, although many other uses fall under this broad category.

The second application—which we call instruction "with" the computer—involves use of the computer as a tool in instruction in courses in all disciplines in the university.

TABLE 7-6 *Courses using the computer, by type of instruction and by level*

	Number of students	*Percentage of students*	*Number of courses*	*Percentage of courses*
Massachusetts survey (1973–74)				
"About" the computer, total	22,984	36.1	392	29.7
Undergraduate	15,784	68.7	266	67.9
Graduate	3,444	15.0	76	19.4
Continuing education	3,756	16.3	50	12.8
"With" the computer, total	40,816	64.0	928	70.3
Undergraduate	26,956	66.0	607	65.4
Graduate	12,560	30.8	296	31.9
Continuing education	1,300	3.2	25	2.7
Total	63,800	100.0	1,320	100.0
Undergraduate	42,740	67.0	872	66.1
Graduate	16,004	25.1	373	28.3
Continuing education	5,056	7.9	75	5.7
SREB national survey (1966–67)				
Total	380,673	100.0	n.a.*	
Undergraduate	324,753	85.3	13,391	
Graduate	55,920	14.7	n.a.	

*Not available.

SOURCE: Comstock (1972*b*, table 28, p. 177).

In Massachusetts, we found that the total expenditure for instructional uses of the computer for the institutions in our study was about $4.5 million. Of this total, the survey showed that about 43 percent was spent on instruction "about" the computer as we have defined it above, and about 57 percent, or about $2.1 million, was spent on instruction "with" computers. For other studies, such as the SREB survey or the California study, only qualitative estimates of this breakdown were made by the authors. In both studies it was reported that far more of the total expenditures were devoted to instruction "about" the computer, although the California study clearly implied that a shift from this position was taking place in 1969.

In fact, the Massachusetts percentage of expenditures for

instruction "with" the computer may tend to understate the shift in this direction. Although there are no comparable data from the previous studies, Table 7-6 shows that about 70 percent of the total courses in Massachusetts that use the computer were using it as a tool in instruction. These courses represented about 64 percent of the students being exposed to the computer through courses. The large percentage of expenditures (relative to the percentage of courses) being allocated to courses "about" the computer is understandable, as these courses generally involve simple program debugging at a continuous, high rate over the course of a semester.

About 86 percent of the courses that we identified came from institutions granting doctoral degrees. These courses included about 69 percent of the total students. Although the latter number seems high, it in fact represents a smaller percentage than Comstock found in the SREB survey. If his figures are adjusted to exclude courses taught at the associate degree level, the corresponding percentage of students from doctoral institutions is 75 percent. It seems that the gradual shift toward institutions offering only bachelor's and master's degrees is taking place as accessibility increases.

Average Costs: Per Student and per School

The 1967 report of the President's Science Advisory Committee (PSAC) recommended an average student expenditure of $60 for instructional uses of the computer. Comstock (1972*b*, p. 163) estimated that in the year set as the deadline for reaching that goal, 1971–72, only 3 classes of institutions out of a total of 40, all of them doctoral institutions, would succeed in reaching that goal. Table 7-7 shows that, on the average, the expenditures per student for instructional computer uses in 1974 was about $17, far less than the goal of $60. However, if one takes into account the increase in computer power per dollar of hardware expenditure (which was roughly doubled each year although effective output is not that great), applies this to the hardware segment of expenditures, and further adjusts for inflation, today's $17 provides much greater computer power than the $60 per student requested by PSAC could provide in 1967.

The $17-per-student figure suffers from the same problem as do all averages, however. Included in this figure are a large number of students who make no use whatever of computer systems in their courses. When one confines the averaging

TABLE 7-7 *Average expenditures for instructional computer use, by degree level (number of schools in parentheses)*

	Enrollment (all schools)	Expenditures for instruction, dollars	Average cost per student, dollars	Average cost per school, dollars
Massachusetts survey (1973–74)				
Bachelor's (21)	19,709	262,305	13	12,491
Master's (37)	87,779	657,750	7	18,047
Doctorate (15)	107,287	3,532,413	33	235,494
TOTAL (73)	260,983	4,452,468	17	60,993
SREB national survey (1966–67)				
Bachelor's (830)	1,028,600	4,064,000	4	4,896
Master's (504)	1,258,150	11,736,000	9	23,286
Doctorate (365)	2,472,550	37,563,000	15	102,912
TOTAL (1,699)	4,759,300	53,363,000	11	31,408
California survey (1968–69)				
Bachelor's (16)		n.a.*		n.a.
Master's (42)		1,376,000		32,762
Doctorate (15)		3,015,000		201,000
TOTAL (73)		>4,391,000		>60,151

*Not available.

SOURCES: SREB national survey data derived from Comstock (1972b, tables 5 and 11, pp. 144, 155). California survey data derived from Comstock (1972a, tables 40 and 62, pp. 196, 230); includes only general institutions; state colleges are included in master's; University of California is included in doctorate.

process to enrollment in courses using computers, the resulting figure is $70 (see Table 7-8). Since many students are enrolled in more than one course that uses computers, this suggests strongly that a small segment of the student population is receiving a large share of the resources.

It is also interesting to note the absolute magnitude of the number of students found in the entire nation who made use of the computer in 1967, compared with comparable data from the 1974 survey of Massachusetts (from Table 7-6). If we use the assumption that the school population of Massachusetts is similar to that of the other states in the nation, it can be conserva-

TABLE 7-8
Average
expenditures per
student enrolled
in courses using
computers

	Enrollment in courses using the computer	Expenditures for instruction, dollars	Average cost per student, dollars
Massachusetts survey (1973–74)			
Bachelor's	4,689	262,305	56
Master's	14,197	657,750	46
Doctorate	44,114	3,532,413	80
TOTAL	63,800	4,452,468	70
SREB national survey (1966–67)			
Bachelor's	32,111	4,064,000	127
Master's	60,259	11,736,000	195
Doctorate	281,161	37,563,000	134
TOTAL	373,531	55,363,000	148

SOURCE: Data derived from Comstock (1972*b*, tables 11, 31, and 32, pp. 155, 182, 183).

tively estimated that the number of students in courses using the computer nationally is over 1.5 million, an increase of about 400 percent. This represents a compounded annual growth rate since 1967 of 26 percent.

Summary

We found rather extensive use of the computer in instruction, an increasing share of which is being devoted to instruction using the computer as a tool (instruction "with" the computer). The average expenditure per student enrolled has about doubled since 1967, although the average expenditure for students actually using the computer in courses has dropped markedly.

WHERE IS THE COMPUTER BEING USED? As Comstock found in both the California survey and the SREB national survey, dividing the total expenditures on computers by most universities into functional category (research, administration, etc.) or academic field is extremely difficult. Accounting and cost control at computer centers is usually done by user identification number rather than by functional category. Another problem is that in many schools, the computer is

TABLE 7-9   *Instructional computer use, by academic field: Massachusetts survey, 1973–74*

	Undergraduates			Graduates		
Field	Number of courses	Number of students	Percent of students	Number of courses	Number of students	Percent of students
Engineering	198	8,782	20.6	73	1,882	11.8
Computer science	97	5,092	12.0	20	355	2.2
Business	116	9,985	23.5	81	8,556	53.7
Mathematics	167	6,399	15.0	36	978	6.1
Physical science	123	4,586	10.8	13	140	0.9
Social science	78	4,495	10.6	41	1,028	6.4
Psychology	29	620	1.5	35	725	4.5
Education	11	382	0.9	11	274	1.7
Agriculture	5	184	0.4	11	98	0.6
Biological science	5	166	0.4	4	65	0.4
Health	8	147	0.4	6	140	0.9
Humanities	10	268	0.6	12	162	1.0
Military	1	120	0.3	5	0	0
Architecture	3	140	0.3	3	239	1.5
English	0	0	0	0	0	0
Law	0	0	0	0	0	0
Home economics	0	0	0	3	30	0.2
Unidentified	18	1,199	2.8	20	1,273	7.8
TOTAL	869	42,565	100.0	374	15,945	100.0

NOTE: Percentages are of column totals.

treated as a free resource for the academic community, which tends to inhibit the development of effective cost-allocation algorithms, even for the internal cost control of the computer center.

In obtaining information about expenditures in the instructional area, therefore, the problems are particularly acute. The data on *expenditures* that are presented in this chapter are derived by extrapolating data from schools where cost information was available to the school population as a whole. The information should be interpreted with this in mind.

Continuing education			Total				
Number of courses	*Number of students*	*Percent of students*	*Number of courses*	*Number of students*	*Percent of students*	*Expenditures, thousands of dollars*	*Percent of expenditures*
8	190	3.8	284	11,088	17.4	1,258	28.0
9	108	3.3	126	5,615	8.8	1,097	24.4
24	3,027	59.9	221	21,568	33.8	789	17.6
7	270	5.3	210	7,647	12.0	714	15.9
12	441	8.7	148	5,167	8.1	251	5.6
			119	5,523	8.7	236	5.3
			64	1,345	2.1	20	0.4
			22	656	1.0	17	0.5
			16	282	0.4	11	0.1
			9	231	0.4	8	0.2
			14	287	0.4	10	0.2
			22	430	0.2	42	0.3
			1	120	0.2	44	0.3
			8	379	0.6	14	0.1
			0	0	0		
			0	0	0		
			3	30	0.04	1	0.02
15	960	19.0	53	3,432	5.4	19	1.3
75	5,056	100.0	1,320	63,800	100.0	4,594	100.0

Tables 7-9 and 7-10 show which academic fields are making most use of the computer. They present the total number of courses, the total number of students, and the percentage of students in these courses for each academic field in 1973–74 and 1966–67, respectively. As in 1967, engineering departments in 1974 contain the greatest number of courses, and they continue to spend the most money. Unlike the 1967 survey, the Massachusetts survey suggests that business courses have far more students in their computer-using courses than any other field (about 34 percent of the total), even though they have only the

TABLE 7-10 *Instructional computer use, by academic field: SREB national survey, 1966–67*

Field	Undergraduates			Graduates		
	Number of courses	Number of students	Percent of students	Number of courses	Number of students	Percent of students
Engineering	4,557	114,367	35.2		18,460	33.0
Computer science	2,040	75,489	23.2		9,120	16.3
Business	2,088	84,545	26.0		1,471	2.6
Mathematics	1,347	7,091	2.2		7,133	12.8
Physical science	1,168	15,700	4.8		4,572	8.2
Social science	708	8,293	2.6		4,136	7.4
Psychology	332	4,060	1.2		1,792	3.2
Education	309	2,863	0.9		3,833	6.8
Agriculture	231	4,282	1.3		2,045	3.6
Biological science	258	2,703	0.8		723	1.3
Health	114	412	0.1		1,741	3.1
Humanities	85	1,308	0.4		299	0.5
Military	23	425	0.1			
Architecture	71	1,056	0.3		321	0.6
English	34	317	0.1		246	0.4
Law	2	2	0		6	0.01
Home economics	24	1,835	0.6		22	0.03
Unidentified	0	0	0		0	0
TOTAL	13,391	324,753	100.0		55,920	100.0

*No data for this category.
†No overhead allowance.
NOTE: Percentages are of column totals.
SOURCE: Comstock (1972*b*, table 28, p. 177).

second largest course offering and the third largest budget (about 18 percent of the total), behind computer science. There seems to be less dispersion of computer-using courses among academic fields in 1974 than there was in 1967. Much activity continues to take place in psychology and in the social sciences, as it did in 1967. Other than these two categories, representing 11 percent of the students using computers, the primary sources of instructional uses are exactly where one would expect them to be: engineering, computer science, physical science, mathe-

Continuing education*			Total			
Number of courses	Number of students	Percent of students	Number of students	Percent of students	Expenditures, thousands of dollars †	Percent of expenditures
			132,827	34.9	6,951	24.5
			84,609	22.2	6,823	24.0
			86,016	22.6	5,118	18.0
			14,224	3.7	3,586	12.6
			20,272	5.3	2,206	7.8
			12,429	3.3	854	3.0
			5,852	1.5	738	2.6
			6,696	1.8	611	2.2
			6,327	1.7	524	1.8
			3,431	0.9	399	1.4
			2,153	0.6	273	1.0
			1,607	0.4	148	0.5
			425	0.1	57	0.2
			1,377	0.4	47	0.2
			563	0.1	26	0.1
			8	0	20	0.1
			1,857	0.5	17	0.05
			0	0	0	0
			380,673	100.0	28,398	100.0

matics, and business. In fact, the concentration in these areas has increased.

Even though the engineering field continues to offer the most courses using computers, there has clearly been a shift away from engineering and toward the other disciplines mentioned above. This may be due to shifts away from engineering caused by the economy, but it also reflects a growing interest in computers on the part of other departments.

There has also been a relative decline in the number of

TABLE 7-11
Average
expenditures
per student using
the computer (in
dollars)

	Massachusetts survey, 1973–74	SREB national survey, 1966–67
Engineering	113	52
Computer science	195	81
Business	36	60
Mathematics	93	252
Physical science	49	109
Social science	43	69
Psychology	15	126
Education	26	91
Agriculture	37	83
Biological science	37	116
Health	35	127
Humanities	99	92
Military	37	134
Architecture	37	34
English		46
Law		2,500
Home economics	37	9
Total	70	75

SOURCE: Data for 1966–67 calculated from Comstock (1972*b*, table 30, p. 180).

courses offered in computer science. However, even though computer science has relatively fewer students (a drop from 22 percent of the total in 1967 to only 9 percent of the total in 1973), its proportion of the total instructional budget has remained constant at about 24 percent. This suggests that the new applications being utilized in business and social science courses tend to be less expensive in any given course than in older computer-utilizing fields such as math and computer science. This hypothesis is confirmed by the data in Table 7-11, which shows the average expenditure per student for each academic field in 1973–74, compared with data from the SREB survey of 1966–67. Current data indicate that cost per student in social science and in psychology is less than half the cost in engineering, mathematics, and computer science. They also indicate a ing, mathematics, and computer science. They also indicate a large decrease in cost per student in mathematics relative to computer science and engineering. The decrease in mathematics may be due in part to a reorganization of computer science as a separate department from one of its common birthplaces, the mathematics department. It may also reflect a phenomenon common to all disciplines—increasing student exposure to marginally inexpensive applications.

If we narrow our focus to courses that teach "with" the computer and exclude courses teaching "about" the computer, Tables 7-12 and 7-13 show that the dispersion of courses among academic fields becomes much greater. In terms of student exposure, only business, with its very large graduate use (56 percent of the total number of graduate students), dominates

TABLE 7-12 *Courses teaching "with" the computer, by academic field: Massachusetts survey, 1973–74*

Field	Undergraduate		Graduate		Continuing education		Total	
	Courses	Students	Courses	Students	Courses	Students	Courses	Students
Engineering	162	5,671	48	911	2	40	213	6,647
Computer science	4	62	4	42	0	0	8	104
Business	91	7,038	68	7,070	5	264	164	14,372
Mathematics	91	4,285	28	875	0	0	119	5,160
Physical science	102	2,965	13	140	3	36	118	3,141
Social science	74	4,075	40	1,005			114	5,080
Psychology	28	600	33	687			61	1,287
Education	11	382	9	258			20	640
Agriculture	5	184	11	98			16	282
Biology	5	166	4	65			9	231
Health	8	147	5	60			13	207
Humanities	8	179	12	162			20	341
Military	1	120	0	0			1	120
Architecture	2	138	3	18			5	320
English	0	0	0	0			0	0
Law	0	0	0	0			0	0
Home economics	0	0	3	30			3	30
Unidentified	14	919	15	975	15	960	44	4,027
TOTAL	606	26,931	296	12,560	25	1,300	928	41,394

TABLE 7-13 *Percentages of students taught "with" the computer, by academic field: Massachusetts survey, 1973–74*

Field	Undergraduate	Graduate	Continuing education	Total
Engineering	21.1	7.3	3.1	16.1
Computer science	0.2	0.3	0	0.3
Business	26.1	56.3	20.3	34.7
Mathematics	15.9	7.0	0	12.5
Physical science	11.0	1.1	2.8	7.6
Social science	15.1	8.0		12.3
Psychology	2.2	5.5		3.1
Education	1.4	2.1		1.5
Agriculture	0.7	0.8		0.7
Biology	0.6	0.5		0.6
Health	0.5	0.5		0.5
Humanities	0.7	1.3		0.8
Military	0.4	0		0.3
Architecture	0.5	0.1		0.8
English	0	0		0
Law	0	0		0
Home economics	0	0.2		0.1
Unidentified	3.4	7.8	73.8	9.7
TOTAL	100.0	100.0	100.0	100.0

the others. All other fields that were heavy users in all courses—engineering, mathematics, physical and social science—share courses equally. Computer science has a very minor portion of these courses.

To identify which types of institutions were using the computer in instruction, we broke down courses and students by the highest degree offered at their respective institutions. Table 7-14 shows that over 71 percent of all students in courses using the computer came from doctoral institutions. Comstock generated a similar table from his California survey of 1969, and this is also shown in Table 7-14. His figures for doctoral institutions are surprisingly low—less than 36 percent of all students in

TABLE 7-14 **Instructional** **use, by highest** **degree offered** **at institution** **(percentages of** **students)**	*Type of* *institution*	*Massachusetts survey,* *1973–74**	*California survey,* *1968–69**	*SREB survey,* *1966–67*

Type of institution	Massachusetts survey, 1973–74*	California survey, 1968–69*	SREB survey, 1966–67
Doctorate	71.2	<36.4	75.3
Master's	22.4	<61.1	16.1
Bachelor's	4.5	n.a.	8.6
TOTAL	98.1	97.5	100.0

*For purposes of comparison, professional schools are not included in the Massachusetts and California data, as the SREB survey did not use these categories.

SOURCES: California survey data derived from Comstock (1972a, table 49, p. 214); state colleges are included as master's institutions; University of California included as doctorate. SREB survey data derived from Comstock (1972b, tables 31 and 32, pp. 182, 183); includes professional schools (medical, theological, art/music).

four-year institutions who used the computer came from doctoral institutions. On the other hand, the SREB survey showed that 281,161 students of a total of 373,531 using the computer, or 75 percent, were from doctoral institutions. It seems, at least in this case, that California is an exception to the rule.

HOW IS THE COMPUTER BEING USED? In our survey of the colleges in Massachusetts, each institution was asked to provide a list of courses using the computer. If the course involved instruction "with" the computer, its primary application of the computer was identified as one of the following six:

- Tutorial—CAI, programmed instruction, etc.
- Drill and practice—using the computer to try out, or to become more skilled at, concepts and techniques acquired from another learning aid
- Problem solving—using the computer as a calculator or data analyzer, etc.
- Simulation—constructing models to gain insight about real-world phenomena
- Games—simulations that involve competition between two or more "players"
- Inquiry/retrieval—accessing data bases[2]

[2]For further discussion of this categorization, see Chapter 5.

TABLE 7-15 Courses teaching "with" the computer, by type of application: Massachusetts survey, 1973–74

	Tutorial	Drill and practice	Problem solving	Simulation	Games	Inquiry and retrieval	Unidentified
Number of courses, total	7	322	393	127	31	4	44
Undergraduate	6	219	261	84	19	4	14
Graduate	1	98	131	42	9	0	15
Percentage of courses, total	0.8	35.8	43.7	14.1	3.4	0.4	4.7
Undergraduate	0.7	24.3	29.0	9.3	2.1	0.4	1.5
Graduate	0.1	10.9	14.6	4.7	1.0	0	1.6
Number of students, total	511	15,630	12,712	5,843	3,051	215	2,854
Undergraduate	295	11,595	8,487	4,002	1,443	215	919
Graduate	216	3,892	4,195	1,831	1,451	0	975
Percentage of students, total	1.3	38.3	31.1	14.3	7.5	0.5	7.0
Undergraduate	0.7	28.4	20.8	9.8	3.5	0.5	2.3
Graduate	0.5	9.5	10.3	4.5	3.6	0	2.4

As shown in Table 7-15, in most courses (393), the computer was used as a problem solver, although more students were involved in courses that used the computer primarily for drill and practice. The most common use after these two major categories was simulation, which accounted for 14 percent of both courses and students. We found almost no inquiry and retrieval and very few tutorial applications as we have defined them here. In fact, the only reported instances of tutorial use were in remedial programs or situations that offered preparation for specific examinations—such as licensing examinations.

Table 7-16 helps to illustrate the dispersion of applications among different institutional groups. A comparison of the 1973–74 data with the data collected in 1969 in California indicates that more institutions are making use of the computer in all categories of application than was true in 1969. The most notable increase in users seems to have taken place within those institutions offering less than a doctorate. It should be noted that the categories of computer application are slightly different in this table to facilitate comparison between the two studies.

To identify the principal users in various types of applications, it is useful to examine Tables 7-17 and 7-18, which show the number of courses and the number of students in each academic field for each type of application. If we first examine the dispersion of courses of any given discipline across categories of application, it is apparent that business is the only academic field that makes some use of the computer in every category, although the physical sciences, the social sciences, and the humanities all make use of the computer in five categories. In fact, 12 of the 15 fields using the computer in some way showed activity in three or more categories, a fact that suggests the versatility of the computer as an instructional aid.

Examining the dispersion of computer applications across academic fields, we find that drill and practice and problem solving both share a universality of sorts, which we would expect. Almost every field made use of these applications. Also interesting is the apparent universality of simulation, which seems to have found a (limited) role in almost every discipline.

Tables 7-19 and 7-20 provide some additional information about three of the largest academic computer users—physical science, social science, and engineering. In the physical sci-

TABLE 7-16 *How the computer is used for instruction in higher education (as percentages of total institutions in each category)*

	Massachusetts survey, 1973–74				California survey, 1968–69			
	Computer science	Problem solving	Tutorial*	Simulation†	Computer science	Problem solving	Tutorial	Simulation
General institutions								
Doctorate	92	85	92	92	100	100	20	93
Master's	82	71	64	54	57	60	12	52
Bachelor's	62	62	62	38	10	0	0	0
Total, general	78	71	69	58	68	45	10	37
Other								
Medical					100	100	50	75
Specialized professional and technical		25	13	25	29	29	14	0
Music/art	0	17	0	0	0	0	0	0
Total	64	58	56	47	61	42	10	33

*Includes programmed instruction and drill and practice.

†Includes gaming.

SOURCE: California survey data derived from Comstock (1972a, table 42, pp. 200–201). State colleges are included in master's category; University of California included in doctorate.

TABLE 7-17 *Computer use in instruction, by academic field (number of students)*

	Tutorial	Drill and practice	Problem solving	Simulation	Games	Inquiry/ retrieval	Unidentified
Engineering		2,077	3,533	892	145		
Computer science		82		22			
Business	216	5,291	3,591	2,504	2,703	67	
Mathematics	77	4,011	943	129			
Physical science	76	357	1,966	642	100		
Social science		2,368	1,124	1,365	95	128	
Psychology		513	682	92			
Education		484	136			20	
Agriculture		72	174	36			
Biology		45	112	74			
Health		122	85				
Humanities	22	78	211	22	8		
Military	120						
Architecture		100	155	65			
English							
Law							
Home economics		30					
Unidentified							
TOTAL	511	15,630	12,712	5,843	3,051	215	

ences, physics uses the computer almost entirely for problem solving, while users in chemistry are a bit more diverse. Other physical sciences, such as astronomy, exploit the computer's potential as an aid in instruction. Within the social sciences, economics clearly dominates the drill-and-practice and the simulation categories. The drill-and-practice mode is almost exclusively used for practice in econometrics and in statistics. Simulation is primarily used to model economies on a macro-level, both to illustrate the implications of economic theory and to gain experience with problems of monetary and fiscal policy.

Engineering is homogeneous across all fields—a great deal of problem solving and other applications in moderation. The

TABLE 7-18 *Computer use in instruction, by academic field (number of courses)*

	Tutorial	Drill and practice	Problem solving	Simulation	Games	Inquiry/ retrieval	Unidentified
Engineering		65	115	29	4		
Computer science		6		2			
Business	1	56	49	34	23	1	
Mathematics	2	80	33	4			
Physical science	2	14	79	22	1		
Social science		45	46	19	2	2	
Psychology		19	36	6			
Education		15	4			1	
Agriculture		6	6	4			
Biology		1	5	3			
Health		8	5				
Humanities	1	3	13	2	1		
Military	1						
Architecture		1	2	2			
English							
Law							
Home economics		3					
Unidentified	—	—	—	—	—	—	44
TOTAL	7	322	393	127	31	4	44

diversity in "other engineering" is due primarily to the inclusion of some operations research under this heading (in industrial engineering departments).

Summary

Growth in the use of the computer in instruction has been characterized by high activity levels outside of computer science and engineering, with relative declines in use being evident in these latter disciplines. Most students involved in instruction "with" the computer use the machine to reinforce concepts and to practice skills (drill and practice), although problem solving is also a major use. These two applications,

TABLE 7-19 *Instruction "with" the computer, by type of use, in selected academic fields: Massachusetts survey, 1973–74 (in number of courses)*

	Tutorial	Drill and practice	Problem solving	Simulation	Games	Inquiry/ retrieval
Physical science						
Physics		1	33			
Chemistry	1	4	27	3		
Other		9	19	9	1	
Social science						
Economics		32	19	14	2	
Political science		4	11	3		2
Other		9	16	3		
Engineering						
Electrical		13	23	5		
Mechanical		16	40	5		
Civil		11	36	3		
Chemical		8	12	5		
Other	1	17	4	11	4	

together with simulation, are evident in almost all disciplines using the computer.

CONCLUSIONS The institutions surveyed in Massachusetts in 1974 represent a small, nonrandom sample of American colleges and universities. The extrapolation from this sample to a description of all four-year institutions in the United States in these categories is considerable, and tempers the absolute accuracy of the data. However, in order to make comparisons with other surveys it has been necessary and, we think, important if not "accurate" to do this extrapolation. With this in mind, the conclusions which may be drawn from the 1974 survey represent trends in the use of computers in instruction by institutions of higher education. Four major trends are evident:

- *High growth* The uses of the computer in higher education have grown rapidly over the past seven years, with administrative uses of the computer growing fastest of all. Nationally, a conservative estimate of this seven-year growth is an annual rate of about 16 percent. In

TABLE 7-20   *Instruction "with" the computer, by type of use, in selected academic fields: Massachusetts survey, 1973–74 (in number of students)*

	Tutorial	Drill and practice	Problem solving	Simulation	Games	Inquiry/ retrieval
Physical science						
Physics		25	719	373		
Chemistry	26	173	745	57		
Other		159	502	212	100	
Social science						
Economics		1,941	612	1,293	95	
Political science		105	254	58		128
Other		322	258	44		
Engineering						
Electrical		699	786	90		
Mechanical		433	1,143	179		
Civil		411	1,153	76		
Chemical		204	305	140		
Other	50	330	146	407	145	

instruction, the number of students who are being exposed to the computer through courses has grown during the same period at a rate more than 20 percent per year. Allowing for inflation but adjusting for the increase in computer power per dollar, it is clear that significantly more computer power is being devoted to instruction—both "with" and "about" the computer.

- *More teaching "with" the computer*   The percentage of computer-using courses teaching "with" the computer is estimated to be about 70 to 75 percent of the total number of courses using computers. There is an evident swing from the use of the computer primarily as a tool to teach "about" the computer to teaching "with" it.

- *Greater dispersion of courses across academic fields*   In particular, physical sciences, social sciences, business, and mathematics have increased their share of use.

- *Bulk of application: drill and practice, problem solving, and simulation*   Each of these applications was found in most of the departments reporting use of the computer. By contrast, there were very few instances of tutorial or inquiry/retrieval uses. The use of games was sparse, with this application concentrated in schools of business or departments of management.

In summary, the *current use* of the computer in Massachusetts institutions is clearly tending to increase and to *cluster in the types of uses that fit areas II, III, and IV* (see Chapter 6). The type of tutorial assistance that would fit area I just was not found to be in use. It appears that individual professors are devoting their efforts toward the type of computer assistance to learning that our normative model would suggest. It is important to note, however, that most of their efforts are in support of areas II and III. The use of simulation, gaming, and inquiry that is supportive of area IV is much less common today. It will be interesting to look at this situation in another seven years, however.

8. Environmental Considerations

The preceding chapters have suggested that the computer *can be* utilized effectively in support of particular areas of the learning process. We now turn to the equally interesting question of whether the computer *will be* effectively utilized in these areas. To attempt to grip the answer to this question, one must turn to an investigation of the major forces evident in the environment of higher education.

This chapter introduces a macro look at the environmental forces which will directly affect higher education over the next two decades—and thus will directly or indirectly affect the use of computer technology in higher education. It is only after a look at each of these forces—and the probable setting for higher education which will evolve from their interaction—that one can begin to estimate the opportunity that computers will have to influence the educational process in the 1980s. In this chapter we enumerate the forces which we believe to be significant and provide our estimate of their impact on technology in higher education in the 1980s.

AN ENVIRONMENTAL MODEL OF HIGHER EDUCATION   A simplified model of the environment of higher education is shown in Figure 8-1. The left-hand side shows *primary factors* that will significantly affect the opportunities available to, and the constraints upon, higher education in the next decade. In the second column are the *modes of influence* these primary factors can have on four-year institutions. The influence of the primary factors is exerted through a set of *intermediate institutions* (column 3). The intermediate institutions fall into two categories. There are those that both regulate and finance and those that provide competition by making alternative forms of higher education available.

FIGURE 8-1   *The environment of four-year higher education*

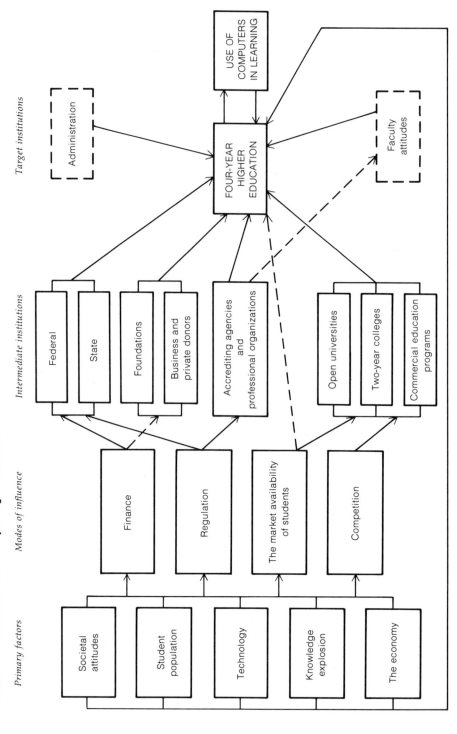

The set of organizations at the top of the third column comprises five major institutional types which affect higher education through both *regulation* and *finance*—two of the modes of influence shown in the second column. The second set of intermediate institutions provides *alternate methods* of higher education. We have chosen to classify these alternate sources of education into two-year colleges (a group of institutions that both compete with and feed the 1,800 four-year colleges, universities, and graduate schools), open universities, and private higher education training programs. This last category also includes courses run by businesses both for their own employees and as profit-making educational institutions.

All factors affect the latitude available to the *target institutions* of this report—four-year colleges, universities, and graduate schools whose components are indicated in column 4. The fifth and final column of Figure 8-1 suggests that the impact of all these forces on the colleges and universities will have much to do with the ultimate use of computer technology within these institutions.

The use of computers in institutions of higher education will have feedback effects upon the institutions themselves. The double arrows to and from column 5 illustrate this. Figure 8-1 could be made more true to life, at the risk of loss of clarity, by showing a much larger number of these feedback effects. The activities within formal higher education (column 4), for example, have distinct effects upon the knowledge explosion shown in column 1. Other feedbacks, although not as strikingly clear, certainly exist. They are not shown in this figure, however, in order to model the process as simply and clearly as possible. (For further discussion, see Demb, 1973.)

SOCIETAL AIMS AND ATTITUDES
In estimating the direction and magnitude of each of the forces shown in Figure 8-1, it is perhaps appropriate to begin with a look at one very basic factor—the attitudes toward higher education of the American public as a whole. The attitudes of the American people toward all things change with time. Higher education is no exception to this principle. Important changes appear to be taking place today in some of the key attitudes of American society toward higher education. At the same time, other, traditional attitudes are being more heavily reinforced.

Historically Americans have been very positive in their attitude toward higher education. Three strong beliefs about education have served as a basis for this overall viewpoint and as a guide for individual action. First, a college degree has been perceived as an initial step of very significant dimensions toward both economic and social success. Second, higher education has been seen as a major force in equalizing opportunity in the United States. Finally, a traditional, a correct path to higher education has been perceived to exist. The route to success has been seen as a straight line, with the student moving unerringly from secondary school graduation to the attainment of a four-year university or college degree. The student is to earn his degree in the minimum possible time while in residence at the most prestigious university or college possible.

Education and success

In recent years, beliefs concerning the link between financial success and college degrees have been enhanced by reports of authorities in the field. In 1966 available statistics showed that a college degree led to lifetime earnings, on the average, of $17,-000 more than those attained by a high school graduate. And increased income due to education clearly rose with advanced degrees. For example, in 1970 a chemical engineer with a bachelor's degree started at $900 a month, while his counterpart with a master's degree started at $1,030 and his counterpart with a doctor's degree started at $1,375. This "obvious" link between education and financial success has become less clear and has more recently been called into question, however.

It is emphatically clear today that a college degree is *not* a virtual "open sesame" to fame and fortune. In the last few years some four-year liberal arts graduates have literally been walking the streets or accepting low-paying, low-prestige jobs. Highly trained engineers, physicists, and chemists with Ph.D. degrees have joined their less well educated brethren in the ranks of the unemployed. At the same time, the wages of high school graduates who "work with their hands" have risen impressively. Electricians, plumbers, and TV repairmen today can afford a more than comfortable life-style. While this may be a temporary situation, some of the economic luster has worn off the gilding of the college degree.

Yet the previous beliefs concerning college degrees and "the good life" appear to continue—and with good reason. Although many have now—aided by the above evidence—challenged the discriminating power of a college degree with regard to economic success, no one has yet seriously challenged the notion that, for most people, higher education leads to a better life from an overall economic and social viewpoint. Despite its detractors, higher education is still seen by the vast majority of the American public to be a very desirable commodity.

Higher education and equality of opportunity

The second major influential societal attitude—the desire to utilize higher education as a social tool to further equality of opportunity—has had, and is increasingly having, a strong impact upon colleges and universities. The impact is twofold. First, in recent years there has been increasing pressure for educational institutions to accept a greater number of "disadvantaged" students, whose education often requires greater financial support. Legislation has provided more "need-based" scholarship grants and loans; however, dollars are more often awarded to students rather than institutions, thus requiring institutional expenditures for recruiting such students. Further, although federal and state moneys are available for student support, the funds represent moneys drawn from other educational areas, rather than new allocations. The financial burden that results from these interactions has produced strain on the resources of many universities.

Moreover, attitudes toward the need for equality of opportunity and for utilizing higher education as a means to provide this equality have been reinforced in recent years. The riots in our cities four years ago brought the issue of equality of opportunity into the general consciousness. The death of Martin Luther King, Jr., certainly underlined the need and desirability for greater integration of blacks into the mainstream of American economic and social life. In the last few years, institutional leaders have recognized that it is necessary to make a major effort to undo the effects of centuries of discrimination against minority communities. Large numbers of minority students previously unaffected by the mainstream of higher education have been recruited into the colleges.

The implications of higher education's taking on an increased role with regard to equality of opportunity are many, but perhaps most evident are the financial and pedagogic strains. With the growing recognition that many people have been limited by poor early education as a consequence of social and cultural background and the prejudices within our society against minority groups, "colleges and universities have felt internal and external pressures to take on the incredibly difficult task of compensating, after the fact, for society's failing. This has led to increased pressure for remedial courses" (Pake, 1971, p. 915). It is clear that additional remedial courses require extra dollars for their development and implementation. The public, with only a few dissenting voices, has applauded this move. The trend is unlikely to be diverted.

"The one true path" to higher education

We now turn to perhaps the most severely shaken of the three major attitudes cited at the start of this section—the traditional attitudes concerning the desirability of the "straight line" toward a four-year college degree. Many developments have led the most recent generation of university-age students to question the validity of attending a traditional university for four consecutive years. Prime among these factors has been their doubt, in an age of Vietnam and Watergate, of the validity of traditional approaches in general. The aforementioned paucity of jobs for some graduates has played a part. In addition, students, and many parents, have increasingly questioned the relevance of most education to the real world. And with the cost of education increasing annually at a rate of 8 percent, these questions have become more than merely academic to the average student and his family.

Moreover, this increased questioning of the "rightness" of our current primary method of higher education draws strength from a more universal dissatisfaction with social services in general. To many, such programs as welfare and Medicaid and other health care have been demonstratively ineffective. From this, it is a possible step to challenge the benefits received from education. At the very least, there is today a "new level of concern with the effectiveness of higher education and a new search for alternative ways of organizing the process"—and of taking part in it, too (Rivlin, 1971, p. 68).

Some Implica-tions of Today's Attitudes

There are, of course, many other attitudes toward higher education that, in a very complex world, could be cited. The ones noted, however, are the ones we believe to have the major implications for higher education in the next several years. With public attitudes toward higher education as a pathway to success bruised but essentially whole, it appears logical that the percentage of high school students going on to higher education will continue to grow, *if at a slower rate*. Many, like Ashby (1971, pp. 3–6), believe that the trend has not been altered in the least. "American higher education seems to be flowing toward a conclusion with the inevitability of the plot in Tolstoy's *War and Peace*. The conclusion is universal higher education. . . ." The rate of flow may have been slowed. Yet even if universal higher education does not literally come into being in the next decade, the trend toward it will, at the least, continue. This suggests that the flow of students will continue to increase, interrupted only by population changes.

In addition, the *diversity* of the student body has increased. "The measured academic aptitude of student bodies, especially those of highly selective institutions, has shifted from a modal to a bi-modal profile" (Mayhew, 1972, pp. 215–216). There is a need to adapt to this new, and quite probably continuing, diversity in the student body. This process of adaptation is a costly one—in both human and financial terms. In many institutions, the greater diversity of the student body has led to pressure for a more diverse set of courses to meet the needs of new types of students. The financial, pedagogic, and social impacts of this push for stretching the available curriculum have not been minor.

Finally, the current state of our third attitude—an increasing disenchantment with the single-path approach to higher education—makes it clear that "the American system of higher education, like most others, will have to come to terms in the next decade with new demands for *flexible access*. More and more people will enter the system of formal education and leave before the 'prescribed' period, only to reenter the system at a later time" (Hodgkinson, 1971, p. 8). According to recent estimates, "as many as one third" of all undergraduates on campus are now "stopping out"—taking a leave of absence from the campus at some point in their academic career ("Colleges Plug in . . .," 1973). Many others are searching for alternative forms of education—such as the open university or junior colleges—better suited to their needs.

Universities have already begun to adapt to a flexible access pattern. Students move in and out of regular enrollment with an alacrity unknown 10 years ago. Such programs as Dartmouth's "Campuses Away from the Campus" are starting to flourish. Diversity along both *temporal* and *spatial* lines has clearly developed in American higher education. If anything, this trend will accelerate. One significant impact of this trend will be on traditional "sequences" of courses—and the timing of course offerings. Key courses will have to be offered every term—since it will be impossible to depend on student attendance in any particular term. The strain on resources arising from this quarter is clearly just one more resource drain on the university caused by changing public attitudes toward higher education.

AVAILABILITY OF STUDENTS
The second significant factor that will affect higher education in the future is the sheer availability of students. The market for higher education is a function of two variables: the number of college-age youth and, as was noted in the previous section, the percentage taking advantage of higher education. Each is changing. As recently as 1945, only one out of seven high school graduates went on to college. Today, some 45 percent of college-age young people enter an institution of higher education. As noted previously, the concept of education as a privilege is rapidly disappearing from the American scene. Ashby (1971) estimates that universal access by the year 2000 will result in an estimated enrollment "in some form of higher education of as many as 14 million students" (p. 91), which will be about two-thirds of the college-age group. (The others presumably will have decided not to go [rare], will have left college, or will be on "leave status" between years of a diversified education.)

Between now and the year 2000, however, advances and declines in the number of students "available" to the halls of higher education will put great stresses on the educational establishment. One student of these demographic trends and their implications for higher education has been Allan M. Cartter. Although some challenge his figures (e.g., Vaughan &

Sjoberg, 1972), Cartter's estimates of growth in the college-age group, high school graduates, and college enrollment for the years from 1970 to 1990 (Table 8-1) have profound implications for American higher education.

The entering college population is expected to grow, although at a steadily decreasing rate, through the year 1982. At that time it will begin a steady slide to about 86 percent of its

TABLE 8-1 *Projected growth in college-age group, high school graduates, and college enrollment, 1970–1990 (in thousands)*

| Year | Age | | | High school graduates | College enrollment | |
	18	18 to 21	Annual change		First time	Total full-time equivalent
1970	3,703	14,371	153	2,969	1,836	6,303
1971	3,847	14,680	309	3,039	1,915	6,755
1972	3,926	15,119	439	3,141	2,010	7,115
1973	4,030	15,532	413	3,264	2,122	7,489
1974	4,057	15,884	352	3,327	2,196	7,831
1975	4,168	16,206	322	3,459	2,300	8,197
1976	4,187	16,465	259	3,517	2,356	8,525
1977	4,204	16,641	176	3,573	2,410	8,799
1978	4,207	16,790	149	3,618	2,460	9,050
1979	4,344	16,967	177	3,779	2,589	9,324
1980	4,254	17,033	66	3,743	2,582	9,539
1981	4,182	17,011	−22	3,722	2,585	9,705
1982	4,120	16,924	−87	3,708	2,596	9,834
1983	3,945	16,525	−399	3,551	2,486	9,746
1984	3,728	16,000	−525	3,355	2,348	9,514
1985	3,625	15,445	−555	3,263	2,284	9,228
1986	3,509	14,821	−624	3,158	2,210	8,862
1987	3,575	14,442	−379	3,218	2,252	8,639
1988	3,564	14,273	−169	3,207	2,245	8,541
1989	3,631	14,279	6	3,268	2,288	8,545
1990	3,723	14,493	214	3,351	2,346	8,674

SOURCE: Cartter (1971, p. 133).

previous high. This will occur in 1989, at which time enrollment will begin to grow again. Most other forecasts predict approximately the same pattern. (See, for example, National Commission on the Financing of Postsecondary Education, 1973, pp. 22–23.)

The implications of this contraction of the student market are many. The clearest ones are increased competition for students among existing institutions and a shrinking need for faculty at all institutions. We shall leave discussion of these two *very* significant implications until later.

TECHNOLOGY This third major exogenous factor has been treated in two of its major aspects in Chapters 3 and 4. On the most macroscopic level increasingly better technology will be available in the United States to assist the learning process. The prime implication of this is that computers and other technology will offer ever more seductive alternatives to professor-oriented education over the next few years.

THE KNOWLEDGE EXPLOSION Concomitant with the growth in technology has been an almost terrifying increase in the amount of knowledge available to man. "Prior to 1500 by the most optimistic estimates, Europe was producing books at a rate of 1000 titles per year . . . by 1950, four and a half centuries later, the rate had accelerated so sharply that Europe was producing 120,000 titles a year—and by the mid-sixties, the output of books on a world scale, Europe included, approached the prodigious figure of 1000 titles per day" (Toffler, 1970, p. 30).

"Today the U.S. government alone generates 100,000 reports each year, plus 45,000 articles, books, and papers. On a worldwide basis, scientific and technical literature mounts at a rate of some 60,000,000 pages per year" (ibid., p. 31).

"Ninety percent of all scientists and technologists who ever lived are alive and at work today. In the first 500 years from Gutenberg, from 1450–1950, some 30 million printed books were published in the world. In the last 25 years alone, an equal number has appeared" (Drucker, 1969, p. 263).

This knowledge explosion has several major implications for American education in both the 1970s and the 1980s. The first is a need for the continual redesign of courses to allow the most pertinent subset of the available material to be taught within the limited time devoted to formal education. This process of redesign is nothing new for American education—but it is increasingly more difficult.

A second consequence of the knowledge explosion is a need to fund, and to control, rising university costs for libraries. The exponential growth in published materials has put every university library in an almost impossible race to keep up with the rate of publication of books, periodicals, and public reports. "A maximum effort means that the particular institution falls behind less rapidly than the others do" (Pake, 1971, p. 913). The cost of attempts to keep pace with the knowledge explosion through expansion of libraries is very significant. Attempts thus far to utilize the computer to store, condense, and manipulate the available information for students have met with little cost-effective success.

Perhaps the most important implication, however, is the need to teach material most effectively and efficiently. Increasing attention must be paid to productivity in the learning process, so that students may keep to a minimum the amount of time spent in educational institutions.

THE ECONOMY For the next decade the interplay of economic, social, and political factors on the United States economy will produce peaks and valleys of activity, but two major trends are evident. First, the GNP will climb. Second, and more important for our purposes, inflation will be a continuing part of the economic scene for several underlying structural and political reasons. As Arthur Burns has noted:

The current inflationary problem has no close parallel in economic history. In the past, inflation in the United States was associated with military outlays during wars or with investment booms in peacetime.

Over the past quarter century, a rather different pattern of wage and price behavior has emerged. The average level of prices hardly ever declines and the average level of wages seems to rise inexorably across the industrial range. The hard fact is that market forces no longer can be counted on to check the upward course of wages and prices.

Cost-push inflation, while a comparatively new phenomenon on the American scene, has been altering the economic environment. For when prices are pulled up by expanding demands in times of prosperity and are also pushed up by rising costs during slack periods, economic decisions are apt to be dominated by expectations of inflation (*U.S. News and World Report,* 1953).

The prime implications of continuing inflation for a man-power-intensive industry, such as higher education, are clear. Wage demands will grow with the inflation. Costs will therefore grow. And the recognition of these costs will lead to increasing pressure from the public and state legislatures for greater productivity in the classroom. Faced with this pressure, already manifested in several states, universities will tend to look with greater favor on technologies that promise to increase productivity—or at least to "improve the learning process" so that higher education costs can be "justified."

These, then, are the five major independent *primary factors* that will affect the use of the computer in higher education in the future: societal aims and attitudes, the size of the student population, technology, the knowledge explosion, and the state of the economy. As noted in Figure 8-1, the impacts of these primary factors can be categorized into four major areas. We turn now to finance and regulation and examine more closely those institutions whose actions translate environmental forces into impacts on higher education.

THE REGULAT-ING AND FINANCING INSTITUTIONS The five principal institutions shown at the top of column 3 in Figure 8-1 make up the set of organizations that play a major part in "regulating and financing" higher education. Of these, undoubtedly the most powerful is the federal government. It, like the other institutions in this group, will be influenced in varying ways by the primary forces noted in the previous pages. It most often reacts slowly to these forces, but it does react—and powerfully.

The federal government
The federal government has had a major hand in the growth and shaping of the colleges and universities in this country over the past few decades—and especially in the 10 years ending in 1969. In many ways the sixties were a very special period.

The decade of the 1960s was characterized by the most rapid growth and development of institutions of higher education in American history. As the postwar babies reached college age, not only did the college-age population rise to unprecedented numbers, but the proportion of these young people seeking higher education also rose steadily. In the post-Sputnik era, moreover, there was a heightened appreciation of the contribution of higher education to national growth and scientific development, which encouraged rising state government appropriations, massive federal aid programs, expanded private gifts, and increased student fees. Thus, institutions of higher education were equipped financially to absorb swelling enrollment of students (Kerr, 1971, p. vii).

Leading the way in financing the expansion of higher education during the decade of the sixties was the central government. The mid-sixties saw the greatest gains. In 1964 federal funds given to all universities and colleges increased 15 percent over 1963. In 1965 they grew an additional 41.9 percent and in 1966 by 30.6 percent. Finally, in 1967, the rate of growth of federal spending began to level off with a year-to-year gain of 10 percent.

Since 1968, federal funds obligated to higher education have been in a downtrend. In that year, the rate of growth decreased to 2 percent less than the increase in the price level, and that rate continued in fiscal year 1969. In fiscal year 1970, federal support of higher education dropped by 7 percent. Although funding has risen in the past three years, the uptrend has been at a far lower rate than that of the sixties. The reasons for this slowdown were many. Student rioting undoubtedly played some part. Perhaps more important was the strikingly evident overblown nature of the graduate programs that were mushrooming on most campuses and producing a glut of Ph.D.'s.

This post-1967 emphatic tightening of the federal purse did not lead (nor does it appear that it *shall* lead) to any outcry from the general public. Many prominent figures in academia wrung their hands, but the public—experiencing both a disenchantment with students and new misgivings about the value of higher education—was in no mood to agitate strongly on behalf of the universities. Nor is public support apt to come. Rising tax rates at all levels—federal, state, and local—have led to a public mood that is not likely to erupt spontaneously in favor of greater funding for higher education. If any desire or willingness to increase the tax burden remains, other areas of concern—the ghettos, the environment, and other "attractive" problems—are apt to gain more attention than an education establishment that at the present time appears neither especially needy nor especially troublesome.

Present federal legislation appears aimed at providing grants to *needy students* rather than to institutions, in an effort to further "democratize" higher education (Wentworth, 1972). Moreover, most of the remaining institutional funding, especially under the Nixon administration, appears aimed at urging institutions to support reforms and innovations in higher education. To assure reforms and innovations in higher education, such institutions as the National Institute of Education have been legislated into existence—and funds authorized, though largely uncommitted—to put greater emphasis on educational research and development. In the past, some of these funds would have gone directly to institutions to deal with as they saw fit. "Indeed, if the new legislation contains any one message for college presidents, trustees, and budget officers, it is simply this: Tighten your belts; the Federal Government isn't about to spoon-feed you" (ibid., p. 39). With no current apparent need to expand higher education further, it appears that "frugality" is the essence of the federal message to colleges for at least the next several years. Whether this will change significantly with future administrations is highly questionable.

Together with this financial message, there is another, no less important imperative from the federal government. Universities and colleges have been told quite clearly that they must expand their activities with regard to minority groups. Affirmative action plans with regard to the hiring of women and blacks and other minority groups are a very real "must" for higher education over the next several years.

State governments

The trends toward financial restriction and increasing regulation which are evident at the federal level are, unfortunately, also clearly visible at the state level. With regard to regulation, the present situation can be summarized simply. "The nation's colleges and universities are losing their traditional independence. They are increasingly subject to government intervention by both courts and the legislatures, which for years held the academic community in awe and difference." This is the stark conclusion of a study entitled *The Courts, Government, and Higher Education,* performed by Robert O'Neil (1972), vice-president and provost of the University of Cincinnati, and sponsored by the Committee for Economic Development. The study also predicts that regulation of academic life by legislature is likely to continue, although there appears to be a sharp decrease in student activism in the 1970s.

In one sense, however, increasing state regulation was imposed in the early 1970s as a reaction to campus disruption and merely reflected the prevailing public attitude about higher education that was generated in 1968 and 1969. The *Journal of the House of the State of Michigan* (May 26, 1970, p. 1936) reports the chairman of the House Appropriations Committee as saying, "If I had my way, I'd cut the hell out of them (appropriations) until these kids decide they want to go to school." He promised he would "push for further cuts in state appropriations to universities unless 'student agitators' and 'gutless administrators' change their attitudes" (Cheit, 1971, p. 19).

Today, in two-thirds of the states, the proportion of the budget allocated to higher education is declining. The rampant expansion of higher education that took place in the last decade placed increased burdens on almost all state tax systems. Concerns about the costs of higher education were perhaps most apparent in California around the turn of the present decade. As a result of actions by the Legislature, the California system went through three consecutive years without pay boosts for its faculty. Pressure was exerted upon the universities to increase the percentage of faculty time actually spent teaching in the classroom. Again, the Legislature reflected a growing public mood. In California and other states the taxpayers' revolt against bond issues for education has been intensifying. In June 1970, a proposal for capital support of the medical school and health sciences in California was voted down in 55 of the state's 58 counties (ibid., p. 10).

One evident result of the increasing pressure to regulate colleges and universities and to control financial expenditures has been the creation of new statewide *coordinating boards.* A coordinating board is an agency, normally appointed by the governor, that is superimposed on the existing governing boards of the educational institutions. Coordinating boards are awarded specific powers in their enabling acts, powers that in most cases are taken away from the institutions themselves. For the most part, the boards have been created to "optimize" the use of state funds and "to plan for the orderly development of the whole of higher education in the state" (Glenny, 1972, p. 17). With this mandate their actions affect both public and private institutions, although it is the public institutions that experience direct controls.

As of early 1971 29 states had governing boards in existence (ibid., p. 18). Two years later the number had risen to 41. Most function through budgetary programs, or power of degree approval. In most states the boards have the power, for example, to limit some universities to undergraduate work and to "reward" others with the authority to grant advanced degrees. New degree programs, in most states, cannot be started without the approval of the coordinating body. But the power of these bodies varies significantly from state to state. In theory, the coordinating boards are only in an advisory role to the governor and legislature—but in many states their advice is overriding.

The power of the states over private institutions is also steadily growing. Not surprisingly, private universities—some faced with a struggle for mere survival—are forming larger configurations and placing themselves willingly under the jurisdiction of statewide agencies. There are three reasons for this trend. The first, and dominant, reason is financial stress. Second, there is a belief in the efficiencies of scale. Finally, and perhaps most positively, there is the educational belief that institutional diversity is desirable and that such diversity can best be assured when there is an agency to assign different roles to universities according to the need of higher education in a state or region.

Whatever the motives, the resulting trend is toward a state-controlled higher education establishment. The concept of the single-campus institution has, in many states, given way to a concept of state or regional systems of institutions, a growing suprainstitutional bureaucracy, and, unfortunately from many viewpoints, a central structure more totally subject to the whims of the legislature.

An inadvertent outcome of the recognition of the interdependence of institutions of education is the more evident infighting between public and private institutions for scarce funds. In such states as Massachusetts the battle lines are being clearly drawn. In early 1973, the *Boston Globe* reported that "a top ranking spokesman for UMASS today warned the state's more than 50 private colleges and universities that only the fittest may survive the upcoming battle for public support of higher education" (Cohen, 1972). If interinstitutional exposures of each other's weaknesses burst into the open, as some are bound to do during the next decade when competition for students must increase, charges and countercharges by warring institutions may contribute to ever-increasing pressures to skeletonize budgets at all institutions.

The O'Neil report has summarized several of these factors. "With increased support will probably come increased governmental control and regulation of the private sector, mounting tension between once autonomous private campuses and state coordinating boards. . . . There will surely be continued competition between public and private institutions for scarce funds" (O'Neil, 1972). In sum, the role of state governments in higher education in the next several years appears clear. There will be *somewhat* increased financing of higher education and *vastly* increased regulation.

Foundations

The third major set of actors in this group of intermediate institutions, whose actions are felt almost completely on the financing side, is the foundations. According to estimates prepared by the Council for Financial Aid to Education, foundation support for education (at all levels) increased 500 percent between 1954–55 and 1964–65—from an annual rate of $70 million to a peak of $358 million. Throughout most of the rest of the sixties foundation support dipped absolutely. By 1972 it had grown to $427 million (see National Commission on the Financing of Postsecondary Education, 1973, p. 122), but when adjusted for the inflation in recent years, this apparently greater figure actually represents a real decrease in funding.

There is little doubt that, with the increasing government regulation of the foundations themselves (ensuring a high payout of foundation income), the stream of funding for higher education will continue. Yet there is no reason to expect substantial increases in funding from this source. Moreover, foundation support is rarely broad-gauge in its impact. It is primarily targeted support, aimed at inducing progressive change in the educational system. Most recently, this support has been aimed either at egalitarianism or at the development of innovations in learning methodologies.

Much recent support has gone to black institutions. Other support has been targeted at institutions serving other disadvantaged minority groups and at programs designed to open up educational opportunities for other previously unserved population segments (e.g., older persons with rich experience but lacking in formal prerequisite degrees). With an eye toward this last arena, increasing foundation support appears to be going today to educational innovation that can distribute educational opportunity more widely—and thus allow people of all ages and callings to select a vehicle of study from as broad as possible a spectrum of methods and places.

This trend toward targeting aid to providing increased access to education is important for our analysis. It is clear that the current predominant mode of education, without the backing of technology, cannot provide this access. As a result, the emphasis in foundation grants is increasingly on methods of learning via television, videotape, and off-campus learning methods of all types. As more and more technology becomes widely available (such as cable TV), we can expect this trend of foundation support to continue and probably accelerate.

In summary, the quantity of foundation support will continue to grow during the decade of the seventies—but roughly in pace with the growth of the economy itself. From the viewpoint of educational technology, the significant factor is the share of the total that will be targeted at assisting the development of learning technology. For the reasons noted above, this share can be expected to grow.

Business and private donors

The business community remains, essentially, only peripherally involved with higher education. Funds are given, sometimes in major amounts. In 1966, corporate gifts to higher education amounted to $213 million. In 1972 they were $223 million. Yet less than one-half of 1 percent of pretax income goes to education at all levels (Patrick & Eells, 1969). There are few, if any, indications of major changes in business support of higher education in the coming years.

There is little reason to expect that the public, the other major source of private funds, will greatly change its attitude toward giving to higher education. Alumni and other public supporters have played a significant and stable role in the support of the private segment of higher education in the past few decades. Approximately $800 million was contributed in 1971–72. Giving has grown steadily through the years approximately as the economy has grown. There is no reason to believe that this role will change significantly in the next decade either in its magnitude or direction. Alumni giving varies somewhat both with the state of the economy (which at the time of this writing is highly unstable with high rates of both inflation and unemployment) and the "state of the campus." But it has not shown any tendency to deviate significantly from its long-term trend of providing approximately 45 to 50 percent of all "voluntary" support to higher education (National Commission on the Financing of Postsecondary Education, 1973, p. 122).

Accrediting agencies and professional organizations
The final set of institutions involved with regulating and financing higher education is the accrediting agencies. These agencies, with their staffs of professionals who review and recommend university programs, are an increasingly significant factor on the American educational scene. Their impact is overwhelmingly on the regulation side—but they do influence finance.

Originally developed to ensure similar standards among institutions and to eliminate the early diploma mills, these agencies are of two principal types today. Some accredit a whole institution; others accredit only a particular professional program. All are voluntary associations. They include six major regional associations formed and controlled by the educational institutions themselves, and approximately 50 professional associations that accredit individual programs with institutions. These latter associations consist of practitioners and the professors who prepare the practitioners. As a result, the institutions themselves have little control over such associations, which are increasingly requiring universities to conform to higher and more expensive standards of education.

While this accreditation process barely affects many major institutions, it can be especially binding on smaller, less well established institutions. The trend, from the viewpoint of educational quality, is undoubtedly healthy. It is another factor, however, that will limit the ability of administrators to distribute resources at will to either encourage or discourage the growth of educational technology. The impact of accreditation will have to be assessed through careful observation during the coming years.

THE COMPETI-
TION

A third effect of the primary factors is the creation of a competitive environment for traditional higher education by the encouragement of alternative methods of delivering education. The institutions that are now competing with four-year institutions include two-year colleges, newly instituted open universities, and private, commercial training programs.

Two-year colleges

The most pervasive alternative to the four-year university now available to a secondary school graduate is the two-year college. More than 1,100 two-year colleges are scattered throughout the United States. As diverse as the nation itself in their goal structures, curricula, and pedagogic methods, these institutions currently account for more than 30 percent of all undergraduate students enrolled in institutions of higher education.

Two-year schools—which include public community colleges and private independent two-year colleges (often called junior colleges)—were a relatively minor factor in education until the end of World War II. At that point, a unique set of circumstances gave impetus to explosive growth in the two-year college sector—in number of institutions, in students enrolled and in educational functions. As Medsker & Tillery summarize it:

Several factors were responsible. First, an expanding job market— particularly based in the broad area of industrial technology— required new training programs of varied intensity and scope. Here, the measured retraining of returning military personnel who had attended vocational schools in the services became a highlight of the new occupational curricula. Second, the passage of Public Law 16—the so-called G.I. Bill of Rights—heavily augmented the enrollments of existing colleges and universities. In the first postwar year of 1946, for example, public and private institutions in the United States enrolled approximately one and a half million students of whom 462,000 were returned military personnel. In the same year, community colleges moved quickly to absorb the enrollment spill-over of crowded four-year institutions.

Finally, the global aspect of a war recently fought on many fronts increased the interest for enlightened, comprehensive education. Aspirations to learn more about the world and its ways as well as the desire for occupational upgrading were reflected in the rapid growth of continuing education programs at the community college. Adults—citizens who never before had considered a "college" education—looked increasingly to local colleges as community centers which could provide a wide spectrum of educational and cultural activities (Medsker & Tillery, 1971, p. 15).

From approximately 200,000 students in 1940 (ibid., chart 1, p. 17), enrollment in two-year colleges has grown by a factor of 10 in 30 years. Four-year colleges, by comparison, grew approximately three times in undergraduate enrollment. For a period of months in the late 1960s, new two-year colleges opened their doors at the rate of one each week.

As Figure 8-2 shows, the decade of the sixties was one of

FIGURE 8-2 *Enrollment in two-year colleges, United States, 1930–1970*

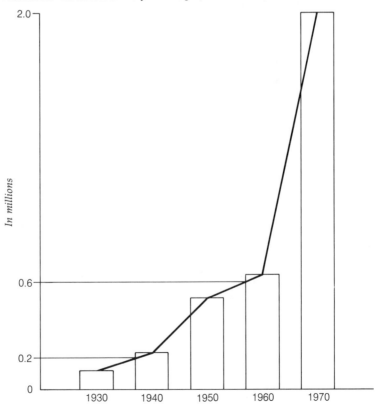

SOURCE: Medsker & Tillery (1971, p. 17).

phenomenal growth—with enrollment more than doubling. It is expected by Medsker & Tillery (ibid., p. 13) to double again—to more than 4 million by 1980. This rapid growth has occurred and is occurring because the two-year colleges, three-fourths of which are now public, serve several needed functions in higher education. First, they provide convenient, local, low-cost education—generally with an open admissions policy. Second, they have adopted many diverse forms, and taken on many functions, to serve a diversified clientele. Instead of following a set format, they have demonstrated a unique ability to merge and blend with—as well as to support—the needs of their particular communities.

This chameleon quality appears to be changing, however. At the present time, the functions of the community colleges can be described as (1) preparation for advanced study, (2) career education, (3) career guidance of students, (4) remedial education, (5) general education of the "whole man," and (6) community service. While each of the last four of these is being pursued to a significant degree, they are far less significant than the first two. The area of preparing students for further study at four-year colleges draws most of the effort in the two-year schools. This is so for a multitude of reasons. Most important among these is the fact that three-fourths of the students matriculating do so with the stated desire to go on to four-year colleges.[1] Many statewide systems of higher education are now being built with this function of preparation for advanced education specifically in mind. Approximately 80 percent of all public and private higher educational institutions in the state of California are two-year colleges (Medsker & Tillery, 1971, p. 12).

Perhaps another major factor in this emphasis is the attitude of the faculty at these institutions. With the current overproduction of Ph.D.'s the proportion of faculty holding doctoral degrees in junior colleges is growing. It is likely that this "new" faculty is aiding and abetting the emphasis toward preparation for advanced training by turning current programs into more academically oriented programs.

At the same time, although of less importance in terms of

[1]Although only a third of these actually do go on to four-year schools (Ashby, 1971, p. 11).

student enrollment, the two-year colleges also provide strong two-year career training programs. A significant factor in developing this area is the pragmatic nature of the administration of many of these schools. Sometimes working from a different point of view from that of the faculty, administrators often devote much time and effort to seeking out and understanding the needs of the employment market in their locality.

Students in the two-year colleges tend to be older than the average—more than half being over 21. And the faculty tend to hold fewer degrees. Medsker & Tillery report that in 1969 fewer than 10 percent held a Ph.D., and approximately 80 percent held a master's degree. Four percent were working on less than a bachelor's. But, to the student's benefit, the faculty in these schools are teaching-oriented. Research, as it is known in the four-year colleges and universities, is a negligible activity.

What this all comes down to is that the two-year colleges provide a low-cost alternative (both with regard to tuition and the student's ability to live at home). Furthermore, they are growing rapidly in their capacity to handle students. As noted above, and as emphasized by Harold Hodgkinson in his *Institutions in Transition* (1971), the two-year schools, with their emphasis on lower-division academic work, increasingly tend to resemble the first two years of the four-year schools. And with the current upgrading of faculty, they are becoming an ever more desirable alternative for many students.

A second factor concerning two-year schools is important for our purposes. In the private institutions, more than 64 percent of income comes from tuition. There is therefore a need, as well as an opportunity, to work vigorously at the business of improving the efficiency and effectiveness of teaching through any possible method—including new technology. Some of this work is evident in two-year colleges today, and it is not unreasonable to suspect that more may be in the future. It is entirely possible that sheer competitiveness and a demonstration effect from these institutions may aid the acceptance of technology in the four-year schools in the next decade.

The open university

The two-year colleges are not the only alternative source of higher education today. The wide availability of television, the development of the concept of self-paced study, and an increased recognition of the ability of the learner to propel himself through the learning process given adequate, if remote, supervision have all led to the development of "the open university." These facilitative factors have combined with previously noted public desire to make education more widely available to people who have heretofore been unable to attend university campuses.

Perhaps the major test of this educational opportunity is being carried out in the United Kingdom. "Britain's new open university, a non-residential system that has expanded higher education opportunities for working adults, began with its first freshman class in 1971. Chartered by the British government, the system enables students to learn through course lectures on BBC radio and television, and through tutorial work and testing at 220 regional centers" ("Open University Put to the Test," 1973, p. 2).

The British Open University produces its own course materials. Some 300 books, 400 films, and 200 audio tapes for first- and second-year students have been developed already. The full-time central academic staff numbers approximately 200, who are divided into six faculties of science, humanities, social science, mathematics, educational studies, and technology. The full-time faculty is aided by an associate staff of the Institute of Educational Technology, who assist the full-time faculty in developing educational technology and in monitoring the results.

To administer the system, the country is divided into 12 regions. Each of these has a small full-time academic and administrative staff. Spread among the regions are more than 250 local study centers (usually in universities, colleges, or schools) at which students may receive counseling or face-to-face instruction. These centers also provide the opportunity for students who have missed scheduled TV or radio broadcasts on the national network to see films or listen to tapes of them. The tutorial and counseling functions are handled by more than 3,000 part-time academics of three types: *counselors* who offer personal and operational advice on the learning system, *class tutors* who lecture and conduct seminars, and *correspondence tutors* who grade student assignments and offer academic advice in writing or by telephone.

"Each week's study (each 'unit') nominally requires about ten hours' work—six hours of self-instruction, a half hour of TV, a half hour of radio, a half hour of self-assessment tests, about a half hour for 'subjective' assignments to be graded later by tutors, about an hour of 'objective' assignments to be graded later by computer, and in science about an hour for home experiments" (Smith, 1972, p. 47). In addition, one week of full-time "summer school" is compulsory for each student for each course of studies.

In the first year 15,823 students took 17,664 examinations; 16,346 credits were awarded for course completion. Although the drop-out rate was high, this is a significant figure for a nation in which only a quarter-million students (under 16 percent of the university-age group) are in school (*Education in Britain*, 1971). The Ford Foundation estimates that approximately 43,000 students were studying in the open university as of early 1973.

As expected, the system has some detractors. These focus primarily on the quality of education offered by the open university. This is, of course, open to question. Many point out that the initial student population was heavily biased toward teachers attempting to improve their own skills—and was far from a representative sample of the population group hoped to be reached by the open university. On the positive side, one very significant factor is apparent, however. On the scale on which it is operated in Britain the open university produces a graduate at about 20 percent of the cost of a conventional university graduate. With attention to educational cost increasing in every country, close attention is being paid to the British effort. More important, perhaps, is that education is being offered in Britain to a great number who have not had a chance previously to obtain it, and that "the new technology" is being used.

The open university today is spreading in the United States, too. Several such universities are in various degrees of development or operation. Two examples of this development are:

Campus-Free College   This private open university was actually the first institution of its type to begin operation in the United States. Within three months of its opening in September 1971, program advisers (mainly college faculty) had agreed to work with students in more than 100 locations in the United States and Canada. Beginning with only 10 students, CFC now has 50, and its network of advisers spans 34 states. Centered in Arlington, Massachusetts, the college itself does not produce any materials. Rather, "learning opportunities" (internships, courses at other colleges, job experience, and special programs) earn credits from the college, which will also grant a degree once it is recommended by a council composed of academics from various fields. Paid in quarterly installments, tuition at the college is $1,000 per year.

The open university in Massachusetts   One example of progress toward the public open university concept is in Massachusetts. Four state colleges are currently offering differing forms of open university programming. One, Salem State, has modeled its program after the British Open University and is using the British teaching materials.

As of late 1973, the Massachusetts program had fewer than 100 students, but a substantial increase in size has been recommended by an Educational Testing Service (ETS) task force that was engaged to evaluate the four pilot projects.

Several other programs, many of them larger in actual or intended scope, are currently under way. The significant points for our analysis are two. First, the open university concept appears destined to grow and to compete for students with more traditional higher education. At present this growth appears to be small, at least with regard to four-year higher education's traditional market, high school graduates. More significant, however, may be the inroads made into a group of students who are now a *potential* market for the four-year college services, adults desiring to continue education—an educational market that could become more important as the "supply" of high school graduates diminishes in the next 10 years.

The second, and perhaps more significant, effect of the open universities may eventually be to demonstrate widely the applicability and effectiveness of nontraditional, often technology-based methods of education. This demonstration effect should help decrease existing barriers to the use of technology-assisted education in the traditional four-year schools.

Commercial alternatives

The third factor that presages increasing competition for our target institutions is the gradually increasing attractiveness of proprietary institutions as alternative sources of education. As noted in the first part of this chapter, students today are much more knowledgeable about what universities *can* and *cannot* do for them. And they have definite thoughts about what universities should do. They are increasingly suspicious of non-relevant education and the ivory tower. As Gould (1970) notes, "they have begun to look on the university as a bold adventurer would regard an unnecessarily fussy, well-meaning aunt who keeps warning him about wearing his galoshes during rainstorms when the adventurer is already busy putting on his space suit" (p. 44).

The stately pace of progress in many universities toward curricula that students feel are relevant to them is increasingly viewed as too slow an adaption to pressing needs. This leaves the door open for alternate sources of education. As noted above, the more quickly adaptable two-year colleges are enjoying rapid growth. But even they are academic. Private entrepreneurs are not unaware of the potential. As Gould put it, "the contemporary university now runs the danger of being replaced in what it always thought was one of its most important functions, that of imparting information. Here it may be in a losing battle with the media and the other outsiders, since it is not so deeply motivated as are the business, military, or the corporate organizations in searching for new avenues of profit, superiority, and status" (ibid.). There is already some evidence for what Cosand terms "a transfer of confidence among citizens from educators to business and industry on the basis of pragmatism" (Medsker & Tillery, 1971, p. 157).

During the past few years, many publishing houses, electronic industries, commercial film makers, and others have entered the field of knowledge dissemination. There have been some withdrawals from the field of combat as commercial institutions found their efforts unwise. However, new entrants have added themselves to a private nonuniversity educational industry that has long had deep roots in the American economy. For many years, IBM has taught both employees and customers for many more student-hours than many recognized educational institutions. Private secretarial schools, computer training schools, and the like have long been an important part of the American economy.

On top of this, a new trend appears to be nascent. Many

private commercial courses have long been recognized by industrial employers as the equivalent of university programs. Now some of these courses are being recognized by the states and given formal degree credit. As the United Press reported on March 18, 1973:

Arthur D. Little's Management Education Institute has been authorized to award a graduate Master's degree in Industrial Development for Developing Countries. The Massachusetts Board of Higher Education granted the research and engineering firm the right to issue degrees in the science of administration contingent upon the appointment of an independent board of trustees for the school ("Research Firm . . .," 1973).

It is true that this program has been small and limited to a single specialty, and may presage no further action upon the part of Arthur D. Little. Yet the concept of an engineering firm granting degrees in university-rich Massachusetts is something to be pondered.

We see no overwhelming trend toward a "take-over" of higher education by the industrial sector. Yet competition from this source may provide an additional spur, no matter how small, toward greater use of technology in education.

ASSESSING THE IMPACT OF FACTORS The several environmental influences discussed in the last few pages will have varying impacts on higher education in general and its tendency to utilize technology in particular. As Figure 8-1 shows, some of these forces will impact four-year universities and colleges directly, but the major impacts can be summarized in four classes of general influences that we have termed *modes of influence*. The ultimate impact of each of these forces, for our purposes, will be to increase or decrease the propensity of institutions of higher education to utilize the available technology. The direction and magnitude of each of these forces is summarized in the "Likert force field diagram" shown in Figure 8-3.

Direct Impacts Of the dozen or so environmental influences previously described, two will impact the four-year institutions of higher education most directly. The knowledge explosion, which is making it increasingly difficult for educators to fully cover the knowledge requirements of students by merely utilizing traditional pedagogic methods, will, as shown in Figure 8-3, exert a reasonably strong positive force toward the utilization of more technology in the education process. Even today, educators are turning to technology to assist them in providing basic material outside of class so that classroom time can be spent more effectively on newly discovered material. This trend is expected to continue.

The impact of the availability of increasingly better technology will also be a strongly positive force, as shown by arrow 2 in Figure 8-3. As the technology becomes cheaper and better, it will become an increasingly desirable alternative for institutions looking to cut costs, improve access to educational materials, or otherwise increase the effectiveness of the learning process.

Indirect Impacts *Economic and financial impacts*

The overall financial picture for higher education, as pointed out in previous sections, can be summarized as distinctly less cheerful than it was in the 1960s. William Bowen (1968) found that during the 1960s the cost per student grew significantly because of the growing costs arising from the universities' increased involvement in research programs, broader community responsibilities, and a shift toward more expensive graduate instruction. Combined with the effects of inflation, these increased expenditures led Bowen to predict that, in general, education expenditures would continue to rise at a compound average rate of $7\frac{1}{2}$ percent a year per student for the decade ending in the mid-seventies.

Although cost cutting has recently reduced this growth rate of costs, general-purpose income, as noted in detail earlier, whether it be from student tuition, from federal or foundation grants and requests, or from state legislature sources for the public institutions, will be increasingly hard to come by during the next several years. As a result, there has been and will be much less discretionary money for administrators to spend. As noted, many universities have been forced to cut back in many areas, making expenditures for technology highly debatable unless clearly justified by cost savings—and even then, quite possibly, subject to direct faculty resistance. As a result, arrow 3

FIGURE 8-3 *The direction and an estimate of the relative strength of the pertinent forces affecting the use of educational technology in higher education*

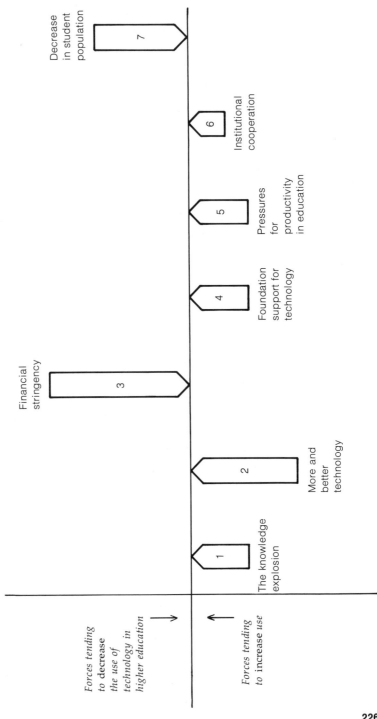

FIGURE 8-3 (continued)

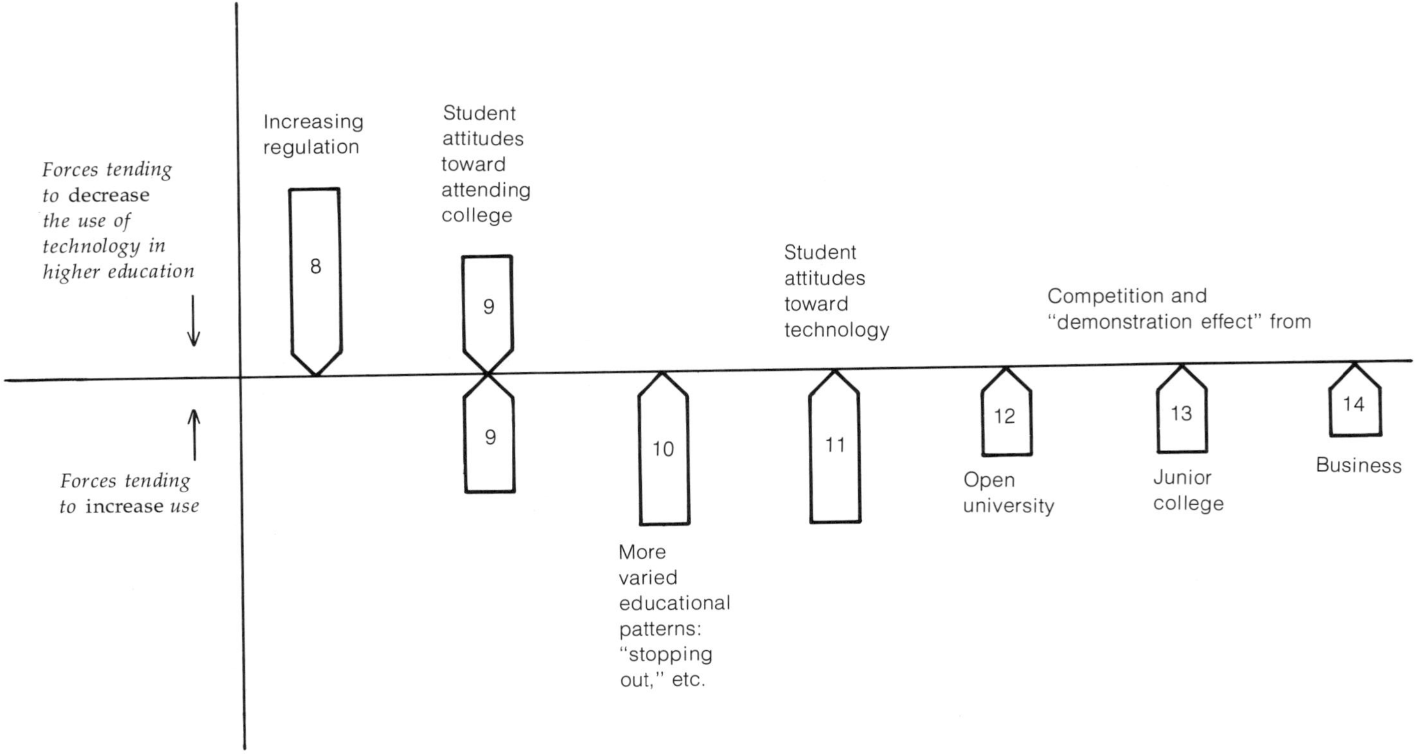

Forces tending
to decrease
the use of
technology in
higher education

Forces tending
to increase use

Increasing
regulation

8

Student
attitudes
toward
attending
college

9

9

More
varied
educational
patterns:
"stopping
out," etc.

10

Student
attitudes
toward
technology

11

Open
university

12

Competition and
"demonstration effect" from

Junior
college

13

Business

14

in Figure 8-3 shows a strong negative pressure vis-à-vis instructional technology, caused by financial stringency.

Countervailing this negative pressure will be several economic and financial pressures to use more instructional technology. Among these is the fact that funding from foundations will be targeted, in some reasonable proportion, directly at innovative technology (arrow 4). In addition, with legislatures taking an increasingly critical view toward educational costs, there will be pressure for greater productivity within educational institutions—which can be at least partially satisfied by a greater use of technology (arrow 5). The very manpower-intensive nature of these institutions in a time of inflation will make increased productivity highly desirable.

Finally, on the positive side, the previously noted efforts by institutions of higher learning toward cooperation will lead to larger-scale institutions, or groupings of institutions, which will provide more fertile soil for an increased use of technology (arrow 6). (In most cases educational technology, like other tec_.nologies, requires large initial investments, and the larger the population of students that this investment can be distributed across, the easier the move to the technology.) The availability of "utilities" offering these technologies to smaller colleges, however, makes this force a minor one as shown.

Offsetting these positive trends somewhat will be a decrease in student population in the 1980s, which (arrow 7) will constitute a drag on the introduction of technology. There will be, with a large percentage of tenured professors, intensive economic and financial pressures to utilize the available manpower capacity rather than to introduce new technology.

Regulation

As previously noted, it now appears that much federal funding to universities will be tied to specific purposes. Included among these are scholarships for disadvantaged students and other "opportunity-opening" mechanisms. In addition, the federal government is increasingly restricting the latitude of administrators by insisting upon grants being dependent on affirmative action and other administrative requirements. Increasing regulation is also evident from the state level. The trend toward statewide coordination of higher education, both public and private, is clear. The increasing trend to interuniversity cooperation noted above will also tend to regulate the freedom of individual administrations. Finally, pressure from accrediting agencies also tends to limit administrative power.

In sum, as shown by arrow 8, the steady increase from all quarters of regulations that limit the initiative of the administrators of institutions of higher learning will tend, we believe, to place these administrations in a much less powerful position with respect to assisting or urging faculty to initiate technological innovation. The increase in the (explicit and implicit) number of levels necessary for each decision will, at least, impede progress toward technological innovation.

The student market

Another significant compendium of forces affecting the rate of introduction of technology into four-year institutions of higher education will be student attitudes. One group of these attitudes centers around the decision of potential students as to whether they should go on to college at all. On one hand, it is clear that college in the past has been "the place to go." There is no reason to suspect that large numbers of potential students will change their minds about this. As noted previously, Ashby and others believe that the proportion of students will actually increase.

On the other hand, there are current "suspicions" of higher education, as we have noted. In addition, Ashby notes (1971, p. 29) that approximately 15 percent of today's college population are on campus against their will. The increasing distrust of higher education among their peers may make it respectable for this group to *not* go on to college. The exact result of this factor, as shown by the equal arrows (9) on both sides of the line in Figure 8-3, is uncertain. Student attitudes are changing now— and will probably change again in the next several years. Clearly, however, the academic administration must make a bet on a long-term trend of college attendance in the United States. Should student attitudes interrupt the continuing trend toward higher education, it would be a blow to the introduction of more learning technology, since yet another source of financial support would be weakened.

One consequence of present student attitudes, however, that will strongly *aid* the introduction of technology is the trend toward taking a year or more off from college, or "stopping out." In addition, the increase of summer sessions, education away from the campus, and other factors are making it increasingly necessary to provide wider access, both spatially and temporarily, to existing courses. This can only aid (arrow 10) the introduction of more technology.

Finally, it can be expected that the more mature, more realistic students of today and tomorrow will better *perceive* and *demand* the efficiencies and greater effectiveness possible in the learning process through the use of recent technology. We believe this positive student attitude toward the technology (arrow 11) will add a relatively minor, but positive, thrust toward the introduction of such technology.

Competition

Although they probably will not be very powerful forces vis-à-vis technology (as shown by the relatively small size of arrows 12, 13, and 14), the presence of increasing competition from two-year schools, the open university, and commercially based education should assist in providing a positive incentive toward the introduction of more technology into four-year schools. With a relatively decreased student population, competition among institutions and therefore a need to improve current methods will be somewhat greater. In addition, some of these competitive teaching-oriented institutions will undoubtedly turn to technology as a competitive wedge—and will therefore provide a demonstration effect of the benefits of technology. Both these factors will lead to increasing pressure on our target institutions to better utilize the available technology.

At this point Figure 8-3 appears heavily weighted toward increasing acceptance of educational technology in higher education. But the analysis is as yet incomplete. Two other major factors will also bear heavily on the rate of acceptance of technology in higher education: the attitudes of faculty and administration attitudes. These will be discussed in the next chapter, in which we turn from the external environment to the internal environment of higher education.

9. Internal Factors: The Administration and the Faculty

In the previous chapter we noted an extensive set of pressures on institutions of higher learning, pressures that stem from the environment in which these institutions are situated. Yet pressures do not affect institutions as such. They affect individuals. The individuals who comprise existing institutions of higher learning are members of four groups—administration, faculty, trustees, and students. This chapter will take a look at the pressures, both environmental and internal, that affect these various groups. A prognosis for their reactions to these pressures and the subsequent effect on the introduction of computer technology into the learning process will emerge from this discussion.

Let us look at each of the four groups. Two of them, students and trustees, will be dismissed rather quickly, since we have stressed the importance of the attitudes of the former group in the previous chapter and believe the input of the latter to the future of educational technology will be minor. More time will be spent on the administration, but by far the bulk of this chapter will be devoted to the faculty—for it is here that the power lies with regard to the ultimate rate of increase of learning technology.

Students There is little doubt that, for a variety of reasons, including the demonstration effect of seeing the two-year schools and other institutions utilizing more and more new technology in the

ACKNOWLEDGMENT: The latter two-thirds of this chapter are taken, in many cases word for word, from a working paper by Jarrod Wilcox, a former faculty member at the Sloan School, now with the Bank County Group. Wilcox has been kind enough to let us use most of his text (see Wilcox, 1972). All subjective conclusions in the chapter are our own, however.

learning process, students in the four-year schools will provide a positive force toward the utilization of additional technology in the learning process. Students do come and go. In this country they have not been a major force on the governance of academia. With the exception of their relatively brief Vietnam-oriented outburst, they have had little effect on university policy. Nor does the evidence of the last year or two suggest that they will have a great effect in the future, despite some claims to the contrary. Yet, as noted in Chapter 8, they will provide a positive force toward a greater use of technology.

Administration The increasing binds, both fiscal and regulatory, that academic administrations find themselves in today was stressed in the previous chapter. Throughout the seventies there will not be a great deal of excess cash available to administrators. Without this discretionary money, one of the major tools in the hands of an administration oriented toward improving the teaching process is blunted. In addition, financial crises—or even semi-crises—tend to hold the attention and overutilize the time of key administrators, thus diverting their energies from selling the faculty on the need for improving today's teaching process.

Nor would many administrations act decisively to promote technological improvement in the teaching-learning process even were additional funds available. This type of action would violate the traditional university mode of operation, which is based heavily on decentralized decision making and the recognized responsibility of each group of professors to set its own standards in teaching and research. In dealing with professors, the administration is dealing with *professionals*. And professionals have long resisted external control—whether by university administration or by anyone else. As Blau & Scott (1962) put it, "The final characteristic of the professions is a distinctive control structure, which is fundamentally different from the hierarchical control exercised in bureaucratic organizations. Professionals typically organize themselves in a voluntary association for purposes of self-control" (pp. 62–63). Blau and Scott continue to point out that "every member of the group, *but nobody else,* is assumed to be qualified to make professional judgments" (ibid., p. 63; italics ours). In other words, professors are socialized toward professional standards that include resisting administrative attempts to exert control in any direction whatsoever. What is more, conditions in the last 10 to 15 years have led to a professoriate with a highly developed sense of autonomy. "An historical analysis of government's trends during the twentieth century clearly shows a weakening of central institutional controls and an especially sharp rise in the power of the professoriate" (Ikenberry, 1972, p. 23).

In the 1960s, universities chased after faculty research "stars" and rewarded their transfer with higher salaries, reduced teaching hours, and early tenure. Today, with universities starting to cut back on faculties, the proportion of the faculty with a high degree of personal security, symbolized by tenure, is growing. The larger this proportion gets, the less the power of the administration. For, although most faculties decide among themselves on the promotion of their members, deans and presidents do have some leverage. For a faculty that is heavily tenured, they have much less. The bear market in academia for professorial jobs today may weaken the power of the *non*tenured faculty— vis-à-vis the power of the administration—but the increasing proportion of tenured faculty members quite ably offsets this market condition. In most major universities, the ability of administrators to vastly influence faculties to change their ways of providing learning assistance is dubious at best.

Moreover, it has been traditionally difficult to get decisions made in favor of *any* new steps on the campus. As Clark Kerr says, "There is a lot of negative power on campus. It is located with veto groups" (in Graves, 1971, p. 2). Fred Hechinger, writing in the *New York Times,* puts it in this manner: "Leadership, under such conditions, becomes negative. Faculty, administration, and students all talk about power and the need to let everybody participate in its exercise. Behind the slogans looms the reality of a general lack of positive powers. If the faculty insists, as it always has, that it ought to be the central power, the fact is that at present it is exercising mainly the negative power of the veto" (ibid., p. 2). This is terribly important for our analysis because "negative power paralyzes constructive action, prevents an institution from being effectively pro-active or reactive in fulfilling its mission or in dealing with crisis" (ibid.).

This multiplicity of veto groups has led to a very weak decision-making apparatus in universities. A second major problem with regard to decisive decision making, moreover, is the difficulty in agreeing upon operational goals within the university setting. Particular courses of action have differential results with respect to teaching, research, and/or public service. With the goals of the university in each area stated in quite fuzzy terms and with no clearly stated priorities between areas, it is often difficult to justify new policy. Detractors may attack from a variety of positions setting their own ground rules. Educational technology is not exempted as a target.

The case for administrative weakness is perhaps overstated. But perhaps not, for—even if this is not correct—university administrators have most often acted as though it were true. "Most important, administrators have frequently failed to achieve what is essential if they are to be effective in the crucial task of facilitating the employment of resources and meeting needs; that is, they have failed to articulate a vision worth pursuing—providing enough of a sense of what the institution is about to enable its individual members to see how their objectives relate to the institution's overall character, and to engender a sense of loyalty to that character" (Gorovitz, 1972, p. 588). Without a well-defined sense of mission and reasonably well-defined strategies, an institution is no more than the sum of the individual faculty members—which is essentially the case today. In summary, administrators generally—despite their possession of at least a few tools—are seen as not a very powerful force with regard to influencing teaching methods as well as many other actions of the universities.

Trustees   Despite their august positions, trustees of most universities have wielded little power, nor are they apt to wield much more in the future. In the first place, many trustees do not understand universities very well. Most trustees are selected for reasons far different from their ability to provide wise aid and counsel to the university president and/or deans. In general, they do not spend the time to learn how a university really functions. Whereas most outside directors of major corporations have a reasonable understanding of the structure, power relationships, and objectives of the commercial organizations on whose boards they serve, the same is far from true with university trustees (Kornfeld, 1970). Except in unusual cases, the trustee is not expected to make a real contribution to the governance or operating policies of the university. We thus leave this group with no further discussion.

Faculty By the process of elimination, the prognosis for increased use of technology in the learning process thus comes down to the will of the faculty. George Pake, like many others, stresses this point. "Whether it is possible at all to understand the present state of U.S. universities is debatable. But anyone who even hopes to understand universities must recognize that the faculty holds the de facto power in a university. Trustees, presidents with their administrative colleagues, and students each, as a group, have a modicum of power. But they can scarcely wield that power without the backing of the faculty, or at least a substantial portion of the faculty" (Pake, 1971, p. 908).

What, then, would one expect the attitude of university and college faculties to be toward technological innovation in the learning process? What are the forces that will tend to push the further use of educational technology, and what are those that will tend to decrease or oppose the use of further technology in the learning process over the next decade?

FACTORS TENDING TO INCREASE FACULTY USE OF TECHNOL-OGY *Innovative zeal* Perhaps the greatest force pushing introduction of more and better technology into the learning process is the spirit of the "goodness and rightness" of innovation among many university professors. The spirit of inquiry which lies behind a great deal of academia also occasionally flourishes with regard to the teaching process itself. As we shall note below, it is easy to overstate this zeal. Yet it is an important factor.

Research by-products In many fields, professors and their graduate students have worked hard to develop computer models to assist them in varying research projects. In many cases, it is realized only after the completion of these projects that the models developed—though often with some necessary embellishments—can be effectively utilized for teaching purposes in the areas that were being researched. This type of fallout from research to the learning process is far from insignificant in several fields.

Dedicated teachers Despite the thoughts that are noted below with regard to the primary orientation of most faculty members to research, there exists a reasonable cadre of professors who are dedicated to the teaching process. Much innovation in utilizing computers and other technological aids to education will come from this group over the next several years.

Demonstration effects As time goes on, faculty members will note in the literature and at conferences the availability of increased amounts of technology to aid higher education. These demonstration effects cannot help but provide some impetus to an infusion of new techniques and technology in the learning process.

Other factors will also tend to influence faculty members toward positive efforts to utilize computers and other technology. Included among these will be student pressure, the availability of cheaper technology, and perhaps improved methods of rewarding faculty members for developing better computer programs to assist the learning process (e.g., royalties and, more important, academic "credit" toward promotion similar to those received for published textbooks). But these, as well as the three or four major factors cited just above, will not, we believe, tend to offset the factors which will tend to restrain faculty efforts in this direction. We now turn to these restraining factors.

FACTORS TEND-ING TO MINIMIZE FACULTY USE OF TECHNOLOGY Eight major factors, we believe, will tend to minimize the amount of new technology introduced into the learning process in higher education over the next several years. These are:

1. *The research orientation of faculty*
The words "publish or perish" are not taken lightly in academia. Although every university or college has a three-part mission—teaching, research, and public service—the three are far from equal. Especially in the major universities, faculty members realize that their research productivity is the major criterion of success. It is at research that promotion committees tend to look most closely. And professors, like other men and women, are apt to spend most of their time and effort in areas that will be directly rewarded. As a result, as James Korn (1972)

puts it, "The promotion committee is the key to the success of any scheme for improving teaching effectiveness because its actions constitute an operational definition of the department's objectives" (p. 131). Where these objectives are clearly and strongly research-oriented, faculty efforts toward improving teaching—and especially teaching innovation with or without new technology—become secondary. Unfortunately, this is the case in many universities.

In addition, a professor's *real* reputation is not built on teaching (which is purely a local activity), but rather on research. It is for research contributions that he builds a national or international reputation. And it is for research that he gets the applause of his peers.

For reasons of both promotion and peer reputation (which are not unrelated), the introduction of new teaching technology is apt to take a secondary place to research in most major colleges and universities. It is unfortunate that this is so, because the very professors who are at the forefront of their professions in research could well be those doing an equally innovative job in improving the teaching-learning process. But this is the situation. It is perhaps the prime reason we expect the introduction of educational technology to advance in the universities at a lower rate than is theoretically possible.

2. *The need to learn a new discipline*

To make use of educational technology, whether it be motion pictures or computer-assisted learning, requires that the professor acquire new expertise. The technological tools and techniques must be well fitted into the regular curriculum and must be responsive to the needs of the materials. As a result, it is impossible to totally delegate the technological part of a particular learning scheme—although the professor can get assistance from technicians. So if they are to use it effectively, professors must *learn* about the new technology. However, effective researchers are most often people who are not especially interested in things outside their own discipline. To be an effective researcher is in some sense to be a superspecialist. The desire to learn broadly about educational technology is not totally incompatible with the instincts of the area specialist, but neither are they a natural match. Quite often, the effective researcher in a particular subspecialty is just not motivated to learn about technology that could assist his teaching process.

3. *Laziness*

Although we mean to demean no one else by this factor, we note in ourselves at many times a disinterest in improving our lectures through the use of technology. Lectures, as noted in Chapter 3, have many advantages for the professor. These include minimal advance planning, minimal equipment worries, minimal need to coordinate with other people about the lecture, and the ability to adapt the lecture to one's current interest. The lecture is basically an "easy form"—especially for those professors who enjoy some charismatic ability.

To use technology in learning, however, all the above must be reversed. Careful planning must be done ahead of time. The material must be laid out exactly so that the computer or movie technician can be told exactly what is wanted. Equipment must be scheduled and available. In sum, the investment for any particular lecture is high—and the effect uncertain. As a result, it takes a very motivated professor to put in the additional energy that is most often necessary to develop and use educational technology of any sort. At best, after working hard at it, he can look forward only to an uncertain result—as he replaces what, for him, has been a tried and true lecture tool.

4. *The diminishing student market*

As the previous chapter noted, the student pool will decrease relatively over the next few years. As a result, decisions will have to be made as to whether money for instructional purposes is to be spent for faculty or for technology. Professors will tend, consciously or unconsciously, not to replace themselves with machines.

5. *Unionization*

Innovation in most unionized industries is a difficult, time-consuming process. One can expect any changes in work roles through technology to ultimately be passed under a faculty union microscope. Today, about one-third of all faculty work in a unionized situation. As Mayhew (1972) suggests, "While the full effects of unionization on educational change cannot be known, analysis suggests that negotiated contracts protective of faculty economic privilege will not favor innovation" (p. 220).

6. *Inherent faculty conservatism*

In a very persuasive article, Edgar Schein (1970) discusses the unwillingness of professors to take action because of their role socialization. Professors have been trained toward the scientific approach, or scholarly analysis, and this affects not only their research but every action of their life. As Schein puts it, "The method of scholarly analysis . . . leads to a detailed fragmentation of every phenomenon under analysis in order to get at its underlying structure. As one of my colleagues puts it, professors are professional hairsplitters.' They do not want to take action until they are absolutely sure that they understand the consequences. Being right is terribly important; being wrong leads to gradual disqualification as a scholar" (Schein, 1970, p. 42). For whatever reason, and the above discussion pinpoints yet another, inaction is observable in academic life. Innovation thus suffers.

7. *Role overload*

In his article, Schein suggests another major factor that tends to hold back innovation in the learning process. He terms this "role overload." As Schein puts it, the professor "is simultaneously a scholar/researcher, teacher, and in some cases, a helper in solving practical problems" (ibid., p. 44). The combined expectations of the "clients" of each role far exceed what the professor is able to do. This factor is highly observable by anyone who has spent even a short period of time dealing with faculties. In an overloaded situation, no person willingly delegates significant amounts of time to areas that do not have high pay-off. Some professors who make educational technology their research will devote such time. But for the mass, whose research interests are elsewhere, the very fact of role overload will tend to minimize—if not completely negate—any time or effort spent on learning innovation.

8. *The "teach it my own way" syndrome*

For decades, faculty members in charge of a course have designed or redesigned the course to teach it in the way they felt it would be best taught. Individual control of course content and methods has many virtues. It ensures that the course is kept up to date. It also allows the professor to teach in the manner in which he is most comfortable—and presumably most effective. Perhaps most important, it encourages the professor's feelings of autonomy and responsibility with regard to the course.

However, from the viewpoint of encouraging the innovation of new technology into a course, this practice of individual autonomy has three disastrous effects. First, it discourages hard work and innovation on the part of an individual professor— since the odds are good his "computer model" or "self-study component" will not be carried out when someone else takes over the course. Second, it allows a professor freely to discard technology—as he takes over a course—if it does not "fit" with his conception on how to teach the course. Finally, and perhaps most significant, it almost ensures that the dollars that go into the development and implementation of a new learning-assistance tool most probably cannot be amortized over a series of years—and a large number of students!

SOME EVIDENCE It is clear, at least to us, that for the key person—the faculty member—the negative factors with regard to innovation in the field of learning technology far outweigh those factors that tend to encourage faster adoption of learning technology. A survey done in conjunction with this project (see Wilcox, 1972) not surprisingly suggests that faculty members are *not* optimistic about the introduction of learning technology into the curriculum, and we suggest it is very largely for the above reasons. In essence, faculty members are fairly certain that, despite the probable availability of technology, the rate of introduction into curriculums will be relatively slow.

Two main groups involved in the area of learning technology—the technologists and the users—were considered in the study. The perceptions of both these groups as to the likely timing and impact of new technology provide a measure of expected impact and insights into *differential perceptions*. These perceptions are also important because they help us understand the likely rate of *actual* adoption of new technologies in the typical college or university environment. The research suggests that the general feeling with regard to the probable rate of adoption of new technology, as viewed by professors in the universities now, is pessimistic. They view changes as coming rather slowly and being limited mostly to undergraduate instruction. The research also suggests that the gap between what is feasible and what is perceived as being done is a large one.

To increase understanding of existing perceptions in universities, a survey was conducted[1] in an attempt to determine when people perceived educational technology being applied. One promising approach for making such technological forecasts is the Delphi method of iterated forecasts from a panel of experts using controlled interaction among the panel between the iterations. However, research indicates that most, if not all, the benefits of the Delphi method can be obtained through predictions based on the sample median or mathematical mean of first-round individual questionnaire predictions with no interaction (Kaplan, Skogstad, & Girshick, 1950; Dalkey, 1969). In this chapter, the latter technique is used to estimate adoption dates for a number of new technologies in colleges and universities.

Early in 1971, four different questionnaires were mailed— one to technologists, one to faculty, one to controllers, and one to librarians. We concern ourselves in this chapter only with the first two groups—they are most important for our purposes. The questionnaires for technologists partially overlapped. Their responses were aggregated within each of these four groups to obtain predicted dates of adoption. The following special analyses were also conducted:

1 Estimation of dates of developments in underlying basic technologies

2 Principal components and factor analysis of underlying basic technologies predictions

3 Principal components and factor analysis of applied technologies predictions

4 Regression and nonparametric correlation of underlying basic technology predictions with applied technology adoption predictions

5 Analysis of differences in predictions between technologists and faculty

[1]See Wilcox (1972) for original survey. The rest of the discussion in this chapter is taken from his paper.

6   Summary of obstacles perceived by faculty to technological adoption

7   Analysis of differences in predictions among faculty by size of institution, by type of institution (public versus private), and by academic field (business and education versus fine and liberal arts versus science and engineering)

8   Analysis of differences in predictions among librarians and controllers by size of institution

From these analyses a number of specific findings emerged. These are discussed in the following sections. General conclusions are given at the end of the chapter, together with some additional suggested reasons for the general pessimism expressed by the faculty.

Technologist Questionnaires   Figure 9-1, pages 243–246, shows the questionnaire mailed to technologists. The mailing list was compiled from lists of those participating in various national conferences on new educational technology and on technological forecasting. The list includes many generally recognized experts in these fields.

There were 90 returns out of 147 questionnaires mailed (61 percent).

In the questionnaire shown in Figure 9-1 each response was coded as follows:

	Currently	By 1972	By 1975	By 1980	By 1990	By 2010	Later or never
Code:	1	2	3	4	5	6	7

Superimposed on the questionnaire is an **X** representing the median prediction.

Also shown in Figure 9-1 is the following information: the mean (M) and standard deviation (S) of the codes, a rough interpolation of the mean code in terms of dates (interpolated using Figure 9-2), and the number of responses (N). For this purpose, "later or never" is regarded as equivalent to "by 2050."

For example, the display on item 1, section A, indicates the median prediction was "by 1980," the mean code was 3.9, or about 1979, the standard deviation of the codes was 1.1, and there were 65 responses to the item.

FIGURE 9-1 *Technologist questionnaire*

Introduction

This questionnaire has been distributed to those who have special knowledge of the technological potential for successful development of new technology likely to have an impact on institutions of higher education. The technologically based estimates which will result will be combined and contrasted with user-based estimates prepared from other questionnaires.

Your forecasts should be based when practicable on your own firsthand experiences. Again, immediate impressions are usually nearly as good as long-drawn-out consideration.

Mark an "X" in the time-span column which you visualize as the most likely period during which an event will take place.

Example

If you think event A will not occur until 1982, mark as follows:

Currently	By 1972	By 1975	By 1980	By 1990	By 2010	Later or never
				X		

Section A: Forecast of underlying technological development

	Currently	By 1972	By 1975	By 1980	By 1990	By 2010	Later or never
1. The manufacturing cost of circuitry for computers will be reduced to less than $0.20 per 500-element chip.	M = 3.9 (1979)			X			S = 1.1 N = 65
2. The manufacturing cost of circuitry for computers will be reduced to less than $0.01 per 500-element chip.	M = 5.3 (1995)				X		S = 1.3 N = 64
3. The cost of reliable interactive graphic terminals like IMLAC, ARDS, or Computic will be reduced to $1,000.	M = 3.9 (1979)			X			S = 0.8 N = 75
4. As a result of laser or other technology, the cost of voice-grade communication channels will be reduced to one-tenth of their 1971 cost.	M = 4.7 (1986)				X		S = 1.0 N = 77
5. Computerized search for information on specialized topics will be more effective than typical human search.	M = 3.6 (1978)			X			S = 1.8 N = 89

6. Effective real-time optical memories for computers.	M = 4.4 (1983)			X				S = 1.4 N = 77
7. Effective compatibility of data files and programs across 50 percent of computers and operating systems in use to support instruction in a particular academic field.	M = 4.5 (1984)				X			S = 1.4 N = 88
8. Effective compatibility of data files and programs across 50 percent of computers and operating systems used to support research in a particular academic field.	M = 4.5 (1984)				X			S = 1.4 N = 86
9. Remote computer terminals will be installed in 10 percent of U.S. households.	M = 5.3 (1995)				X			S = 0.9 N = 89
10. Provision for hardcopy or videotape reproduction of incoming TV signals will be installed in 10 percent of U.S. households.	M = 4.9 (1989)				X			S = 0.8 N = 90
11. Advances in printing or reproduction will reduce the manufacturing cost of an average textbook to less than $0.25.	M = 5.9 (2008)						X	S = 1.4 N = 83
12. Inexpensive, safe drug products will be available which will double typical learning and memory abilities.	M = 6.2 (2016)							X S = 1.1 N = 85

Section B: Forecast of user applications

For each of the following forecasts please use as a frame of reference the period by which you visualize new technology used routinely within the typical institution of higher education.

1. *Routine audiovisual techniques*—the classroom use of films, taped lectures shown on closed-circuit television, or of listening laboratories, etc.

Currently	By 1972	By 1975	By 1980	By 1990	By 2010	Later or never
M = 2.8 (1974)		X				S = 1.5 N = 88

2. *Programmed instruction*—the student uses a text or simple supplementary device which uses step-by-step feedback reinforcement techniques to progress through sequentially ordered, structured material. Good examples are programmed texts and self-study language audiotapes.

Currently	By 1972	By 1975	By 1980	By 1990	By 2010	Later or never
M = 3.2 **(1976)**		X				**S = 1.5** **N = 89**

3. *Routine computer-assisted instruction*—the computer is used in the instructional process for either computerized programmed instruction or for drill-and-practice exercises.

Currently	By 1972	By 1975	By 1980	By 1990	By 2010	Later or never
M = 3.9 **(1979)**			X			**S = 1.2** **N = 90**

4. *Computer simulation*—the computer is used in simulation exercises involving student investigation of the properties of a "pseudo-reality" generated by a model of the phenomenon under study.

Currently	By 1972	By 1975	By 1980	By 1990	By 2010	Later or never
M = 3.9 **(1979)**			X			**S = 1.2** **N = 90**

5. *Advanced computer-assisted instruction*—the computer is used in a flexible, individualized way to support student exploration of a well-defined body of knowledge; this may include socratic dialogue, tutorial exercises, and the ability to answer at least some unforeseen student questions.

Currently	By 1972	By 1975	By 1980	By 1990	By 2010	Later or never
M = 4.9 **(1989)**				X		**S = 1.0** **N = 90**

6. *Computer-managed instruction*—measures of the student's performance are monitored and analyzed by the computer; based on this the computer provides aid or direction to the student or teacher as to the most suitable packet of instructional material, such as film, programmed instruction, or live teacher, to be used next.

Currently	By 1972	By 1975	By 1980	By 1990	By 2010	Later or never
M = 4.4 **(1983)**			X			**S = 1.1** **N = 90**

7. *Remote classroom broadcasting and response*—the use of remote television broadcasting from a central location to dispersed classrooms, with at least audio live response or questions from the students.

Currently	By 1972	By 1975	By 1980	By 1990	By 2010	Later or never
M = 3.9 (1979)			X			S = 1.3 N = 89

8. *Student-initiated access to audiovisual recordings*—the use of audio-video recordings in a technological environment sufficiently inexpensive and easy to use to allow individual student-initiated access to recorded lecture or demonstration material.

Currently	By 1972	By 1975	By 1980	By 1990	By 2010	Later or never
M = 3.9 (1979)			X			S = 1.1 N = 90

9. *Computer-aided course design*—the use of computers to record and analyze student responses to instructional packets in computer-assisted and computer-managed instruction in order to provide information for the design of improvements in instructional material.

Currently	By 1972	By 1975	By 1980	By 1990	By 2010	Later or never
M = 4.4 (1983)			X			S = 1.0 N = 87

10. *Remote library browsing*—the ability of users to "browse" through most library materials from a remote location with the aid of a computer and visual display terminal.

Currently	By 1972	By 1975	By 1980	By 1990	By 2010	Later or never
M = 5.2 (1993)				X		S = 1.0 N = 88

11. *Man-machine research support*—the availability to the average researcher of remote time-shared computer consoles, computational support equal to the best available on an experimental basis in 1971.

Currently	By 1972	By 1975	By 1980	By 1990	By 2010	Later or never
M = 3.9 (1979)			X			S = 0.7 N = 88

FIGURE 9-2
Conversion of
codes to years

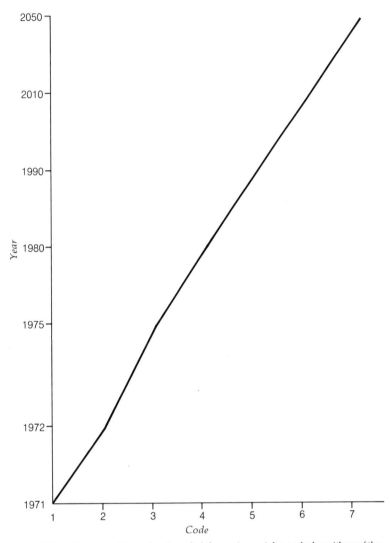

NOTE: Taking the mean of the codes gives slightly varying weights to the logarithms of the various forecast horizons.

The reader should note that the existence of the qualitative "later or never" code might make the interpolation of the mean code in terms of dates suspect. The median is not affected by this possible problem, but has less resolving power. Also, the reader should note that in calculating the mean, roughly equal weights are given to the logarithms of the time intervals from the present to the predicted date. This is in accord with experimental evidence on the tendency toward logarithmic normal distributions of date responses to technological forecasting questions.

Technologists' predictions of underlying technology

Section A of the technologists' questionnaire produced three points of particular interest for this study. The first of these is that the technologists see no breakthrough in communication-channel costs before 1990. (See question 4, section A.) If true, this is an important point, as widespread use of technology in the higher educational system will require extensive use of communication channels.

The second point was the technologists' predictions that effective compatibility of data files and programs across 50 percent of computers and operating systems being used in research would not occur until 1990. A number of suggestions have been made recently (see Levien, 1972) about sharing computer programs for educational support; if the technologists' predictions are true, then these solutions are going to have to solve the compatibility problem before they can be effective.

A third point on which the technologists were generally pessimistic was the date by which a significant number of household computer terminals and videotape or hardcopy facilities would be available. Their forecast date of 1990 is generally consistent with the statements made by the learning corporations.

This lack of breakthrough in communication channels, printing, and household facilities suggests that there is no technical possibility of a radical revision of the organization of the campus toward individual home instruction. However, as we discussed in Chapter 2, one can forecast increased availability of economical computer facilities including much larger memories and inexpensive interactive display terminals as well as low-cost CPUs within the next decade. These will clearly have potential impact within the typical college or university as they will sharply reduce the cost of delivering computer power to the student. However, the forecast of lack of compatibility among computer files and programs means that there is unlikely to be any radical homogenation in instruction via the computer *across* various academic institutions.

The indication, then, is for a continued existence of some kind of campus orientation providing economies of scale in instruction. This is not to say, however, that there may not be significant changes in on-campus instructional technology and perhaps in the relative mixture of different pedagogic techniques used for instruction.

Conclusions on application adoption forecasts

The most interesting aspect of the forecasts of applied technology adoption by the technologists was the relatively early impact foreseen on the typical college or university of many applications. Widespread use of the computer for routine CAI, simulation, and computer-managed instruction was predicted by 1980 as shown in section B, Figure 9-1. Advanced audiovisual systems (remote broadcasting with audio feedback, and student-initiated access to audio-video recordings) were also foreseen by 1980. These *technologist* forecasts would imply widespread changes in teaching methods on the campus during the next 15 years, relying on the existing technology base.

Special analyses of technologist questionnaire responses

A principal components analysis of the responses on the various underlying technologies revealed that about 30 percent of the normalized variance in the coded responses of all 12 items could be accounted for in terms of a single component.[2] This implies a mild technological "halo" effect. That is, individual respondents tended to be somewhat optimistic or pessimistic across a wide range of items rather than to consider them completely independently. The correlations of the 12 items with this principal component are shown in Table 9-1.

When a varimax rotation of principal components of the basic technology predictions was done, however, the only strong local groupings of items were items 1, 2, and 3 (manufacturing cost of chip < $0.20, manufacturing cost of chip < $0.01, and interactive graphics terminal < $1,000) in one factor and items 7 and 8 (instructional computer compatibility and research computer compatibility) in another. This analysis indicates the lack

[2]See Harman (1967) for an explanation of principal components analysis and factor analysis.

TABLE 9-1
Loadings of technologists' "section A" items on their principal component

Correlation coefficient (loading)	Item	Label
Strongly related		
.71	7	Instructional computer compatibility
.70	2	Manuf. cost of chip < $0.01
.66	1	Manuf. cost of chip < $0.20
.61	10	Household hardcopy
.61	11	Printing cost text < $0.25
.59	8	Research computer compatibility
.57	9	Household computer terminals
.55	3	Interactive graphics terminal < $1,000
Not strongly related		
.37	4	Communications channels one-tenth 1971 cost
.37	6	Optical computer memories
.18	5	Effective computer information search
.16	12	Drugs for learning

of strong local interdependencies in the predictions for the other items. The significance to the reader is that whatever technological information he may have relevant to forecasting one item is not likely to be strongly relevant to the other items.

Similarly, a principal components analysis was made of the forecasts of applications of new technology (section B items). This revealed a somewhat stronger "optimistic versus pessimistic" halo. About 37 percent of the total normalized variance of the responses to the 11 applied items in section B could be summarized in a single principal component. Table 9-2 gives the association of each item with this central theme. *All* the items figured at least moderately in this component.

This relatively pervasive component of variation implies a somewhat greater commonality of attitude across the items in section B than across the items in section A for each individual. That is, a particular technologist tends to be uniformly optimistic or pessimistic compared with the group of technologists as a whole.

Correlation coefficient (loading)	Item	Label
.74	3	Routine CAI
.69	6	Computer-managed instruction
.64	7	Remote classroom response
.64	4	Computer simulation
.62	2	Programmed instruction
.62	5	Advanced CAI
.62	9	Computer-aided course design
.60	8	Student access to audiovisual recordings
.53	11	Man-machine research support
.45	1	Routine audiovisual technique
.44	10	Remote library browsing

TABLE 9-2 Loadings of technologists' "section B" items on their principal component

Faculty Questionnaires

Figure 9-3, pages 252–258, shows the questionnaire mailed to faculty and the responses. The mailing list was taken from *The World of Learning,* and represented stratification by size of institution, source of institutional support (private versus public), and academic field. It was aimed at gaining a very broad cross section of faculty views in this country. In this the faculty mailing list differed from that for technologists, which was drawn from a smaller group of nationally well-known activists in new technology. There were 152 returns out of 413 questionnaires mailed (37 percent), based on one mailing. One might suspect that faculty nonrespondents might be on the average more conservative than respondents, but this was not investigated.

Table 9-3 breaks down the questionnaires that were mailed and those that were returned by size of the university and by field of respondent. These categories are used to evaluate some of the responses later on in the analysis.

Preliminary conclusions regarding faculty responses

The first overall conclusion one reaches is that faculty predicted routine adoption of most of the new technology as coming

FIGURE 9-3 *Faculty questionnaire*

Section A: Forecast of instructional technology application

In this section, you are given brief descriptions of various devices and systems which might be used to supplement or supplant the existing teacher-student classroom instruction process. You are asked to roughly estimate the period during which adoption will occur in your general field of specialization and in your institution. We ask that you distinguish between undergraduate and graduate adoption and between adoption as a secondary teaching support and adoption supplanting the traditional teacher.

Place an "X" in the time-span column you visualize as most likely for adoption or other event to be predicted.

Example

If you estimate the event in 1986, mark as follows:

Currently	By 1972	By 1975	By 1980	By 1990	By 2010	Later or never
				X		

The areas of technology covered are audiovisual techniques, programmed instruction, computer-assisted instruction, computer-managed instruction, remote broadcasting, student-initiated access to audiovisual recordings, and advances in the technology of instructional improvement.

I. *Routine audiovisual techniques*—the classroom use of films, taped lectures shown on closed-circuit television, or of listening laboratories, etc.

	Currently	By 1972	By 1975	By 1980	By 1990	By 2010	Later or never
A. Fairly widely available for some courses in my field but not necessarily in my institution	X M = 2.1 (1972)						S = 1.6 N = 136
B. Used routinely in my institution for undergraduate courses in my field	M = 3.0 (1975)		X				S = 1.9 N = 135
C. Used routinely in my institution for graduate courses in my field	M = 4.9 (1989)				X		S = 2.2 N = 135
D. Has largely supplanted the traditional live-teacher classroom instruction in some courses taught by my department	M = 5.6 (2000)						X S = 1.8 N = 132

II. *Programmed instruction*—the student uses a text or simple supplementary device which uses step-by-step feedback reinforcement techniques to progress through sequentially ordered, structured material. Good examples are programmed texts and self-study language audiotapes.

	Currently	By 1972	By 1975	By 1980	By 1990	By 2010	Later or never
A. Fairly widely available for some courses in my field but not necessarily in my institution	M = 3.1 (1975)		X				S = 2.0 N = 142
B. Used routinely in my institution for undergraduate courses in my field	M = 4.2 (1982)			X			S = 2.0 N = 133
C. Used routinely in my institution for graduate courses in my field	M = 6.0 (2010)						X S = 1.5 N = 129
D. Has largely supplanted the traditional live-teacher classroom instruction in some courses taught by my department	M = 6.1 (2013)						X S = 1.4 N = 130

III. *Routine computer-assisted instruction*—the computer is used in the instructional process for either computerized programmed instruction or for drill-and-practice exercises.

	Currently	By 1972	By 1975	By 1980	By 1990	By 2010	Later or never
A. Fairly widely available for some courses in my field but not necessarily in my institution	M = 3.5 (1977)		X				S = 2.0 N = 140
B. Used routinely in my institution for undergraduate courses in my field	M = 4.2 (1982)			X			S = 1.9 N = 134
C. Used routinely in my institution for graduate courses in my field	M = 5.1 (1992)				X		S = 2.1 N = 132
D. Has largely supplanted the traditional live-teacher classroom instruction in some courses taught by my department	M = 6.4 (2023)						X S = 1.1 N = 131

IV. *Computer simulation*—the computer is used in simulation exercises involving student investigation of the properties of a "pseudo-reality" generated by a model of the phenomenon under study.

	Currently	By 1972	By 1975	By 1980	By 1990	By 2010	Later or never
A. Fairly widely available for some courses in my field but not necessarily in my institution	M = 3.8 (1979)			X			S = 2.1 N = 139
B. Used routinely in my institution for undergraduate courses in my field	M = 4.4 (1983)			X			S = 2.1 N = 133
C. Used routinely in my institution for graduate courses in my field	M = 4.6 (1985)				X		S = 2.2 N = 133
D. Has largely supplanted the traditional live-teacher classroom instruction in some courses taught by my department	M = 6.5 (2027)						X S = 1.3 N = 129

V. *Advanced computer-assisted instruction*—the computer is used in a flexible, individualized way to support student exploration of a well-defined body of knowledge; this may include socratic dialogue, tutorial exercises, and the ability to answer at least some unforeseen student questions.

	Currently	By 1972	By 1975	By 1980	By 1990	By 2010	Later or never
A. Fairly widely available for some courses in my field but not necessarily in my institution	M = 4.5 (1984)			X			S = 1.7 N = 140
B. Used routinely in my institution for undergraduate courses in my field	M = 5.1 (1992)				X		S = 1.5 N = 130
C. Used routinely in my institution for graduate courses in my field	M = 5.4 (1996)					X	S = 1.8 N = 128
D. Has largely supplanted the traditional live-teacher classroom instruction in some courses taught by my department	M = 6.5 (2027)						X S = 0.9 N = 127

VI. *Computer-managed instruction*—measures of the student's performance
   are monitored and analyzed by the computer; based on this the computer provides aid or direction to the student or teacher as to the most
   suitable packet of instructional material, such as film, programmed
   instruction, or live teacher, to be used next.

	Currently	By 1972	By 1975	By 1980	By 1990	By 2010	Later or never
A. Fairly widely available for some courses in my field but not necessarily in my institution	M = 4.7 (1986)				X		S = 1.7 N = 139
B. Used routinely in my institution for undergraduate courses in my field	M = 5.3 (1995)				X		S = 1.4 N = 129
C. Used routinely in my institution for graduate courses in my field	M = 5.8 (2005)						X S = 1.4 N = 129
D. Has largely supplanted the traditional live-teacher classroom instruction in some courses taught by my department	M = 6.5 (2027)						X S = 1.0 N = 129

VII. *Remote classroom broadcasting and response*—the use of remote television
   broadcasting from a central location to dispersed classrooms, with at
   least audio live response or questions from the students.

	Currently	By 1972	By 1975	By 1980	By 1990	By 2010	Later or never
A. Fairly widely available for some courses in my field by not necessarily in my institution	M = 2.9 (1974)		X				S = 1.9 N = 143
B. Used routinely in my institution for undergraduate courses in my field	M = 4.5 (1984)			X			S = 1.8 N = 130
C. Used routinely in my institution for graduate courses in my field	M = 5.4 (1996)						X S = 2.0 N = 132
D. Has largely supplanted the traditional live-teacher classroom instruction in some courses taught by my department	M = 6.0 (2010)						X S = 1.6 N = 132

VIII. *Student-initiated access to audiovisual recordings*—the use of audio-video recordings in a technological environment sufficiently inexpensive and easy to use to allow individual student-initiated access to recorded lecture or demonstration material.

	Currently	By 1972	By 1975	By 1980	By 1990	By 2010	Later or never
A. Fairly widely available for some courses in my field but not necessarily in my institution	M = 3.0 (1975)		X				S = 1.5 N = 140
B. Used routinely in my institution for undergraduate courses in my field	M = 3.8 (1979)			X			S = 1.6 N = 133
C. Used routinely in my institution for graduate courses in my field	M = 4.7 (1986)			X			S = 1.9 N = 134
D. Has largely supplanted the traditional live-teacher classroom instruction in some courses taught by my department	M = 6.2 (2016)						X S = 1.5 N = 131

IX. *Computer-aided course design*—the use of computers to record and analyze student responses to instructional packets in computer-assisted and computer-managed instruction in order to provide information for the design of improvements in the instructional material.

	Currently	By 1972	By 1975	By 1980	By 1990	By 2010	Later or never
A. Fairly widely available for some courses in my field but not necessarily in my institution	M = 4.4 (1983)			X			S =1.6 N = 137
B. Used routinely in my institution for undergraduate courses in my field	M = 5.1 (1992)				X		S = 1.5 N = 128
C. Used routinely in my institution for graduate courses in my field	M = 5.7 (2003)					X	S = 1.5 N = 127
D. Has largely supplanted the traditional live-teacher classroom instruction in some courses taught by my department	M = 6.6 (2031)						X S = 0.9 N = 124

Section B: Constraints on the adoption of new instructional technology

Please use the following codes to rate the probable significance of different factors such as funding, attitudes, etc., as obstacles restraining the adoption of new technology in your institution.

Code	Constraint
T	Effectiveness of technology for inducing learning
$	Availability of funds to pay for new technology
F	Attitude of faculty
S	Attitude of students
A	Attitude of administration

Now, use these codes to rate the obstacles facing each group of technologies. For example, if you predicted adoption of audiovisuals in 1975, rate these factors in terms of importance in delaying adoption till that date.

Example

Not a real obstacle					A severe obstacle
	A, T		$, S	F	

Again, your first reaction is probably most useful, so don't spend more than 10 minutes on this part of the questionnaire.

	Not a real obstacle				A severe obstacle
I. Routine audiovisual techniques					
II. Programmed instruction					
III. Routine computer-assisted instruction					
IV. Computer simulation					
V. Advanced computer-aided instruction					
VI. Computer-managed instruction					
VII. Remote classroom broadcasting and response					

VIII. Student-initiated access to audiovisual recordings

IX. Computer-aided course design

Section C

Please indicate when, relative to the adoption of new technologies in your undergraduate courses, you expect the technologies will be used routinely in graduate courses in your discipline.

1	2	3	4	5
				X

| More than 5 years *before* they are used in undergraduate courses | 2–5 years *before* | Within the same year | 2–5 years *later* | More than 5 years *after* they are used in undergraduate courses |

TABLE 9-3
Questionnaire returns by class

By size of institution (in numbers of students)	Overall	Less than 10,000	More than 10,000
Total sent	413	141	272
Returned	152	48	104

By field	Sent	Received
Arts, etc.	164	53
Engineering, science	141	52
Business, education	105	44
Unclassifiable	3	3
TOTAL	413	152

considerably later than did the technologists. See Table 9-4 for a comparison. In all but two areas, the difference is three or more years, with four of the nine areas showing a significant difference at the one percent level on a test of means. Clearly, faculty members are more pessimistic than technologists.

The second striking point is the sharp difference in timing between different degrees of impact. For example, the pre-

TABLE 9-4 *Faculty mean predictions of availability and routine undergraduate use, technologists' mean predictions of routine use*

Item and label	Faculty prediction of availability	Technologist prediction of routine use	Faculty prediction of routine use for undergraduates
1. Routine audiovisual technique	1972	1974	1975
2. Programmed instruction	1975	1976	1982*
3. Routine CAI	1977	1979	1982
4. Computer simulation	1979	1979	1983
5. Advanced CAI	1984	1989	1992
6. Computer-managed instruction	1986	1983	1995*
7. Remote classroom feedback	1974	1979	1984*
8. Student-initiated access to audiovisual recordings	1975	1979	1979
9. Computer-aided course design	1983	1983	1992*

*Difference in means for routine use is significant at .01 level according to large-sample test (two-tailed).

dicted lag from "fairly wide availability" in one's academic field to "routine use in one's own institution for undergraduates" ranges from three or four years for items 1 and 8 (routine audiovisual techniques and student-initiated access to audiovisual recordings) to nine or ten years for items 6, 7, and 9 (computer-managed instruction, remote classroom broadcasting and response, and computer-aided course design). The further lag from predicted "use for undergraduates" to "use for graduates" ranges from two to four years for computer simulation and advanced CAI, through over a decade for routine audiovisual techniques, remote classroom broadcasting, and computer-aided course design, to at least thirty years for programmed instruction. Faculty members are suggesting that despite widespread availability, use by *themselves* will take a while.

Finally, faculty very strongly predict that the traditional live-teacher classroom instruction will *not* be supplanted in even some courses taught by their own departments before 2000. No doubt this latter prediction incorporates some emotion as well as logic, but it is clearly significant.

According to mean faculty predictions, by 1980 routine undergraduate use will come for only routine audiovisual techniques and student-initiated access to audiovisual recordings. A few years later will come programmed instruction, routine CAI, computer simulation, and remote classroom broadcasting and response. Advanced CAI, computer-managed instruction, and computer-aided course design are not predicted until after 1990. Generally summarizing, only those technologies well within the current state of the art are foreseen by faculty as destined for adoption within the next 15 years. Also, as we will see shortly, there are dramatic differences by academic field in the faculty predictions.

Special analyses of faculty questionnaire responses

An analysis was done comparing the prediction responses of faculty by size of institution.[3] Figure 9-4 gives details. In general, faculty of the larger schools predicted adoption of new instructional technology sooner, but the individual item differences were small.

An analysis was also made of faculty responses from private institutions versus public institutions. At least at the broad aggregate level, no significant differences were found.

Finally, faculty responses were analyzed on a sample basis for differences by academic field. Differences among three broad groups were investigated for each technological item and for each degree of impact. As Figure 9-5 indicates, there were highly significant differences. Some of the greater pessimism shown by faculty as opposed to technologists arises from within the liberal and fine arts fields, as would be expected.

Section B of the faculty questionnaire (Figure 9-3) asked for ratings as to the relative difficulty imposed on adoption of new technology by constraints of technology effectiveness, funding, faculty attitudes, student attitudes, and administration attitudes. The responses strongly indicated that faculty ranked these constraints as follows:

1 Funding
2 Faculty attitudes
3 Technology effectiveness

(text continues on p. 268)

[3]The analyses by size and for public versus private were done by Joseph R. Matson based on about 90 percent of the returns.

FIGURE 9-4 *Differences in mean codes of faculty responses, by size of institution*

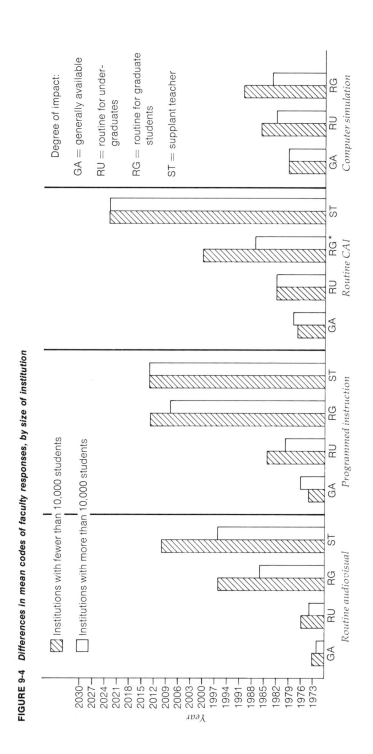

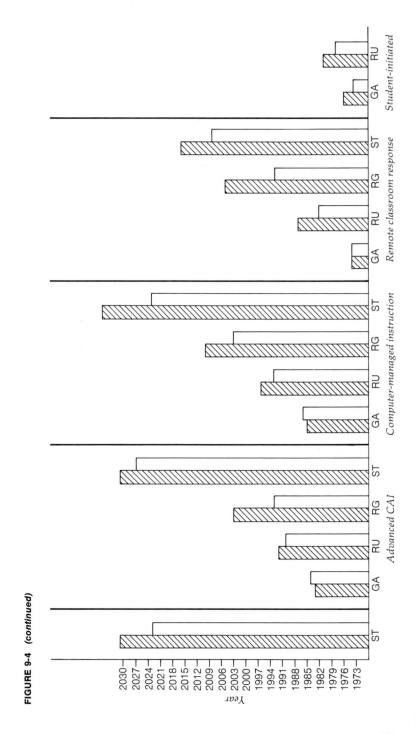

FIGURE 9-4 (continued)

FIGURE 9-4 *(continued)*

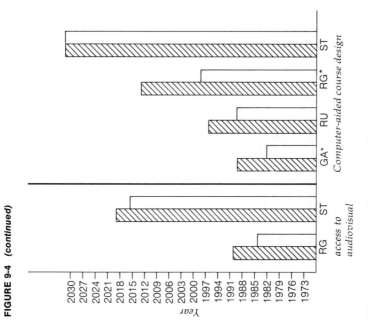

*Differences in means significant at the 0.02 level by two-tailed large-sample test.

FIGURE 9-5 *Differences in mean code responses by academic field*

Degree of impact:

GA = generally available

RU = routine for under-
graduates

RG = routine for graduate
students

ST = supplant teacher

Engineering and science. Includes engineering, physics, chemistry, mathematics, and social sciences.

Business and education. Includes accounting, business administration, and education.

Liberal and fine arts. Includes English, history, geography, philosophy, music, foreign languages, fine arts, and arts and sciences.

Year

2030 2027 2024 2021 2018 2015 2012 2009 2006 2003 2000 1997 1994 1991 1988 1985 1982 1979 1976 1973

Routine audiovisual

GA RU RG ST

Programmed instruction

GA RU RG ST

Routine CAI

GA* RU* RG*

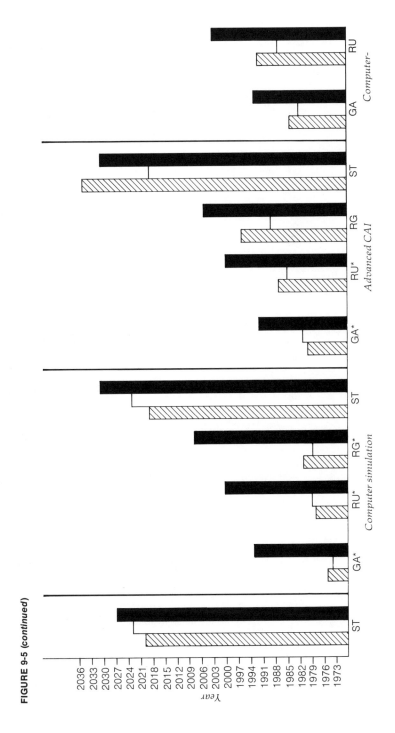

FIGURE 9-5 (continued)

FIGURE 9-5 (continued)

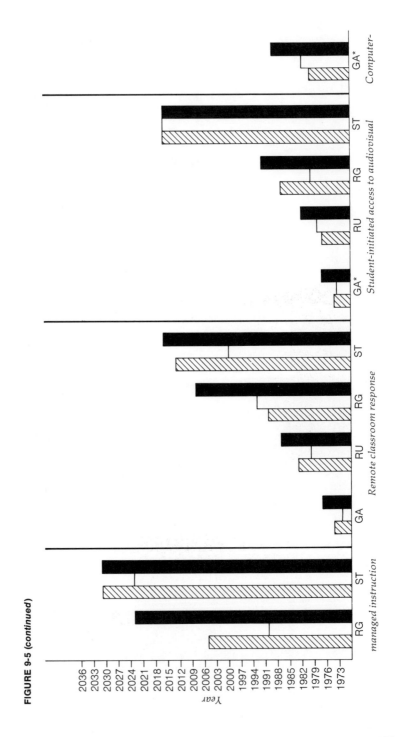

FIGURE 9-5 (continued)

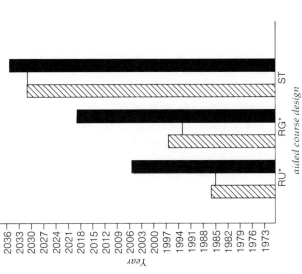

*Difference in means between arts versus engineering and science is significant at the 0.01 level by two-tailed large-sample test.

267

4 Student attitudes

5 Administration attitudes

It is, to us, highly significant that faculty attitudes rank so high. On most questionnaires, faculty attitudes were perceived as a greater obstacle to adoption than was lack of technological effectiveness. This is a significant "admission" for the faculty— and, to us, a very important insight today into a (perhaps *the*) significant obstacle to a rapid spread of technology in higher education.

CONCLUSIONS   Chapter 8 presented several factors pro and con that will affect the introduction of educational technology over the next decade. These factors were selected from the environment *external* to the universities and colleges. This chapter suggested two major further *internal* factors that will affect the introduction of learning technology. These are the attitudes of administrators and faculty. It is suggested that while administration attitudes may be favorable to new technology, this will not have a very great effect on the introduction of learning technology for a variety of reasons. Faculty attitudes, on the other hand, will have a major impact. Unfortunately, we have suggested, the average faculty member will see many more reasons *not* to work toward the introduction of more learning technology than positive factors urging him to work toward its introduction.

The research study cited in this chapter (Wilcox, 1972) tends to confirm our less quantified thoughts about faculty attitudes. Faculty members, in general, tend to see the availability of adequate technology as being further in the future than do a representative sample of technologists. This, of course, may be merely a difference in perspective, but it may also reflect *disinterest* in the field or an inherent *desire* to not have the necessary technology available until further in the future. Perhaps more telling is the fact that faculty members foresee their own institutions as utilizing this technology well after it is widely available. In assessing the reasons for the slow impact of learning technology, the faculty put "faculty attitudes" as the second most significant factor—after only the availability of funds. We suspect that faculty attitudes may well be the predominant factor. And in an environment where faculties control what is and is *not* done in the learning process, a negative—or at best heavily conservative—attitude on the part of faculties does not bode well for early implementation of computer assistance (or any other technology) in the learning process.

As a result, we can now complete the force field diagram initiated in Chapter 8. It is now as shown in Figure 9-6.

The administration will exert positive pressures in total—with some negative pressures coming as a result of its need to keep costs (including technology development costs) down. However, the main thrust of administration efforts will be to further learning technology, both to increase human penetration and to increase the quality of education.

The faculty will provide some positive impetus toward the development and implementation of more and better learning technology for the reasons noted on pages 235–236. On the other hand, the ensemble of negative factors noted on pages 236–240 certainly exists. The scales can be tipped either way in the future by many variables, but at the present time—due to all the external and internal faces discussed in this chapter and the preceding one—we see the faculty as a relatively negative influence on the promotion of educational technology. At best, faculty will inhibit the rate of growth that is technically possible.

FIGURE 9-6 The direction and an estimate of the relative strength of the pertinent forces affecting the use of educational technology in higher education

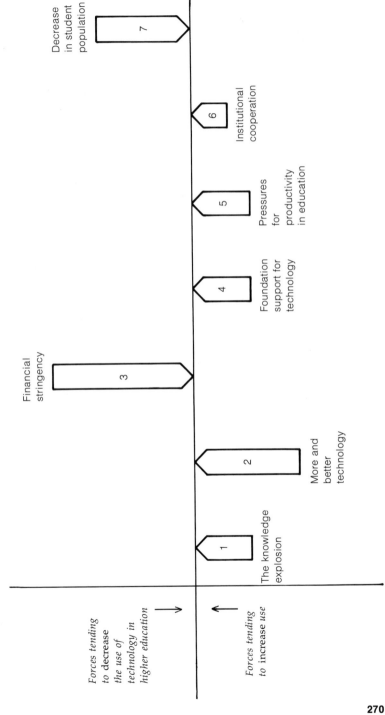

FIGURE 9-6 *(continued)*

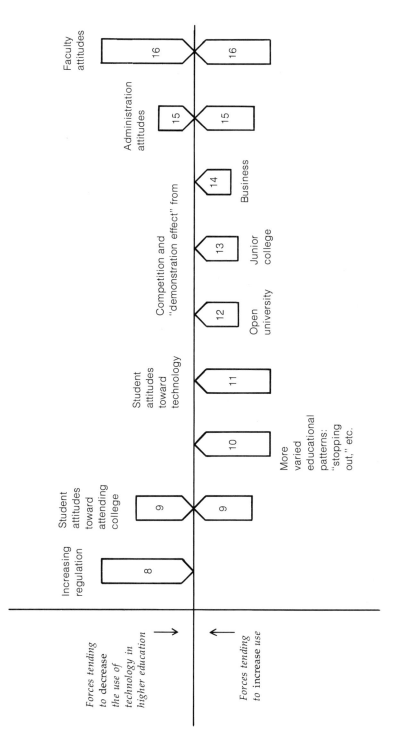

Forces tending
to decrease
the use of
technology in
higher education

Forces tending
to increase use

Increasing
regulation

Student
attitudes
toward
attending
college

More
varied
educational
patterns:
"stopping
out," etc.

Student
attitudes
toward
technology

Competition and
"demonstration effect" from

Open
university

Junior
college

Business

Administration
attitudes

Faculty
attitudes

8

9

9

10

11

12

13

14

15

15

16

16

10. *Conclusions*

One obvious and inevitable conclusion that emerges from this study is that

Technology is continuing to change, and it will continue to have a potential impact on the way we conduct ourselves in higher education. Indeed certain technologies, computers and television in particular, have the potential to have a major impact on the learning process and the structure of the university.

Our analysis suggests that despite this potential, the focus and level of spending on many technologically based projects has not been appropriate. We have been in an era, which seems to be ending, of spending without thinking—some believe we are entering an era of thinking without spending. We need to be on a carefully chosen middle ground. The millions of dollars spent for many massive projects, in computer-based instruction, for example, have thus far left little tangible impact on what actually goes on in institutions of higher learning. At the same time, investment in other areas of high potential impact, areas such as research on the learning process, on efforts aimed at the development of "enrichment systems," and on the impact of such systems, has been minimal.

The continuously changing technology gives special problems to a profession for which innovation itself is relatively new. In computer technology we experienced a wave of new computer systems in the period 1958–1965. There was a series of new machines, of which each had considerable potential and each was more powerful than the one before. By 1965, however, the useful power delivered was still considerably more expensive than the educational techniques it might have replaced.

Having advanced a great deal, computers were still not cost effective in any of the fields of use where traditional mechanisms were entrenched. In other areas, such as using the computer to teach students about the computer, some progress was made. Following the 1958–1965 period of rapid growth was a plateau, roughly from 1966 to 1971. This plateau occurred at the same time that funds became available for new computer-based educational projects, funds that were made available as a result, in part, of the wave of excitement built up by the 1958–1965 period. These funds were to a large extent invested in uninteresting, inadequate hardware. Relatively little money, as reported in the literature at least, was spent on courseware— what was spent was heavily in programmed instruction or in fundamental research on how to organize material so that it could be effectively deployed in the learning process. From these gargantuan efforts we have now learned that standard hardware, delivering standard CAI material to university-level students, was generally not a success—at least not as measured by continued use and growth in the implementation of the concepts developed in the 1966–1971 period.

We are now firmly embarked on a new upswing in computer technology. This is perhaps best exemplified by the sharp drop in costs of large-scale computers, the advent of the minicomputer, and, quite significantly, the development of computer networks. An analogy can be found in the dramatic drop in cost, and increase in performance, in the hand-held-calculator market, which employs substantially the same technology. This upswing in technology, dramatic as it is, has not been matched with an equivalent amount of attention, or funding, on the courseware and learning side. We turn to this below.

A second major technological shift that is clearly on the rise is "live" television, that is, television with a possibility for student feedback. The considerable improvement in the United States communications systems and the rate structure that is developing make television much more attractive than it has been. It has been around long enough that a great many people understand how to communicate through it. The major advance has been live two-way communication. Linking the student, via voice channel, to the lecturer provides the feedback that is central to several stages in the learning process, particularly for all material other than simple facts and skills.

The open university in the United Kingdom has been cited for a successful use of television to expand the reach of the university. Less noticed, but perhaps as far-reaching, are the experiments in the United States with television and two-way voice channels (see "Bringing Graduate School . . . ," 1970). Neither of these is *the* answer, but both are working, and as recently as five years ago few faculty would have given them much chance of success. Looking ahead over the next five years, two technologies, computer and television, clearly dominate. It may well be that they will dominate for 10 or more years. Improved access to libraries via microfiche-like means seems to be the only other active technological area of likely impact on higher education, and here the job is so massive that it will take extraordinary pressure before much progress is visible. In addition, of course, "printed" library material is a one-way form of learning, as no communication is possible with the author, and may therefore not impact learning as much as it may reduce the cost of running libraries.

We have, then, three areas in which technology is changing in an interesting and potentially powerful way—computers and their peripherals; television, particularly two-way; and libraries, in their nonpaper form. We would contend that the technological aspects of these changes are taking place without adequate reference to the process of education. Many other, more powerful forces are shaping and extending these three fields. Space and the military have done much to speed computer developments; companies' needs for data have affected the pricing and form of communications, and the sheer number of books and costs of storage may affect libraries. None of these areas is waiting for educational investment or interest before further development.

The impact of technology on education, therefore, is very much in the hands of the university itself, shaped, of course, by the pressures that beset it. The university can accept and use the technology, which will always be further developed than the university can absorb it, or the university can ignore the technology. The answer does not depend on the technology or the technologist.

Our second contention, that before expending greater effort to apply technology, we need to understand where to apply it and why, has led us to six major propositions. They are:

- *There is a definite need for a robust model of the learning process.* Only through the development of such an explicit model can the targets of opportunity for any particular technology be consistently exploited.

- The development of our model leads us to a clear understanding that no single technology can adequately serve the learner in all stages of the learning process—or across all types of material. *Our prescription therefore is for a "smorgasbord," or portfolio, of learning mechanisms, with specific attention given to the further development of each mechanism in the areas where it has a clear comparative advantage.*

- In light of our model, Skinnerian programmed instruction (or CAI) has had too much effort placed on it in the past. In the areas of learning where it *is* applicable, other technologies dominate along the relevant dimensions.

- Again in light of our model, the primary clear target of opportunity for the computer in higher education is in "enrichment activities." For almost all kinds of material, problem solving, games, and simulation can provide the learner with better methods of *integrating* and *testing* the knowledge that he has acquired than other available technologies.

- *It follows from the above that the real impact of the new technology will for the most part be adding to, rather than replacing, current learning mechanisms.* Some current mechanisms will be displaced, but the new technology will allow two major improvements. First, it will provide opportunities for increased enrichment as noted above. Second, it will provide increased access by university faculty to students formerly outside the geographic limits of the regular educational system.

- Notwithstanding the above, for those interested in directly substituting technology for current functions, the technique of computer-based drill and practice is growing steadily—to aid the embedding process—and will increasingly replace some traditional "written assignment or homework" techniques. However, even this one-for-one replacement process will enrich the curriculum, since the level and timing of the feedback possible under computerized drill and practice is an order of magnitude more beneficial to the learner.

We expand each of these points in the material that follows.

As we demonstrated earlier, there are stages in the learning process. Admittedly they are poorly understood and are a confused, iterative blend of inadequately defined steps, but none-theless "acquiring," "embedding," "integrating," and "test-ing" are not the same things, and there is no reason to suppose that each stage will be supported equally well by the same pedagogic device. Added to this is the fact that students differ sharply in maturity, intelligence, background, and style of learning. Poets do not learn in the same fashion as engineers; it does not seem reasonable that they would find the same peda-gogic tools useful. However, to do an analysis of these differ-ences requires careful use of a learning model and accurate understanding of the attributes and potential impact of the various learning mechanisms—we could use a good deal of research in both these areas. Our present level of understand-ing is primitive.

These arguments suggest that a diversity of pedagogic devices is not only desirable but necessary if we are to be effective. At the moment such diversity must look like a smor-gasbord—an array of teaching devices from lecture, film, and television to multimedia computer-based labs. As we learn more, this diversity can be managed and take on the aspects of a portfolio, a collection of techniques gathered together for a purpose. At the moment we have only the sketchiest of ideas about how to put such a portfolio together.

In earlier days the amount of material to be taught in a university was less than it is now. Pressures to keep costs down were often less. Technology, beyond the printing press, was nonexistent. Thus the human lecturer was ubiquitous. All these factors have changed. Such progress in the use of technology as we have made has been at least partly as a result of being unable to use the lecture mode—given the new material and a class size of several hundred or more—to really develop skills or embed frontier concepts.

Pressures upon us are diverse and our needs are diverse. To expect any one technique to effectively solve our teaching prob-lems is naïve, yet we do not yet know enough to consciously manage the matching of student to material and to teaching method. To develop good teaching portfolios is going to require several years more work. At the Association for Computing Machinery (ACM) conference in 1972 Oliver Selfridge made a similar point.

Another question I'd like to raise is this: I don't really see from the talks where PLATO and TICCIT—treating them as the paradigms, the real large models of what is coming in CAI—fit in with respect to other kinds of education that are probably still needed. That is, suppose PLATO and TICCIT were all we had, and instead of having hundreds of hours of instruction, we really had millions of hours, would books be a breakthrough? I use computers a lot of times to do my ordinary things, but reading is something special in its own way. In spite of the browsing capabilities that these systems have, there is nothing like browsing through a book, and I would like to see it fitted in a little better. (*ACM SIGCUE Bulletin*, 1972, p. 12).

Looking back over 10 to 15 years of computer uses in teaching, it is possible to see the dominance of the Skinnerian model of learning and the tremendous prevalence of the fill-in-the-blank computer page turner. We would contend that this school of thought has dominated for too long. From the arguments above it seems reasonable to argue that it would be a mistake to accept any one view on learning until a lot more good research has been done. At the university level the Skinnerian view seems appropriate for only a very small subset of the material, some of the facts, and only certain of the students. We are unable to judge whether the hard-line Skinnerians are still in charge of research budgets, but even if they have been replaced, or changed their minds, it will be several years before other views are actively felt in the form of working systems. We may be four to five years away from having the evidence needed to assess other approaches. Our very modest attempts to develop a multitechnique approach at MIT took three years to develop and can be considered operational only in part even at this point.

A further factor seen in hindsight is the enormous size of many of the computer-based projects that were funded and the rapidity with which they faded to nothing when the funding disappeared. This suggests that the money did not produce a viable, robust solution. Arguments have been made that this was due to structural or incentive problems—no royalties to the faculty to write CAI programs, hence no incentive, and so forth. Although such problems were possibly a factor, it might also be that the type of teaching technique (typically CAI) and the particular form of the system were not appropriate for the job of educating university students. We contend from the logic in this report that this has often been the case. Massive projects, then, did not produce usable systems as measured by the degree of usage now visible.

Further, in many of these massive projects considerable attention was paid to hardware, and little or none was paid to imaginative courseware or to the measurement of the impact of such systems. Careful unbiased assessment of the reasons for success—or failure—has not been the hallmark of CAI projects to date. As we established earlier, technology is no longer as much of a problem as is understanding how to use it. Given our state of knowledge, a few large projects are substantially less likely to yield insight into a solution to the smorgasbord question than would a number of smaller ones.

Looking at evidence from projects around the country, such as those at Dartmouth, and extending the insight gained from the learning model, we would argue that the computer's unique ability to provide low-cost enrichment represents the most underexploited aspect of the technology. Such work would have substantially greater pay-off than the standard CAI approach. This enrichment ability may take a partial Dartmouth-like form and provide the student with access to computational power, thus allowing him to handle "real" problems, or it may provide access to data banks containing real-world models or data. Such support for learning cannot be easily provided any other way, and it substantially enhances the student's ability to acquire and test certain concepts. The support provided opens up a way of teaching new material and a small amount of our previous material—it is more likely to add to what we do than to replace what we do. Computers are acceptable to faculty and are widely used in such a capacity in part at least because there is no active competitor—it is in areas such as this that usage will be heavy. The evidence from the Massachusetts survey suggests that this type of usage is already developing; we expect it to grow.

THE PACE OF IMPLEMENTATION

A final conclusion emerges from Chapters 8 and 9:

The potential that exists in the new technology to assist (perhaps significantly) the learning process will not be exploited nearly as rapidly as it might be.

The development of additional simulation models, games, and computer practice sets, as well as the increased use of television and other audiovisual aids, could significantly assist learners in better obtaining, integrating, and retaining knowledge. These developments will come to pass. But they will happen over a much more extended time period than is technically possible. The facts behind this statement are clear, and it is important for educators to face this conclusion squarely.

The reasons for this very leisurely pace of implementation of new technology are many. Simply, however, the forces favoring further efforts to design and implement learning systems involving new technology are not nearly as powerful as the opposing forces. On the positive side are such things as student pressure, innovative tendencies of faculties, the availability of better technology, external competition, and some demonstration effects. None of these is terribly powerful. On the negative side—to name only the most significant factors—we find a possibly decreasing number of students, tightness of funding, the relative weakness of university administrators vis-à-vis the faculty, increasing external regulations and internal unionization (both of which tend to squelch innovation), and a faculty reward system that positively discourages innovation in educational technology.

A FINAL WORD The learning process is complex. If nothing else, the availability of educational technology is currently motivating researchers to refocus at least some efforts on understanding more precisely— from either a fundamental or behavioral standpoint—how this process works. This, by itself, can be a major contribution of the new technology.

But this will not be all that the new educational technology does. Both in our own efforts and in those we have observed, we have seen students acquiring, embedding, integrating, and testing material in ways that both we and they believe more effectively and efficiently assist their learning process. These efforts today are too few, too isolated, and too short-lived. But as educators determine more specifically in what areas of the learning process efforts should be focused, as efforts are focused on the proper areas and positive results are achieved, and as the absolute and relative cost of learning technology decreases, technology will take greater hold in the learning process.

Appendix A: Some Efforts to Meet the Needs

A broad understanding can be gained about a field of knowledge through research into the accomplishments and views of others. However, there is no better way to gain perspective on the significant problems and opportunities in an area of technology than to participate in the field of endeavor. As one delves into the muck and mire of the difficulties of actual development and implementation of working systems, insights and understanding are born that can occur in perhaps no other way.

It was partially this need to better come to grips with the true potential for technology in the education process that led our group at MIT to initiate a series of efforts of our own in the educational technology field. We also, however, began these efforts because of the recognition of the gaps in educational technology discussed in Chapter 5 and an attendant desire to investigate the potential for filling these gaps. The work was initiated by, and performed under the direction of, Professor Zenon S. Zannetos, the head of the Planning and Control Area at the Sloan School of Management.

By early 1968 it had become clear that there was a need in the field for two different entities to enable higher education to utilize the potential of technology. On one hand, there was a need for distinctly different and better *individual tools* for the professor to use in the learning process. Equally important, however, was the need for the development of better means of "delivering" these tools to the student—a need that might be termed the requirement for improved *delivery systems*. At the time, the development of improved delivery systems seemed to us to be a matter of better hardware and systems software— tasks better left to others more expert in this area. We thus turned to the development of individual tools. Since our primary focus at that time was on the computer, this meant the development of interesting and effective applications-oriented software.

This appendix presents the natural history of our own efforts in this field. In one sense these efforts were successful. By getting our hands dirty in the development of educational technology, we gained major insights into the process—insights that we are reasonably convinced would have been obtained in no other way. And we did develop some interesting and effective tools (which fitted into perceived gaps).

On the other hand, measured by some of our original objectives, we were certainly less than totally successful. Because of three factors the scope of our original vision in 1967–68 was somewhat too great to be totally realized. These factors were (1) the state of development of available hardware and software technology, (2) the state of development of methods for efficiently transferring material into fully developed applications software, and (3) the state of theory with regard to the learning process. The results of our forays into education technology, both those that were reasonably successful and those that were somewhat less successful, are noted in this appendix and the next. They are presented both as additional background to our stated conclusions in the field of educational technology and as a case study from which some lessons may be drawn.[1]

Our thinking with regard to educational technology went through three very distinct phases. These were:

- An emphasis on general, global systems

- An emphasis on individual, more specific-purpose technological tools

- An emphasis on the utilization of technology in context as only one segment, but a well-orchestrated segment, of the learning process

THE "EFFEC- TIVENESS PHASE": GEN- ERAL, GLOBAL SYSTEMS Our original thoughts were primarily aimed at increasing the "effectiveness" of the educational process—as opposed to the efficiency of the process. It seemed to us that much of the teaching process was disjointed, trivial, redundant, or missed

---

[1]We believe that both the positive and negative aspects of the work presented are of some interest. There is too little reporting in the literature of the reasons behind relative *lack* of success so that others may avoid the same pitfalls.

the mark in a number of other ways. In mid-1968 two of our group (Scott Morton & Zannetos, 1969) wrote with regard to the initial stages of the development of "an associative learning instructional system":

This project has been undertaken in an effort to provide solutions to some critical problems that we are facing in the field of education. In order to solve these problems we have chosen to experiment with a computer driven interactive terminal linked to an associative memory with flexible search procedures. The basic problems as we see them are:

1. The Lack of Integration of Instructional Material within and across Functional Fields

If we examine the management of our educational efforts we find that in spite of the fact that we offer training leading toward professional degrees our curricula are structured in such a fashion that we teach in rigidly defined compartments. Very little effort is devoted to integrating the material in a student's major area of concentration, and even less to integrating across fields. Many of us will readily admit that we are not sure how we would, in fact, integrate this material, because we can neither master all the subject matter involved nor do we fully understand the process of association. As a result of this lack of understanding we fail to do much, if anything, and leave it up to the student to worry about trying to form a cohesive whole out of a series of disjointed parts.

While the student has, under any circumstances, to take an active part in this integration, we would hold that much more must be done on the part of the faculty to help in this process. In short there must exist some formal mechanism which can evolve over time to meet the changing nature of the integrative process.

2. The Uniform Treatment of All Students Irrespective of Background and Individual Speed in Learning

A second major motivation in undertaking this project is the desire to improve the efficiency of the learning process by allowing the student to learn at the speed which is most efficient for himself. To achieve this end we need to develop systems which will allow flexible use of the material rather than a strict guided tour ordained by the teacher. For this reason we need systems which retain the search paths of the students, keep scores, and on the basis of the progress realized identify the next level in the hierarchy of instructional material. In order to guarantee that mismatches between students and programmed material do not interfere with the learning process, the student must be allowed flexibility to switch from highly structured material to an interrogative mode.

The flexibility which we propose will also help the educators learn about learning processes. In this way one can not only obtain a record of the difficulties the students meet, but also trace ingenious student search procedures and solutions. Such information can be of enormous help to us in learning how students proceed to structure problems for solution, and in revising the educational material.

3. The New Material Explosion

Finally we feel an increasing pressure from the rapid growth of new material. In the management field, as with medicine, science and many others, our understanding of the basic processes is growing. The increased research and disciplined observation has resulted in an ever-expanding body of substantive knowledge which must be passed on to students. Ideally we would like to teach in class only that material which is on the boundary of our understanding. That is, spend the class time discussing new concepts, recent research and generally developing sound principles from ill-structured material. This, however, we cannot do, nor can we pursue research effectively, if we have to spend all our time repeating the ever-increasing collection of well-structured material. The basic fundamentals, the well-organized aspects of our understanding, are just those facets of the material that are easiest to assign to some teaching system.

We are convinced that powerful instructional systems can be built that will materially affect the educational process in all three of the aforementioned areas. The development of flexible computer-driven, interactive terminal systems provides a mechanism that links the user to the two key attributes of our system. These are the associative memory with flexible search procedures and the ability of the system to learn and adapt on the basis of experience.

These features, we believe, will allow the student to choose the mode of instruction that is best suited to his learning habits, assimilate and integrate the structured material in a fashion most appropriate for that material and contextually associate it with previously learned matter. As for the educators, the system will provide a management tool that is critically needed, as well as focusing our attention on the instructional process.

While the use of flexible interactive terminals is no automatic panacea, indeed they necessitate the expenditure of considerable effort in material development, it seems to us that this approach has considerable potential. Hence our basic long-run objective is to develop such a terminal system.

In the shorter-run, our objectives are quite specific. We wish to establish a flexible interactive terminal system at the graduate level to be used for experiments aimed at developing our long-term goals. This system is being used initially in the management accounting field.

II. *System characteristics*

Our objective has been stated as a flexible interactive terminal system for use in higher education. We feel that provision of a truly flexible system requires certain fundamental characteristics which have not previously been tested, to our knowledge, in connection with the learning process.[2]

A. *Semantic content association* The first of these is the use of a semantic memory,[3] with associations based on the content of information, not its location. This characteristic provides the necessary flexibility which allows the students to address the system in natural language and to follow paths through the material that are relevant to *their* line of questioning.

The design and use of a semantic memory implies a certain formal structuring of the information content, at least initially. Unfortunately, there has not been enough development in our understanding of the structure of natural language to allow complete freedom to the user. However, with structured material this is not a serious limitation as there is a "natural" formality to the subject matter which does not impose any severe limitations on the user. Often the recognition of key words is a sufficient base from which the system can start.

Potentially a system with semantic memory offers advantages both at the input and output stage. Its associative characteristic can allow automatic reorganization of the data base content entered. Greater efficiency in both storage and retrieval of information is thus assured as all relationships between concepts do not have to be inserted and stored explicitly. Furthermore, the semantic memory can use the stored information as building blocks to provide output that was not specifically entered into the system, and eventually support logical inference. This becomes necessary with any complex body of material as it is clearly inefficient to store all meaningful combinations of factual statements.[4]

This brings us to one of the greatest limitations of present "exhaustive" semantic memories.[5] We have said that semantic memories in

---

[2]These characteristics have been identified as desirable in connection with other problems by Kochen & Wong (1958), Levien (1972), and Zinn (1967), among others.

[3]Some pioneering work on this area has already been carried out. See, for example, Quillian (1966).

[4]Another advantage of a system that is capable of forming relationships on the basis of semantic content and *constructing* answers is that it brings us face to face with weak logic on our part.

[5]We will call "exhaustive" semantic memories those which depend on exhaustive listings of all meanings of each stored concept.

general are efficient in terms of associating new declarative statements with stored information, and also retrieving information that is specifically structured in response to each particular question. That much is true. This capability, however, is based on an exhaustive storage of all the different meanings of each concept. If erroneous or even ambiguous definitions are originally introduced, erroneous relationships among concepts will be constructed. Furthermore, the memory of even the largest computer becomes cluttered with the storage of a score of concepts.

In contrast to designing an exhaustive semantic memory we have concentrated on selectivity. We decided to store only the most appropriate hierarchical relationships among concepts rather than list all the attributes of each concept. In this way we limited the "inventiveness" of the system but achieved efficiency in storage, expanded the breadth of our system and also limited the misleading associations. The system may occasionally present innocuous relationships but these are easily recognizable because of the limitations imposed on the relationships among concepts.

B. *Capability for learning*   The second major distinguishing characteristic of our system is the importance we have attached to the system's ability to learn. It is central to our notions that we build a system that is able to monitor the user, recognize patterns in his behavior and adapt accordingly. This characteristic has been recognized as being desirable by others before us, but we are suggesting something beyond what we think we have seen discussed in the literature. We feel the system can be made to exhibit a certain degree of intelligence. For example, it can monitor the user and retain information on his stated objectives, the types of questions he asks, and also evaluate (or update) the user's performance level by analyzing his responses to the system's questions. In this fashion the system can associate objectives with successful search procedures and guide subsequent users toward an efficient search path.

To achieve this goal the system must have:

1   Pattern recognition capability at a level adequate enough to identify significant patterns in user activity as they develop. This implies the development of a model of the user that is powerful enough to represent his current level of understanding of the material in question.

2   Adaptive characteristics, such that the system can modify its responses on the basis of experience. Thus, not only is pattern recognition required but also identification of the key variables in the learning process and of the specific attributes of the material to be taught so that the two can be matched.

C. *Hardware characteristics* We accepted as a premise, that the physical conditions in the use of the system must not interfere with the user's natural learning process. There must be no inflexibility due to time delays, or awkwardness of specifying *and* receiving responses from the *system*.

III. *Conclusion*

Our fundamental concern is with innovation in the teaching process in an attempt to deal with increasing subject complexity and rising costs. To do a decent job it is obvious that one has to understand something of the way people learn. This understanding of the learning process allows one to design systems using the latest technology in a reasonably optimal fashion. The instructional system described briefly here provides a useful opportunity to conduct research on the learning process itself.

We feel that we must have a mix of pedagogical tools that are appropriate to the particular student, to the subject matter in question and to the stage in the learning process that has been reached. To do this we need systems which provide much greater richness than that offered by traditional programmed instruction.

To meet the above stated objectives, the ALPS (Associative Learning Project System) system was developed in several stages. ALPS was a semantic, memory-based system that provided both tutorial (programmed instruction) capability and a student-assisting, question-answering facility. The basic structure of the system and progress toward our goals were described in the following way in 1970:[6]

Although our progress thus far is modest, the system is operational and can be utilized, studied, and improved following each experiment. Through the medium of the LISP language, a first-stage associative memory has been built which allows the student to ask questions of the type "what is," "where," "how," and "when," and also retrieve information on the relationship among concepts (i.e., what is the relationship between A and B).

For subject matter we have chosen the fundamentals of accounting. The reason for our choice is that the subject is well-defined, and therefore easy to program. . . . We must stress, however, that the basic

[6]Since this is by far the most unusual, and therefore most interesting, system on which we worked, it will be described in far greater detail than the other three systems. The following pages are taken from Rockart, Scott Morton, & Zannetos (1971).

system capabilities do not depend on the subject matter. In other words we are developing a potential general purpose system.

In order to allow the system to handle the dual roles of "lecturer" and "font of knowledge," two major interrelated capabilities are provided. First, the student has the opportunity to respond to the well-known programmed instruction mode of teaching. Secondly, and more uniquely, the system provides the student with the ability to ask questions of it and to receive appropriate responses. . . . Three concepts underlie the basic question-answer ability.

First, by using a simplified version of a semantic memory we have achieved a reasonable degree of *flexible search*. Accounting has some inherent formalism in its terminology so we can use "natural" accounting English language to ask questions of the memory. Capitalizing on this inherent structure, we have been able to construct an adequate working system that appears to the user to be answering questions in natural English language.

Secondly, we have provided the ability for *simple association*. Concepts are stored in the semantic memory with links or pointers associating them to the other concepts to which they are principally related. These associations have been originally chosen on the a priori judgment of the designers of the system. As information on student associative methods is gathered (from data available on the stored trace), however, the associative paths are being reorganized to better meet the learning requirements of the users, and to incorporate new discoveries.

Thirdly, in similar fashion, we have provided for *simple inference*. The system traces through a series of levels in the semantic hierarchy in an attempt to link up the concepts raised by the user. This ability to relate aspects of accounting which have not been directly linked to each other by the programmer will be discussed later under the systems software section.

The student, however, is most often uninterested in the concepts behind the system. To him the question-answer ability means that:

1　If the current programmed instruction frame includes a word or concept which he has previously learned, but has forgotten, he can merely ask a question of the system and have his memory refreshed on the spot. In this sense the system serves as an "exhaustive" indexing device and as a library.

2　If a programmed instruction frame suggests a tangential, but highly interesting, area of inquiry he may ask questions on this new area while the idea and his interest are still fresh. It is well understood that a student learns best when provided with material about a matter in which he is highly interested *at the particular time* at which his interest is blooming.

3 He may guide his own learning experience. We claim no exclusive ability to provide *the* single programmed instruction path which will exactly fit the thought progression of all students. Nor do we have as yet a system which restructures itself to appeal to the individual objectives of each particular user. What we now provide the student is flexibility. He can "escape" if he so wishes from the prescribed path and then return to the spot from where he left, at will. It is felt that this provides the student with a sense of control over his learning process. Rather than being merely led, he now has a chance to lead and to explore; he can become an *active* participant in the educational process rather than merely a passive recipient.

To us the above capabilities of the system mean that ultimately "better paths" may be developed for the user since the system allows teachers to trace the steps which the students take in their efforts to learn. The user "protocols" are actively analyzed for the recognition of significant patterns. As we learn more about how students actually learn, improvements may be made not only in the material used but also in the process of teaching itself.

With the above material as a background we will now turn to the hardware and software of our present system.

Associative Learning Hardware The associative learning programs are currently being run on the Compatible Time Sharing System at M.I.T. This is a very flexible time sharing system with a large number of programming languages available. The machine being used is an IBM 7094 computer with two banks of core each with 32,768 36-bit words of memory. . . .[7]

The terminal that is being used for the project is a Computer Displays Inc. Advanced Remote Display Station (ARDS) the heart of which is a Tektronix $6\frac{1}{2} \times 8$ inch storage tube. The ARDS has the capability to store up to 50 lines of written material (80 characters to the line), or to accept graphical input in stored points and line segments. . . .

Associative Learning Software As previously discussed, the associative learning program operates in two major instructional modes: programmed instruction and question-answer. Because these modes are largely independent, they will be discussed separately, following a section on general file and start up

---

[7]The program was later shifted to the MIT Multics system and reprogrammed in PL1.

procedures. Figure A-1 provides as an overview, the systems files and the major divisions in the core storage "map."

Program initialization

The associative learning program reads from three separate data files during its operation. These are:

"Text"   which contains all the questions for programmed instruction.

"Answer"   which contains all of the answer lists for the programmed instruction. The answers are formatted in blocks of ten answer lists per block.

"User Status"   which contains the names of students who have used the system and the next frame number for each student who has not completed the entire program.

When the student first starts the system, he is asked to type his name. With this name as an input, the "begin" function opens the "Text" and "Answer" files and reads in the proper block of answers. The student is then asked, "WOULD YOU LIKE TO ASK SOME QUESTIONS." If the student answers in the affirmative, the question-answer mode is entered. If he does not wish to ask a question, then the programmed instruction is started.

Programmed instruction mode

The programmed instruction mode (Figure A-2) is supervised by a function called "test." "Test" starts by presenting the first (or next) question to the student. After presenting the question, "test" reads the student's answer and compares it with the answer list that has the same number as the question. If the answer given is correct, "test" prints the first correct answer on the list (the preferred answer) and the words "IS CORRECT" and waits for the student to ask for the next question. The number of this succeeding question is determined from a coded question number following each correct answer in the answer list.

If the answer to any question is incorrect, then "test" prints "YOU ARE INCORRECT—(preferred answer) IS THE CORRECT ANSWER." For incorrect answers, "test" also looks at the answer list for a specially encoded "question" which it presents to the question-answer program (described below). These special questions with the appropriate

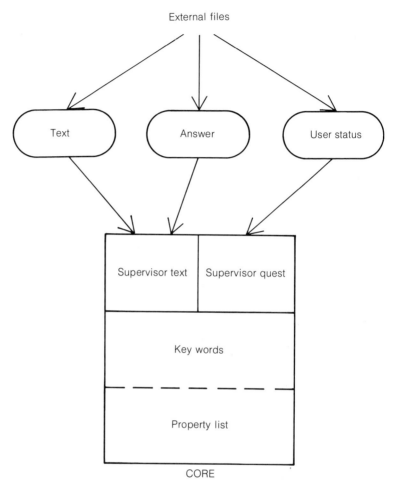

External files

Text

Answer

User status

Supervisor text | Supervisor quest

Key words

Property list

CORE

answers are then presented to the student as remedial material. After an incorrect answer, the next question is determined by a coded number at the end of the answer list.

If during the programmed-instruction mode, the student types the word "quest" between frames, then "test" stores the next frame number and calls the question answer program. If the student types the word "explain" between frames, then "test" gets and displays the block of remedial material for the last frame before going on to the next frame. If the word "stop" is typed between frames, then "test" writes the student's name and the next question number on "User Status" and prints the number of questions that the student answered correctly and incorrectly and ends the session.

FIGURE A-2 *Programmed instruction flowchart*

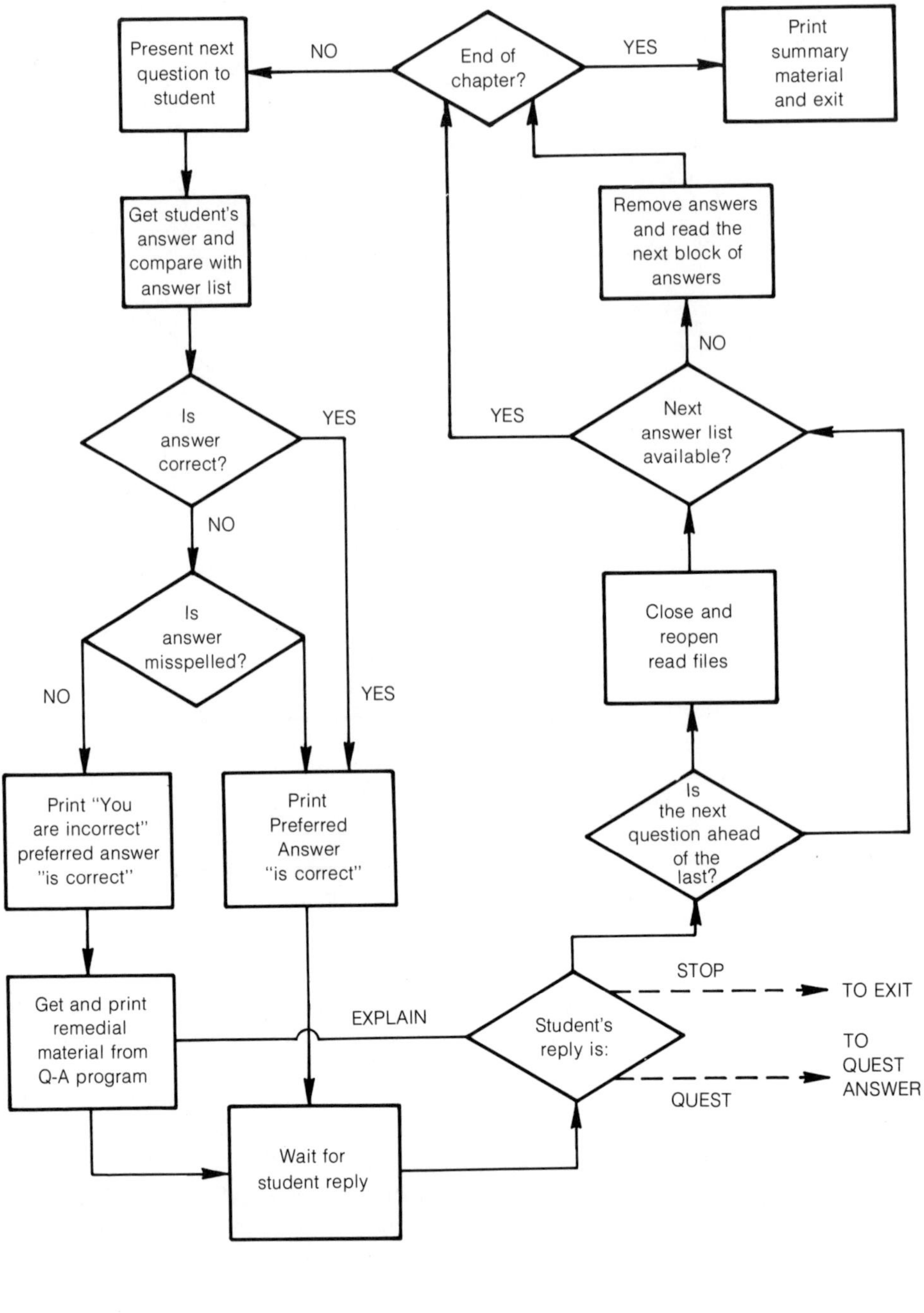

Question-answer mode

The question-answer mode of the system is supervised by a function named "quest." The first operation that "quest" performs is to provide the student with the following message: "PLEASE ASK ANY QUES-TION RELATED TO BASIC ACCOUNTING PRINCIPLES. WHEN YOU WISH TO HAVE THE PROGRAM ASK QUESTIONS AGAIN, TYPE THE WORD 'TEST' AND HIT THE RETURN KEY." Following this, "quest" reads the student's questions, encodes them and has the "analyzer" function answer them. It then presents this answer to the student. . . .

The dictionary

To answer the student's questions, the "analyzer" uses an extensive dictionary of word forms that is stored in core during program execu-tion. This dictionary uses the list structure and list processing capabili-ties of the LISP language to recognize four major types of word forms: keywords, supplementary words, question words and relation words.

The largest section of the dictionary is devoted to nouns and phrases which are used as *keywords* and which enable the system to understand the questions. For each keyword there is stored a *"property-list"* with up to six descriptions (properties) of the word stored on it. These properties are (see Table A-1 for examples):

a. The definition - (DEF)

b. The use of the item - (USE)

c. A time context for the item - (WHEN)

d. A place context for the item - (WHERE)

e. Some examples of the item - (EXPL)

f. The relationship of the keyword to other keywords (REL)

Like an ordinary dictionary the first five keyword properties (a through e) are followed by plain English descriptions of the noun or phrase in that context. The REL property, which is more complex, uses verb forms as *relation words* to relate the various keywords in the dictionary (see Figure A-3 for a diagram of some of these relationships). Since the student may use synonyms or plurals, the system stores these *supple-mentary words* with a pointer to the main keyword and uses the main keyword dictionary entry to answer questions which have been phrased by the use of supplementary words. The program must also recognize *question words* and *phrases* in order to understand the ques-tions being asked. The question words which the program recognizes are "what," "what for," "how used," "when," "where," and "exam-

ASSET — symb = an asset (or form of capital)

DEF = is tangible or intangible property (a form of resources) in the firm's legal possession

USE = can be used to generate future value

WHEN = exists if there is value remaining at balance-sheet time

WHERE = is noted on the left-hand side of a balance sheet

EXPL = can be cash, accounts receivable, inventory, buildings, or machinery

REL = (is a form of *capital*) (is decreased in value by *credit*) (is increased in value by *debit*) (is exemplified by *inventory*) (is economic *value*) (is identified by *title*) (is equivalent to *property*) (is committed by *expenditure*)

T-ACCOUNT — symb = T-account

DEF = is the simplest representation of a ledger account

USE = lists the impact of transactions on that entity. On the left-hand side are all the capital flows, the account received, and on the right-hand side those that it gave.

WHEN = is used when all entries must be transferred from the journal to the ledger accounts prior to constructing a balance sheet

WHERE = is contained in the ledger

REL = (represents [written] *account*) (results in *balance*) (is contained in *income statement*) (is contained in *balance sheet*)

TITLE — symb = a title

DEF = is the name of an account

USE = identifies an account

REL = (identifies *asset*)

VALUE — symb = value

DEF = is the measurement, as amount in dollars, of the worth of an economic good. In accounting, value for assets is the same as cost.

REL = (measures *asset*) (is in terms of *unit of measurement*)

FIGURE A-3 *Section of keyword-relationship map*

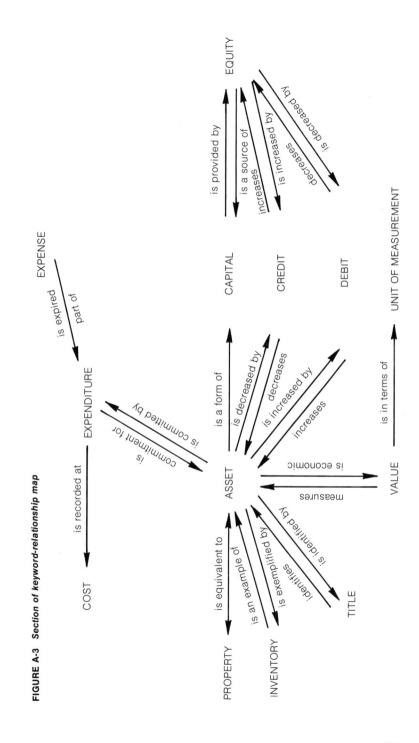

ple" or "examples." Phrases are combinations of words which include keywords.

Question-answering procedure

An overview of the question-answering procedure is diagrammed in Figure A-4. With the various word forms defined and available, the program proceeds as follows: "Quest" determines how many words of each type (keyword, supplementary word, question word, relational word) it can recognize in the student's question. It passes these words to the "analyzer" which in turn proceeds to classify the question as *simple, complex,* or *relational.* Based on this classification, "analyzer" constructs one or more answers to the question and passes these back to "quest." If more than one answer has been constructed, "quest" presents the first one and stores the rest until the student asks for them in sequence by hitting the return key.

A *simple* question contains only one keyword and a question word. These questions are answered by simple dictionary lookup as follows: If the question word is "what" then the answer is the definition followed by the use. If the question word is "what for" or "how used" then the answer is the use property. If the question word is "when" then the answer is the time context of the item. Similarly, "where" draws forth the place context and "example" or "examples" is answered by using the EXPL property. For example, the question "What is an asset" causes "quest" to find the question word "what" and the keyword "asset." "Analyzer" then forms a single answer from the combination of the definition and use properties. The student is then given the answer "AN ASSET (OR FORM OF CAPITAL) IS TANGIBLE OR INTANGIBLE PROPERTY (A FORM OF RESOURCES) IN THE FIRM'S LEGAL POSSESSION."

A *complex* question contains two keywords with or without a question word. To answer this question the "analyzer" uses the relationships associated with the second word to find a relationship path to the first word. This path may contain several intermediate words as it leads from the second keyword to the first keyword. (See Figure A-3.) For example, if the keywords are "assets" and "wealth" the path would be "WEALTH IS ECONOMIC VALUE. VALUE MEASURES AN ASSET." This process is continued until all paths from the first to the second and from the second to the first are discovered and the relationships stored. In addition, if there is a question word in the question, a further answer is developed which is the answer to the simple question made up of the question word and the first keyword. So, for example, if the question is "what is the title of an asset," "quest" finds the question word "what" and the two keywords "title" and "asset" and "analyzer" constructs two answers to be presented to the student.

FIGURE A-4 *Question-answer data flow*

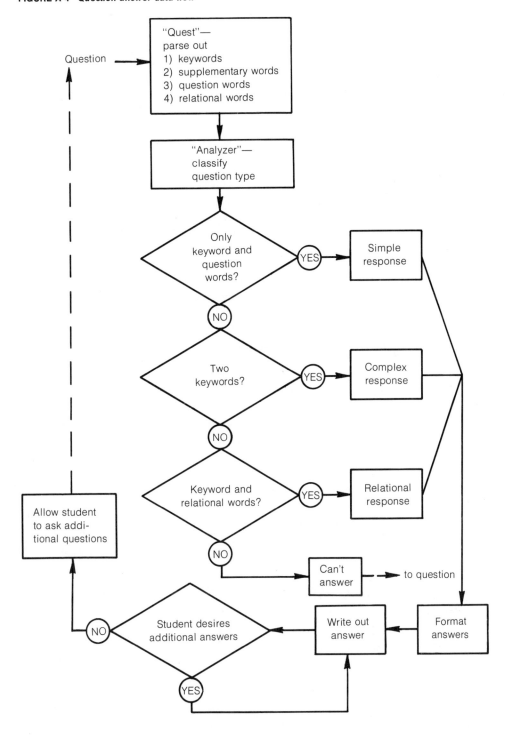

These are: (1) "AN ASSET IS IDENTIFIED BY A TITLE," (2) "A TITLE IS THE NAME OF AN ACCOUNT, WHICH IDENTIFIES AN ACCOUNT." It can be seen from Figure A-2 and Table A-1 that the first answer is the relationship from the second keyword to the first, and the second answer is the DEF and USE properties of the first keyword "title" (i.e., the *simple* question answer). Of course, this is a rather trivial example of a complex question, but it can be seen how this principle can be used to provide some very complex relationships to the student.

The *relational* question has only one keyword, one or more relational words, and an optional question word. The "analyzer" answers this type of question by searching the keyword's REL property to determine if the relation words contained in the question are there. If a relationship is found then the answer provided is this relationship. For example, if the question is "how do you commit an asset," then "quest" recognizes no question words, the relational word "commit," and the keyword "asset." "Analyzer" then provides the relational answer "AN ASSET (OR FORM OF CAPITAL) IS COMMITTED BY AN EXPENDITURE." Since there is no question word in this question (i.e., no "used" with the "how") this is the only answer that is provided. If the question had been "what does an expenditure commit," then there would have been two answers: the *relation* between "expenditure" and "asset," and the *definition* of expenditure.

At least two words must be recognized in order to provide an answer. If the two words are not present or if the particular reference is not in the dictionary, then "quest" replies, "I DO NOT UNDERSTAND—PLEASE REPHRASE YOUR QUESTION."

Throughout the operation of the ALPS program, all interchange of information with the student is also written on the file named "Tutor Users." During programmed instruction operation the question number, the student's answer, and a grade of right or wrong are all encoded on one line. During the question-answer operation, each question and answer is printed verbatim as it is displayed to the student. This is the current methodology to allow the system developer or the teacher to grade the progress of the system or the student at a later date and also to view students' methods of structuring the learning process.

Some Tests, Results, and Conclusions with Regard to the ALPS System

The ALPS system went through two full-scale revisions following its original construction. Each version was tested by allowing students to utilize the system as part of the introductory accounting course. The results of these experiments led to six major conclusions concerning our work with ALPS. These are:

1 The sheer *process* of attempting to specify a field for a computer is an exhausting but hugely worthwhile learning process for the instructor. Many of the ambiguities in accounting texts we had heretofore been utilizing came home to us with crashing emphasis as we attempted to translate their statements into precise, nonredundant, noncircular reasoning for the computer system. The degree of detail and precision necessary for this process necessitated careful thought, which in turn facilitated our deeper understanding of the material to be taught.

2 The automation of traditional programmed instruction texts is, at best, unexciting for the learning process and of dubious cost effectiveness in relation to paper versions of the same material. However, the temporary automation of these texts can significantly assist the process of improving a paper programmed instruction text through careful scanning of student performance as recorded in files such as our "tutor users" file. For example, those questions that are answered incorrectly by a significant proportion of a student test group can be automatically determined and flagged for closer scrutiny to determine the reason(s) for the question's difficulty (e.g., it might be that the question is poorly worded, or that the conceptual jump from the previous question is too large).

3 The current level of understanding concerning the manipulation of the English language in computers is still not adequate to the task of a system such as ALPS, even given our initial premise that, at best, less than total success could be hoped for with an English implementation of a question-answer system. Table A-2 shows a summary of the ability of ALPS to answer student questions on the second and third tests of the system. System answers were marked as "good," "fair," or "poor" for five distinct types of student questions. The ability of the system to provide a "good" answer to a question increased from 44 percent in 1969 to 64 percent in the 1970 test. But we could see little chance of improving this performance without massive revision of the system, and even with massive revision, only an incremental improvement in question-answering ability could be expected.

In addition, it is clear that the system performed best when asked to respond to sheer definitional questions of the order of "What is a . . . . When asked to provide examples, determine relationships, answer questions on the order of "How does one . . . ," or handle other miscellaneous questions, the system was not truly effective even in its latest version. Cost per system use was halved between versions 1 and 3, and question-answering power was doubled. On an absolute scale, however, the system was still not cost effective as an educational tool. In large part, this is due to the difficulty of handling the English language with today's hardware and software.

TABLE A-2
Analysis of
answered
question, ALPS
system

		1969—Test 2		
Question type	Good	Fair	Poor	Total
Definition	19	4	3	26
Example	1	0	0	1
Relational	0	4	9	13
How———	0	0	0	0
Other	0	0	5	5
TOTAL	20	8	17	45

		1970—Test 3		
Question type	Good	Fair	Poor	Total
Definition	61	6	14	81
Example	7	0	4	11
Relational	3	3	5	11
How———	0	0	7	7
Other	1	0	2	3
TOTAL	72	9	32	113

4 The effectiveness of an individual tool is heavily dependent on its delivery system. MIT's Multics, in terms of costs and response time, still leaves much to desire. Application-tool designers must pay great attention to the abilities of their delivery systems.

5 Students are goal-oriented. When they can complete an assignment by following an instructor's path through the material—as provided by the programmed instruction segment of the ALPS system—it is rare that they will search for "richness" in understanding. At least they did not do so in the basic accounting material presented by ALPS. As the programmed instruction material was made better and better from one version to the next, utilization of the question-answer facility dropped (even though the responsiveness of the question-answer facility increased!). On the average, each student in version 3 asked only three questions. It is, of course, possible that in different contexts one would observe different and "questing" behavior. We did not.

6   With regard to the observation and recording (tracing) of the methods by which students search a data-base to learn (the research purpose), the system has greater power. Traces of small samples of students working their way through the material *without* the programmed instruction segment (i.e., only the question-answer facility) showed interesting tendencies in search patterns. Despite the hindrance of a less than completely adequate question-answer facility, ALPS did appear in the analysis to be a good vehicle for understanding what made students tick in their data searching (learning?) process. The trace facility of on-line computer systems is a powerful tool.

PHASE II: A SMORGASBORD OF INDIVIDUAL, MORE SPECIFIC TOOLS   With the dawning realization that the ALPS system as a global, general approach to assisting the learning process would not, *in the near future,* be totally satisfactory, we began to turn our attention in 1970 to developing more specific individual tools tailored to particular felt needs of our initial accounting courses. It was, by that time, clear that much more basic research needed to be performed in the areas of artificial intelligence, learning theory, and methods of inexpensive computer system development and implementation of application programs before the ALPS concept would be of value in the teaching process. We therefore turned some of our efforts to the development of three specific products—IGRAM, CLOSE, and COST. These three systems and some of the results from using them will be briefly described in the following paragraphs.

IGRAM   The original IGRAM (Interactive Graphical Risk Analysis Method) system was based in large part on the writings of Hertz (1969). It was built in response to a felt need in the classroom to allow students to explore the benefits of both interactive computers and the use of probability distributions in decision making. The program, in its fourth version, is now much more general, and has consequently been renamed the Hierarchical Modelling System (HMS).

In general, the system allows a student, for a particular decision-making problem, to enter attribute values on a "deterministic," "probabilistic," or "dependent" basis for all low-order segments of a decision tree. Higher-order tree nodes are then calculated by the program, and reports or probability density graphs are displayed, if desired, for the predicted value of each node. In the early versions, Monte Carlo methods were utilized for this calculation process. Recent versions utilize a more compact and less expensive, in terms of computation time, convolution method.

The basic hypothesis behind HMS is that the decision maker, either through his research staff or by his own judgment, can break a problem into basic elements and describe the relationships between elements. Given this initial step, he can then assign to each element known values or subjective probability estimates for possible outcomes. It is felt that estimation of the individual elements one at a time in a probabilistic manner (with machine computation of the results), based on well-understood mathematical principles, can lead to a better decision than many of the deterministic and/or offhand techniques now utilized for handling hierarchically structured decision problems.

A sample problem will illustrate one basic underlying use of the system. Briefly, the case requires the student to evaluate the prospects for a particular manufactured product given competitive conditions in the industry and a probable four-year life of the equipment available to produce the product. A competitor has offered to buy the equipment. The student is asked to analyze the situation to decide his course of action—either to sell the equipment or to continue producing the product under a selling-price strategy that he must design.

The decision tree for this problem is shown in Figure A-5. With regard to the alternative at left, going out of business, there are two uncertainties involved. The decision maker must estimate (1) how much the present equipment can be sold for, and (2) how much can be recovered from the liquidation of the remaining inventories and accounts receivable.

The model, or problem tree, for this alternative consists of two levels. The lower level contains independent elements for the expected return to the company on the sale of the equipment and for the liquidation of the inventory and accounts receivable. Values for these elements must be entered by the decision maker. The entry may be deterministic—e.g., the price may be stated to be exactly $15,000—or the expected price may be indicated by a cumulative probability function as shown in Table A-3. This table shows that there is no chance that the company will receive less than $15,000 for the equipment, a 25 percent chance that less than $50,000 will be

FIGURE A-5 *System structure for the sample problem*

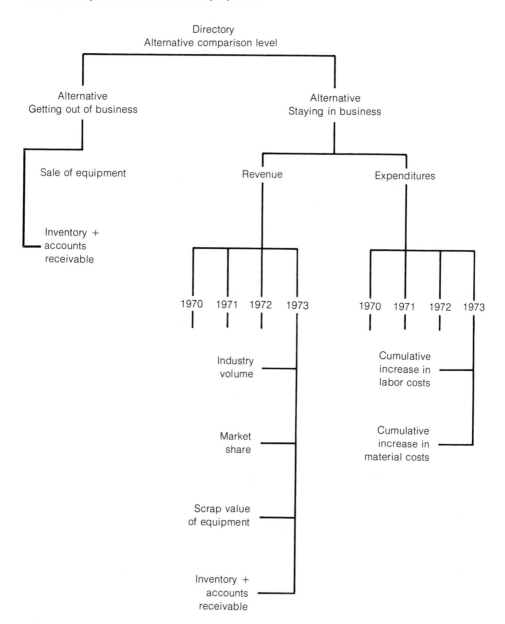

TABLE A-3 Sale of equipment		
Cumulative probability	*Amount received, thousands of dollars*
0.00	15
0.05	20
0.10	35
0.25	50
0.30	60
0.50	75
0.60	85
0.75	105
0.90	120
1.00	200

received, a 60 percent chance that $85,000 or less will be received, etc. The top level contains one element that describes the total expected return to the company if it sells out. This level is calculated by the computer by taking the sum of independently selected values from the distributions of the two independent elements of the model and including a tax allowance based on the difference between the book value of the equipment and the actual sale price.

With regard to the alternative of staying in business, the decision maker must enter such data as his expectations for each of four years for industry volume and the market share for his company (Figure A-5). In addition, initial values for various expense items at varying levels of production must be entered. In most cases some of these data are supplied to the student so that he need merely exercise his judgment in relatively important areas of the problem. In addition, for the last year of the analysis, estimates must be made for the scrap value of the equipment and the expected return to the company for the liquidation of its remaining inventory and accounts receivable. (Again, these estimates may be deterministic or probabilistic.) Estimates must also be made as to the expected percentage change from the initial values incurred for labor and material costs each year after the initial year.

Two sample output graphs that can be displayed on a screen are shown in Figures A-6 and A-7. Several graphs can be

FIGURE A-6
Graph of distribution entered for the sale of equipment

Sale of equipment
Go out of business

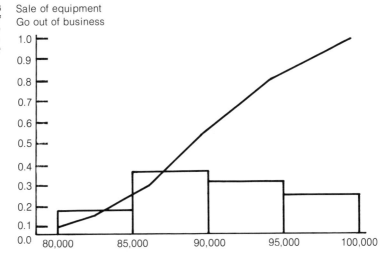

A) Save this graph
B) Continue without save
Type desired option:

FIGURE A-7
Graph of expected return from the alternative of leaving the business

Go out of business
Mean = 177,805   Standard deviation = 5,209

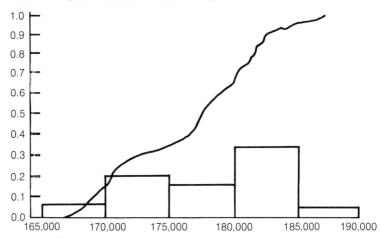

A) Save this graph
B) Continue without save
Type desired option:

displayed on the same screen. The decision maker can then decide on the alternative that fits his degree of risk aversion best. For example, the expected value of leaving the business (50 percent level in Figure A-7) is just less than $180,000. And there is only a 5 percent chance of making more than $185,000. If the cumulative probability graph of staying in business showed an expected value of only $160,000 but a 25 percent chance of making more than $200,000, a "gambling" decision maker might decide to stay in business.

It is just this process of quantifying as much as possible of each element of a hierarchical decision model and inspecting the *distribution* of possible results before making a decision that we attempt to teach our students at Sloan. Students have indicated that the method is helpful to them in learning both to structure problems and to solve them. The system's ability to quickly perform the tedious mathematical calculations and to display results in a graphic form greatly assists the student's ability to "see the forest" instead of having to concentrate on the "dog work" necessary to work through this type of problem by hand. In addition, interesting results concerning the process of individual decision making have been obtained from the use of the system on an experimental basis (Zannetos, Beville, & Wagner, 1970; Herzog, forthcoming).

CLOSE   IGRAM moves into one area that our analysis in Chapter 6 suggests is appropriate for the use of the computer as a learning aid—a model that allows computer-aided problem solving. CLOSE is based on the fact that all the mechanics of financial accounting are built around a simple cycle of posting, adjusting, and closing the books. Students need drill and practice in performing these functions—practice that has historically been provided through written homework.

Traditional homework, however, has some drawbacks as a pedagogic technique. First, simple errors in arithmetic may badly distort not only answers but students' conceptions of the material they are studying. Second, when students run into a conceptual block while performing pencil-and-paper homework, there is no tutor available to ask for help. Frustration may reign and an important learning opportunity be missed as the student "guesses." If his paper is marked correct, he may forget that he did not *understand* the situation; if incorrect, and the paper is received several days later, he may have forgotten what his problem was—or, being further along in the material, be uninterested in fully probing the prior material.

Finally, and perhaps most important, the amount of adding, subtracting, column finding, and other nitty-gritty work that goes into most financial-accounting homework tends to obscure the forest for the trees.

It is to overcome these problems that the CLOSE program was built. CLOSE provides for the student a set of T-accounts at the top of a CRT (cathode-ray tube) screen. An initial balance sheet is provided and the entries are written in the T-accounts. The student is then presented with a set of transactions that must be posted to the books. Examples of each of the three major classes of entries are presented to him, and these initial entries are performed by the computer system. Following each set of computer-performed entries, the student is given a set of entries to perform.

If the student provides a correct answer, the entries are automatically posted to the correct T-account, in the correct amount, for him. Should he make an error, the parts of the answer in error are underlined on the CRT. Should the student continue to err, he may ask for help, and two levels of "hints" are given to him. If he still cannot solve the transaction posting at the third "help," the correct posting is made by the machine.

Account-name misspellings are automatically corrected through a spelling-correction algorithm. The student may also skip through one or several entries if he feels he understands one or more of the three sections well enough to not need further practice.

At the end of the exercise, the system automatically totals the various T-accounts and prints both a balance sheet and a profit and loss statement. No addition errors are possible. Perhaps the most important advantage of the system, in addition to the practice it provides, is its ability to quickly lead the student through the entire technical process comprehended by the first half of this core course. The total flow of the process, learned over a period of days or weeks on a step-by-step basis in most texts, becomes clear in a console session of one to two hours because the student is forced (or enabled) to run through the entire process, see the T-accounts filling up, and see the translation of the entries into period-end statements—all in a short period of time.

It should be clear that most of the problems noted above that are major faults of traditional homework are obviated by this program. It is a somewhat more expensive educational experience than traditional homework, costing $3 to $5 per student (at 1972 Multics rates at MIT). But this is in great part because of an expensive delivery system (Multics), a point to which we return later.

COST   CLOSE provides computer-aided drill and practice encompassing the majority of technical material in the first half of the basic core accounting course at Sloan. In similar fashion, COST was aimed at encompassing, and providing an integrative framework for, the second half of the course, which is concerned with the basic principles and practices of internal cost accounting.

COST, like CLOSE, was designed to provide a drill-and-practice mode in which students could work through the fundamental concepts of this half of the course and ensure, with tutorial assistance, that they understood the material. COST, however, was designed to go one step further. In a second "model" mode it was structured to allow students to check the *sensitivity* of the various decisions that can be made by management concerning cost allocation.

Cost figures are used primarily in a firm as (1) aids in measuring performance, (2) aids in product costing, and (3) inputs to financial accounting. In addition, various cost figures are drawn off as "relevant costs" for decision-making purposes. The development of costs for the first three purposes is illustrated in Figure A-8; a more detailed explanation of this process is shown in Figure A-9, which presents the basic structure of cost accounting as taught in the second half of IDS I.

The COST program made available raw data from a case situation to the student and, in drill-and-practice mode, had him work through each step—correcting errors and providing help where necessary.

The student could, for example, in steps 1a, 1b, and 1c of Figure A-9, determine the basis by which each set of overhead costs (e.g., administrative salaries) would be originally allocated to each department of the firm. In step 2, he could deter-

FIGURE A-8 *Macro flowchart of a pedagogic view of activities and information flows in the management use of cost data*

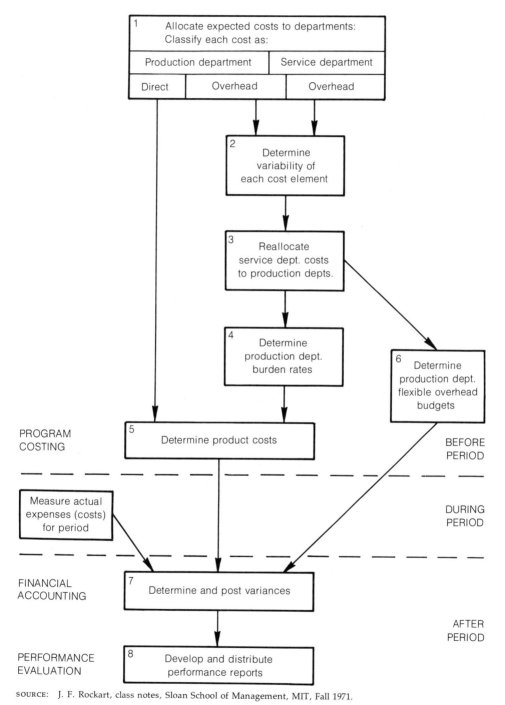

SOURCE: J. F. Rockart, class notes, Sloan School of Management, MIT, Fall 1971.

FIGURE A-9 *Micro flowchart of a pedagogic view of activities and information flows in the management use of cost data*

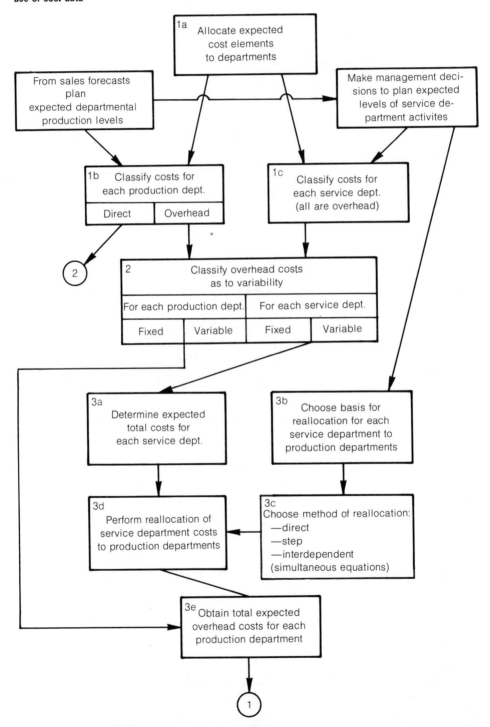

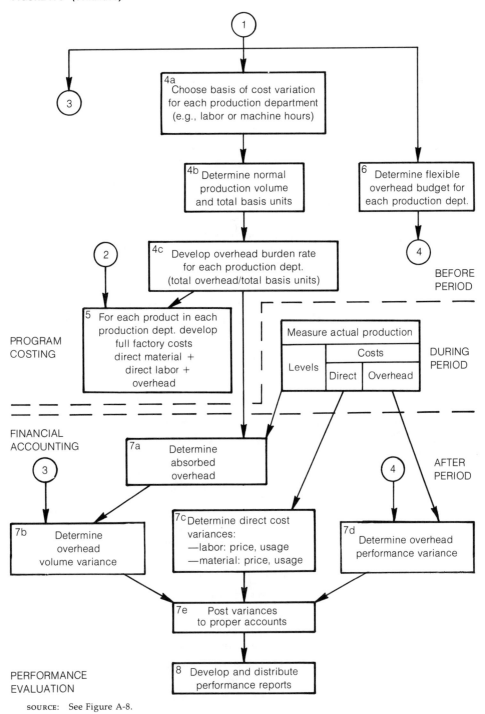

SOURCE: See Figure A-8.

mine whether each of these costs was variable, semivariable, or fixed. Any "errors" in this decision were pointed out—as in CLOSE. Ultimately the student worked through to steps 5, 7, and 8, in which the three major products and the process were developed—from his preceding decisions—and appeared on the CRT. Once again, as in CLOSE, the student had the entire process of the half of the course summarized for him in a drill-and-practice manner, and he could run through it in approximately an hour at the console.

In the "model" mode the student was allowed (urged) to work his way through the same problem trying alternative decisions at each step to see what differences they made in the eventual cost assignments—i.e., the sensitivities of each decision. (For example, in step 3c, Figure A-9, instead of choosing the step-down approach for reallocating overhead for service to producing departments, the student could choose either the "direct" or "interdependent" method side by side with the step method.)

CLOSE has been run with several student groups and is still utilized. COST went into the final stages of software development but was never run with a student group. Development funds ran out, and for many of the reasons noted in Chapter 9, work on this program was dropped. IGRAM is still utilized with students.

PHASE III: DELIV-ERY SYSTEMS During our work in phase II, there was much speculation, as there remains today, on the development of effective delivery systems to facilitate the use of computer technology for the learning process. Multics, as noted earlier, was felt to be cost ineffective for educational use at the time. As noted in Chapters 2 and 3, however, it was clear that more cost-effective computer systems were on the way. Yet more effective *computer* delivery systems were clearly not enough by themselves.

Toward the end of our work as a group under Professor Zannetos, it became increasingly clear that the general concept of matching multiple learning resources to appropriate learning materials was the best approach. (In other words, different types of material—utilized to assist different types of learning—require the use of the particular learning tool best able to assist the student in a particular learning effort.) One must not get lost with information about technology. Rather, it is neces-

sary *first* to define learning objectives; *second,* to determine
what material best meets these objectives; *third,* to determine
the method by which the material is to be delivered to the
learner; and *finally,* to choose the resource that can best aid the
learner. The *course delivery system* will then usually become a
multiresource system—with some combination of human and
technology assistance to learners.

There are three major resources presently available to the
learning process. These are (1) the professor and his assistants,
(2) the student, and (3) various types of technology. The important thing with regard to education today, we believe, is to
design objective-based, multiresource, course-centered delivery systems that maximize the learning possible through the
best utilization of the available resources.

Our initial approach to this is fully spelled out in Appendix
B—taken in its entirety from an article in the *Journal of Higher
Education*—which describes the implementation of this
approach in the fall of 1971 in a basic core course in the Sloan
School. The case, as noted in Appendix B, was successful—and
this success helped firm up many of the ideas that are presented
in this book. (Appendix B can be read at this point by those
who desire to probe this "smorgasbord" approach to learning
assistance in depth.)

SOME CONCLUDING THOUGHTS ON OUR SLOAN SCHOOL EFFORTS As we look back on our original goals, noted in the first paper
from which we quoted early in this appendix, our successes
and failures in attacking the three problems noted in 1968 are
clear, and perhaps instructive.

On the negative side, we have failed completely to integrate
material, through technology or otherwise, across fields. The
task is too large—and it may be that the material changes too
rapidly, although this is doubtful—and the participants, at
least in our cloister, are too individualistic to make this a
feasible task without massive resources. The process of working through the relationships of one item to another in any *one*
field is huge. (We spent on the order of four man-years on the
basic material of one part of our field alone.) To attempt to
integrate the conceptual structures of several fields in a computer data-base can be viewed as a nearly Herculean task at
present.

On the more positive side, as previously noted, the short-run objective of establishing a "flexible interactive terminal system at the graduate level to be used for experiments aimed at developing . . . long term goals" was accomplished. And we learned that there is merit in doing just this. For one thing, it forces the instructor to fully examine his own field, which, in turn, is hugely helpful in the development of effective courses in the field. In addition, the establishment of the terminal system (ALPS), no matter how limited, also led to the fulfillment of another goal—the ability to trace student learning paths and to gain some insights into the learning process. One learning approach we saw by this method was the search for an early overview of the material—an observation that complements some existing literature and has assisted us in course design.

With regard to the aim of better handling the new "material explosion," our success was mixed, but we are not displeased with the outcome. On one hand, we did not cope with the need to take the teaching of well-understood material out of the hands of the professorial resource in the manner we expected— by turning over the teaching process for this type of material to the technology. On the other hand, we did satisfy the objective. In our experimental course described in Appendix B, the professor no longer delivers (teaches) this material. It has been turned over to the learning resource represented by the student himself on a self-study basis. The method has been changed, but the objective has been satisfied. Success, we think.

And what of the original perception? Perhaps too visionary for today, we suspect it will be realized in the future. The necessary breakthroughs in artificial intelligence, English language processing, cost-effective hardware and software, learning theory, and improved ways to analyze course material are in the process of happening. With regard to the first two areas, Winograd (1971) has made some useful strides. The cost of computer hardware and software is continuing in a downward trend that has been evident for the last two decades—made possible by improved technology and very real economies of scale as computers become ubiquitous. The "sciences" of learning theory and the analysis of course material are both very much in their infancy. Yet the need in these areas is clearly perceived, and increasing resources are being devoted to better understanding of both processes. When one speculates on the progress made in other fields in the past 50 years and the increasing attention being turned to the need for change in the process of education, it is reasonable to expect student learning tools on the order of the ALPS system to be available sometime in the next few decades.

Appendix B: A Method for the Integrated Use of Learning Resources in Education

It is no secret that the cost of education has risen much faster in recent years than the cost of living as a whole. At the same time, quality appears to have fallen off—or at least perceived quality has been reduced. Students complain about the size of classes, the dedication of the faculty to research rather than teaching, the dullness of some classes, and many other things.

All these symptoms (despite the recent drop-off in student strikes and other dramatics) may be indicative of what some have termed an "educational crisis." At the very least, they are symptoms of a productivity problem in a labor-intensive industry. While technology has done much to raise output per man in many other industries, it has done little, if anything, in education. A lack of increased productivity not only causes increased costs but also eliminates the possibility of increasing quality at equivalent cost. Under these conditions, resources are most often strained to merely "keep the system going."

It is clear that the productivity problem in education and other knowledge-based industries now is of extreme importance. As Drucker has pointed out, "The bulk of tomorrow's employment will be in service trades, knowledge jobs—in health care, teaching, government . . . and the like. And no one knows much about knowledge work, let alone how to improve it" (Drucker, 1971, p. 39).

Drucker may overstate the case somewhat. This perceived need has certainly called forth a spate of research. In the educa-

NOTE: This appendix first appeared in the *Journal of Higher Education* (see Rockart, 1973). The course discussed herein (illustrated as a specific example) won the 1971–72 Western Electric Fund Award for Educational Innovation in Higher Education for Business Administration of the American Association of Collegiate Schools of Business.

tion area alone (with which we are concerned in this paper), there has been a significant amount of research into new teaching methods. These have ranged from the development of paper programmed instruction textbooks,[1] to computer-assisted instruction (Nordman, 1962; Grubb, 1968, pp. 38–42), to computer-assisted homework (Wilkinson, 1969), to computer-managed instruction, to on-line modeling of significant decision processes (Zannetos et al., 1970).

Other efforts have turned their back on the utilization of new technology and instead focused on the behavioral aspects of the learning process. Chief among these has been self-paced, self-study learning, one of whose chief and earliest advocates was Keller. Working from Skinnerian principles, Keller in 1965 ran a successful application of self-study (Keller, 1968, pp. 78–89). Since then, self-study has grown and flourished, although in universities almost entirely on the undergraduate level.[2]

In addition to these two major trends—computer assistance and self-study—a host of other efforts have taken place. These include the use of videotape, pass-fail courses, smaller classes, larger classes, student teaching, etc.

All the above are efforts to satisfy a felt set of needs which might be enumerated as follows:

1 To increase productivity in the educational process

2 To achieve "higher quality" of learning (although the definition of quality is unclear)

3 To "take the heat off the student" by allowing him to learn material at his own pace

4 To individualize instruction to the needs of the particular student

5 To provide the student with more autonomy by allowing him to study in depth those subjects which are of great interest to him while achieving an unpenalized minimum standard only in other courses

One major failing of these efforts has been the lack of good controlled studies to determine what has been accomplished. In the main, most courses involving new techniques such as self-study have been composed of student volunteers willing to take

[1]See, for example, Dearden (1969).
[2]See, for example, Green (1969) and Ferster (1968).

the educational risks of experimental situations. In addition, many of the new courses are based on techniques which explicitly do not allow comparisons with control groups. Yet there is an evident need to evaluate new forms of education.

Perhaps most interestingly, most educational innovations have focused on the use of one technique at a time as a particular instructor has become enamored with CAI, self-paced study, or some other individual method (Green, 1969; Ferster, 1968). This has been perhaps *the* major failing of the process of innovation in education. Despite much jawboning to the contrary, very seldom has a very detailed look been taken at the existing courses in today's curricula (especially at the graduate level). If this were done, the rudimentary fact would be noted that most courses are composed, and rightly so, of diverse types of material which meet multiple learning objectives. It follows, then, that diverse learning methods should be applied in each course to enable students to best comprehend the diverse material. This paper reports on an experiment in the integration of available methods "delivered" by varying resources to meet the requirements of diverse learning objectives and the resulting diverse materials in a single course.

The objectives-material-methods-resources development process of an experimental course is illustrated in the next major section of this paper. Much has been written about the need for clear course objectives, the decision process with regard to course material, and the pros and cons of different teaching (or learning) techniques. We have tried to avoid repeating all this methodology here. Rather, these factors are presented in only as much detail as necessary to illustrate the development of the particular course in issue, which in turn is done primarily as an illustration of the major point of this paper. That point is simply that it is necessary to define carefully the role of each major resource (professor, student, and technology) so that it is compatible with the prior choices of course objectives, type of material, and learning methods. The choice of the most effective and efficient resource to be utilized in each part of the learning process, it is suggested, can lead to both greater productivity and increased quality in education. The second major section of the paper presents the resulting course design, and the final section reviews the results obtained with regard to this course design in a controlled experiment.

The course with which we experimented, entitled Information and Decision Systems I, was taught to both undergraduate and graduate students at the Sloan School of Management at MIT. The subject is a core course in both curricula. It is intended to provide students with an in-depth grounding in the principles and application of accounting for management decision-making purposes. It introduces financial- and cost-accounting systems as one major segment of corporate information systems.

Objectives of the course   The course has several objectives. It is felt that the student should learn:

1   The principles which underlie the development and use of accounting data

2   The general process of management decision making in which accounting data are used

3   The accounting system and the detailed knowledge necessary to actually perform journalizing, adjusting, and closing entries to the corporate books

4   The process of cost distribution, the use of accounting data for product pricing, performance analysis, and capital budgeting

5   The concepts underlying "management planning and control"—the other area of major use of accounting data

6   The subjectivity and imprecision inherent in many of the cost and financial data used by management

7   The basic concepts concerning data collection and the "fit" of the accounting system within a model corporate information system

Pedagogic groupings of course material   With regard to the learning process, the course objectives were operationally translated into teaching material which divided fairly clearly into the following six pedagogic subsets:

1   Material illustrating the management process—especially the decision-making process. The target course is the initial "functional" course in management for most of the master's candidates. (Most of the other courses taken in the first term are disciplinary courses.) Some idea of the management process must be depicted. Emphasis is placed on the primary role of decision making.

2   Motivating material. Accounting methodologies, no matter how important, can be dull. There is a need to insert material which

illustrates the absolute need for managers to understand cost and other financial data.

3   Material concerned with the "language," "principles," and "procedures" of accounting. Making up the bulk of the course, this material is well described, although in highly varying ways, by diverse authors.[3] Although far from "cut and dried," this material is clearly set forth in understandable form. It varies in content or form only slightly from year to year.

4   Material on which the student can test his detailed knowledge and understanding of accounting techniques. This is "practice" material, best popularly exemplified by "homework."

5   Material highlighting "gray areas" or "major issues" which face developers and users of financial information. The language and procedures of accounting leave a great deal of latitude to the individual company accountant in the development of financial results for any period and in the development of cost data. While it is important that the student understand the basic postulates and principles underlying accounting and the results they produce, it is perhaps more important that he understand the "failings" of these man-made principles. It is important that the student have a deeper knowledge of the material in order to ponder such notions as replacement-cost depreciation, the results in product costing of various methods of overhead distribution, and the effect on the balance sheet of current accounting rules in times of inflation.

6   Material which is "timely," has changed during the period of the course, or offers new perspectives on the process. In general, this is material which cannot be (or has not been) put into writing prior to the start of the course. It is material, however, which often adds greatly to student understanding of the course, or which makes the course material "live" through relating it to current events or to ideas which the professor has recently developed and is excited about.

Available learning methods   The material above is diverse. It therefore demands diverse treatments. At the very least, it demands a careful matching of the way that each type of material can best be assimilated against the repertoire of teaching techniques available. If the learning process were better understood, instead of being a coin-flipping process for the theory which one wishes to select, an unambiguous material-to-tech-

---

[3]Since we wished to illustrate varying views as well as take the best from each author, we utilized various sources (Anthony, 1970; Horngren, 1970; Gordon & Shillinglaw, 1964) in different parts of the course.

nique matching process could take place. Unfortunately, it is not that simple. Today each professor must employ his own heuristics to select techniques for each type of material to be learned.

A learning method may be defined as a procedure, process, or technique by which material is presented to a student with the expectation that the student will gain in the knowledge, understanding, or skill encompassed by the material. Many learning methods are available. Use was made in the new course of 11 of the most ubiquitous methods. These 11 learning methods—and some of their cardinal attributes from our point of view—are as follows:

1 Listening to lectures: Excellent for communicating new or ill-defined material. Very poor for the transmission of well-understood facts which are available in books, since reading speed is several times faster than verbal communication.

2-3 Case discussion and class discussion of readings: Excellent for the involvement which they provide, the requirement which they place on the student to "think through" the material—no matter how cloudy the issue—and the need this method poses for the student to determine his own position and to defend it. Good for the absorption of all sides of major issues and for the exposition of all sides of "gray areas." Poor for learning facts, because of the inefficiency (verbosity and nondirectedness) of presentation.

4 Reading of textbooks: Excellent for the transmission of facts and well-understood, well-digested material for the reasons noted just above (comprehension speed and efficiency of presentation).

5 Reading of programmed instruction (paper): A first-rate alternative for some students to traditional textbooks for the transmission of facts. Some students consider this a highly efficient method of learning (Zannetos, 1967).

6 Following instructional modules: As developed for self-study courses, modules are "instructor's guides" to sets of materials. When well written, they provide directions as to how to go about the efficient assimilation of material provided by others of the above learning methods.

7-8 Performing homework and taking marked (but ungraded) quizzes: These can allow the student to test his knowledge of each segment of the work and get feedback on his degree of knowledge.

9 Taking part in "question sessions": These are class sessions in which the professor or a teaching assistant may be present, but which are

designed to be "run" by the students, who introduce the topics for discussion. Only those topics which meet the needs of the students at the time are discussed. The agenda is the student's, not the professor's. Excellent process for original learning or reinforcement of knowledge for some students. (Our view on these sessions has been shaped by feedback from students, most of whom cite the major value of these sessions as "tutorial" in the sense that they allow the removal of specific learning "blocks"; i.e., they allow students to clear up difficult points or misconceptions and to continue the learning process.)

10 Computer-assisted learning: Very poor, to date, as a replacement for textbooks or paper programmed instruction for original learning of most material on a cost-benefit basis. Highly worthwhile, if the programs are well developed, in allowing students to test their understanding of material or explore the effects of certain choices in a simulated world represented by a computer model.[4]

11 Self-paced, self-study: A "metamethod"—incorporating many of the above techniques—which is excellent for the transmission of facts and techniques which are well understood and where the material or adequate guidelines to its comprehension can be adequately presented in written form (Keller, 1968, pp. 78–89; Wilkinson, 1969). Self-study suffers, however, in areas where many views must be heard to illustrate the multiple facets of an important issue.

As previously noted, there are additional learning methods not discussed just above. And we have only begun to scratch the surface in developing the multiple attributes of some of these methods. The prime point, however, is that diverse learning methods do have diverse strengths and weaknesses. These attributes of each method must be matched against the attributes of each type of material to be presented within each particular course. To expect that one learning technique can be stretched to cover all types of material is to deny students the benefits of the application of the correct tool at the correct time. It is similar to a dentist who uses a single cutting bit, or a golfer playing with only his five iron. The task can be accomplished, but with far less than optimal results—both in terms of output and aesthetics.

[4]Although some would challenge them, Professor Z. S. Zannetos and we ourselves have found these comments on computer assistance to learning to be true in our work in this field. See, for example, Rockart, Scott Morton & Zannetos (1971).

From methods to resources　Interestingly, the 11 teaching methods just presented can be broken down into three major classes along the lines of the three major resources available today to the learning process. The methods fall into classes of those that are professor-dominated, those that are heavily dependent on the student for attainment in the learning process, and those in which technology plays a major part. The initial class, which we term *professor-intensive,* is characterized by class sessions in which the professor takes the responsibility for delivering the material or shaping the discussion. In *student-intensive* learning, to the contrary, the professor either is not present at the learning site or merely acts as a resource for the learning student. In *technology-intensive* learning the prime actor guiding the process is some form of technology—today usually a computer.

From a resource point of view, a curriculum developer can selectively utilize the strengths of these three major actors. In sum, one can choose among:

a. Professors—whose major comparative advantage is not in sheer "information transfer," but rather in the development of motivation,

		Classroom-oriented sessions	
		Professor intensive	
Classes of material	Lecture	Case discussion	Class discussion
(1) *Decision making and managerial process*		x	x
(2) *Motivational*		x	x
(3) *Language, principles, and procedures of accounting*			
(4) *Material to test understanding of (3)*			
(5) *"Issues," "gray areas"*	x	x	x
(6) *Timely, changing material*	x		

TABLE B-1
Specific course design

in the leading of discussions of issues to which there are no "right answers" but whose significance must be comprehended, and in the guiding of the student's learning process through intelligent interaction with students.

b. Students—whom it has been shown are capable of "active" learning of well-understood, well-documented material on their own when properly directed and relieved of the need to sit "passively" in class.

c. Technology—which, it is believed, can take the place of previous professor- or student-intensive methods where patient "answer checking," exploration of a simulated environment, or simple tutoring assistance is necessary.

SPECIFIC COURSE DESIGN
The traditional method of teaching the course described earlier had been 24 classes of 1.5 hours each based on both lecture and class-discussion techniques. As a result of the above-described process, the new course structure was developed; it can be summarized as shown in Table B-1. This table illustrates the matching of the types of material to be presented in the target course (rows) with learning methods (columns) and with major resources (groups of columns). It is a sparse matrix, since only

		Self-study sessions				
		Student intensive				Technolgoy intensive
Text-books	Programmed instruction	Instructional modules	Home-work	Feedback quizzes	Question sessions	Computer models
X	X	X				
			X	X	X	X

the *most* applicable learning methods (the methods used) are noted for each type of material. Following the resource lines shown in Table B-1, the new syllabus was divided into two basic types of pedagogy. These were a *classroom-oriented* set of sessions (professor-intensive) and a *self-study* set (student- and technology-intensive) as shown at the top of Table B-1 and described below.

1 A classroom-oriented set of sessions: To take best advantage of the professorial resource, eight classroom sessions remained "required." These sessions (four at the start of the course, two in the middle, and two at the end) were timed and designed to make maximum use of professorial skills. The start-of-the-course sessions were used to motivate the students with regard to the material, to provide examples from the instructors' background of the material's importance to managers, to provide an "overview" of the course, and to develop the decision-making setting in which the material is utilized by managers. Basically, the initial sessions were used to provide the students with a "feel," from a managerial viewpoint, of the material they were about to master. The later classroom sessions were utilized to discuss case situations, providing further perspective on basic material previously learned, as well as linking the material to other areas of management knowledge.

All these classroom sessions were designed around the instructors' comparative advantage over other learning media. In particular, instructors—as previously noted—have advantages in terms of motivation toward material; providing students with insights into "issues" in the course; exposing "gray areas" in the material; and finally, in making managerial case situations "live," further explicating and providing depth to the material. Material sets 1, 2, 5, and 6 from Table B-1 were therefore taught in this manner.

2 Self-study-oriented sessions: The remaining two-thirds of the scheduled course time was devoted to a self-study mode. Material sets 3 and 4 were included here. As noted below, all the student-intensive and one form of technology-intensive learning methods were utilized in this section of the course.

It is relevant to note that self-study was utilized—not self-paced self-study. The students were paced by the course examinations. It is felt that in their coming professional world, the students will be paced by externally imposed deadlines which they will have to meet by working on their own. There is good reason to provide them with experience in doing exactly this in the academic setting.

For these 16 self-study sessions, students were expected to study the basic course material on their own. This self-study was assisted, however, by the following:

a. Nine written guides to the instructional modules (averaging approximately 10 pages each): These provided information as to the particular concepts to be learned, reading to be done of particular material in the texts (both required and optional), the instructor's comments concerning the material (which ranged from such things as putting stress on particularly important aspects of the reading to further explanation), and homework to be handed in and/or other exercises to be performed, e.g., on the computer.

b. Optional attendance at "question sessions": Replacing the 16 class sessions which would ordinarily have been held were 12 question sessions at which the instructor was present solely to answer student questions on the assignments and to respond to any other questions concerning management in general which the students wished to discuss. Attendance at these sessions averaged 25 percent of each class (approximately 10 students per session). Some two-thirds of each session turned out to be concerned with questions on the material. The remaining third varied widely over general management subjects, reflecting particular student interests.

c. Homework: This was marked by the instructor and by teaching assistants. The teaching assistants also answered student questions during their office hours. TAs are traditionally used in this course.

d. Feedback examinations: These were brief, informal, marked but nongraded "quizzes" which students could take after completing modules 2, 4, 6, and 8 to allow them to gauge their progress in the course. The exams were immediately marked and could be discussed with the teaching assistant.

e. An interactive computer program—CLOSE: This on-line computer program allowed the student to review, whenever he wished to do so, the complete material of the first half of the course. Financial accounting (the major material of the first half) breaks down into a simple posting-adjusting-closing cycle of events. Using computer graphic capability on a CRT screen, students were able to test their ability to perform financial-accounting entries throughout this entire cycle. The interactive program assisted them by performing arithmetic, by displaying for them the up-to-date status of the books, and by tutoring whenever a mistake was made. (In this last "tutor" mode, the program indicates each entry which is made in error—pointing to the exact part of the entry in error. In addition, it provides hints to the student to enable him to derive the correct answer, but only if the student asks for help. Many other similar features of the program provide it with an ability to reasonably replicate the actions of a human tutor.)

The most important point about the program, however, is that it enables a student thoroughly to test his ability to actually perform all the accounting functions which he has learned in one relatively short session at the computer console. In this way the student can check his detailed and overall understanding of the material in a short session with the computer. The student can test and retest his knowledge by himself, at a time of his own choosing, with or without tutoring assistance.

The material included in the original version of CLOSE was simple for the best students—but of greater challenge to the less well prepared students to whom it is most particularly addressed. A version with advanced subject material has been prepared.

Process objectives for the experiment The experimental course was designed with five "process" objectives clearly in mind. These were:

1 To improve academic productivity by making optimum use of the strengths of all the resources available to the learning (not teaching) process.

2 To increase student satisfaction with the learning process by allowing pupils greater flexibility in the use of their time and greater initiative in the learning process through the above methodology.

3 To increase the quality of the learning process by providing, for those students who desired it in the particular subject, more meaningful access to the professor. (It is felt that not all students want, or can handle, great depth in all courses—but greater depth and breadth should be available to those who desire it in any particular course.)

4 To allow (and encourage) the students to feel a greater responsibility for their own education by putting the emphasis, through self-study and optional learning-feedback mechanisms, on active learning on the part of the student, rather than on passive classroom-based absorption of material.

5 To thoroughly test the validity of the innovative course by both quantitative and qualitative means. Measures of success were therefore

designed and control sections run so that sound experimental results could be derived.

The course was run for the first time in the fall term of 1971. There were seven sections of the course. Four sections were taught in the "regular" fashion—a combination of lecture and class discussion. Three of the sections utilized the innovative program. (Hereinafter these sections are referred to as self-study or SS, and regular sections are sometimes referred to as REG.)

Students selected particular sections in accordance with their schedules. Notification of which sections would be self-study was not given ahead of time. In addition, every attempt was made to play down the "experimental" nature of the course. Although there is undoubtedly some Hawthorne effect in every innovation, it is felt that there was as little as possible involved in the experimental results.

In order to check the value of the program in an objective, quantitative manner, the three self-study sections and the four regular sections were given the same midterm and final examinations. In addition, a questionnaire was distributed to all students in both the self-study and regular sections at the end of the course to determine their subjective feelings about the course.

Results, both in terms of relative performance of SS versus REG sections on the examinations and in terms of student "feelings" about the course as noted on the 70-question questionnaire, suggest that the objectives-material-methods-resource matching approach to the course was a definite success. The results were as follows:

Objective evidence from examination results: All students in the course, both REG and SS, took the same two examinations (midterm and final) at the same time. The results were as shown in Tables B-2 and B-3.

The objective evidence from the examinations, both midterm and final, is clear. The self-study sections outperformed the regular sections. There is no reason to suspect that the two groups were not homogeneous in mental ability and background at the start of the course. Teaching ability undoubtedly makes some unmeasurable differences, but the average number of years of teaching experience in this course of the instructors

TABLE B-2 *Relative* *performance:* *midterm exam*		*Regular* *sections*	*Self-study* *sections*
Undergraduate			
	Mean	42.27	52.02
	Standard *deviation*	9.62	11.28
	N	(67)	(23)
Graduate			
	Mean	51.54	52.09
	Standard *deviation*	8.84	10.56
	N	(60)	(82)
Total			
	Mean	46.65	52.08
	Standard *deviation*	10.22	10.67
	N	(127)	(105)

TABLE B-3 *Relative* *performance:* *final exam*		*Regular* *sections*	*Self-study* *sections*
Undergraduate			
	Mean	87.66	101.55
	Standard *deviation*	19.48	21.36
	N	(57)	(21)
Graduate			
	Mean	102.17	105.10
	Standard *deviation*	20.1	25.45
	N	(57)	(82)
Total			
	Mean	94.91	104.37
	Standard *deviation*	21.02	24.61
	N	(114)	(103)

for both SS and REG sections was approximately the same.[5]

The differences for the total (both undergraduate and graduate) scores of SS versus regular (52.08 versus 46.65 on the midterm and 104.37 versus 94.91 on the final) is highly significant at the .01 level on a t-test. On both examinations, SS undergraduates and graduates outperformed their REG counterparts. The difference is most striking with regard to undergraduates. However, when a group of graduates who took the course in a regular section as an elective (and who therefore might be expected to be more motivated toward the material) is removed from the data, the examination results show a significant difference in the graduate ranks in favor of self-study, also!

Subjective evidence from questionnaires: In the free-form section of the course, self-study students provided some logic behind the above results. Some of the ideas frequently expressed were:

I felt the responsibility for learning the material had been transferred, under self-study, from the professor to me.

Self-study is a lot more productive. I didn't have to waste time in class on things I already understood . . . or spend time in class when I was too far behind for the class to do me any good.

The computer program enabled me to check on my own learning of the entire first half of the course when *I was ready to do so*. That's great. You ought to have a program for the second half, too, if you can design one. It helps to be able to review *all* the material—for integrated understanding—in two to three hours on the computer.

The instructors liked it, too. One self-study instructor summarized his views by saying:

I've never enjoyed teaching so much. I taught only those things which require a professor. Self-study removed the "transmission" of a lot of the dreary details which can be learned from a book. The question sessions, above all, were challenging and fun. Only those students who were motivated to come showed up—and our discussions were always lively.

---

[5]Still, one suspects that the teaching factor may have played a definite role, since significant differences in results caused by learning method alone are almost impossible to find in the literature. See Grayson (1972, p. 12–19) and Guetzkow, Kelley & McKeachie (1954, pp. 193–207).

We got to discuss, in addition to the strict course material, things like management in general, and philosophies of life—both mine and theirs. These were things one would hesitate to tie up a class of forty on—but with ten to twelve interested students, these discussions came naturally.

The variety of possible questions, some of which I could not answer (students could ask *anything*), somehow made me appear more human, I think . . . a bit less the "authority" and a bit more an "assistor in the learning process." This is the only way to teach.

The students who *want* personal contact get more attention than they would otherwise get (ten people in question sessions vs. forty). Those who are satisfied merely with picking up the basic knowledge alone in this particular course are left alone to do so most easily and efficiently.

More quantitative assessments of these feelings are available from the course questionnaire data. Student answers to nine of the questions tell much of the story[6] (Figure B-1).

The course design and the materials for implementation purposes required approximately four man-months of effort. As noted below, the resulting increase in academic production can quickly amortize this investment.[7]

Relationship to academic productivity   The course allows a 50 percent increase in academic productivity. One instructor can now handle three sections instead of two. This potential gain will be implemented the next time the course is taught.

This statement concerning productivity is based on the conclusion that the average number of students in each *question session* can be increased from 10 to 15 with little effect. Thus one instructor can lecture three sections and combine them into two for question-session purposes, providing an exactly equivalent teaching-hour load for the instructor as in the past with a 50 percent increase in sections taught. Briefly:

During this term there was evidence that the increase in students in the question sessions from an average of 10 to an average of 15 was highly feasible. A very few sessions did, in

---

[6]Seven-point scales were used. For clearer exposition and to allow chi square analysis, the points were grouped to a three-point scale.

[7]In addition, some course redesign takes place each year. Therefore, the four months of curriculum development effort is not all "extra" effort.

FIGURE B-1 *Significant questionnaire results (a pertinent set of 9 out of the 70 questions)*

"For learning the material in this course, self-study is a preferable mode."

	Strongly agree	Uncertain	Strongly disagree
SS	71	21	8
REG	41	42	17

Chi square significance level .005

"This course will be *more* useful to me in the future—compared with other courses."

	Strongly agree	Uncertain	Strongly disagree
SS	50	40	10
REG	35	49	16

Chi square significance level NS

"During the course my knowledge of management techniques changed considerably."

	Strongly agree	Uncertain	Strongly disagree
SS	70	28	2
REG	49	46	5

Chi square significance level NS

"During the course my knowledge of management principles changed considerably."

	Strongly agree	Uncertain	Strongly disagree
SS	59	35	6
REG	49	45	6

Chi square significance level NS

"In this course the professor stimulates students to think about the issues."

	Strongly agree	Uncertain	Strongly disagree
SS	46	51	3
REG	19	56	25

Chi square significance level .005

"Professor has a clear plan for the semester's work."

	No	Uncertain	Yes
SS	4	16	80
REG	25	42	33

Chi square significance level .005

"Class sessions are always interesting."

	No	Uncertain	Yes
SS	25	50	25
REG	49	49	2

Chi square significance level .005

"Professor motivates student interest in the material."

	No	Uncertain	Yes
SS	7	44	48
REG	46	49	5

Chi square significance level .005

"Professor is available for outside assistance."

	No	Uncertain	Yes
SS	13	34	53
REG	28	57	15

Chi square significance level .01

NOTE: NS = not significant.

Old system (2 sections)		New system (3 sections)	
Sections	= 2	Lecture sections	= 3
Class sessions	= 24	Lecture class sessions	= 8
Hours per session	= 1.5	Hours per session	= 1.5
(2 × 24 × 1.5)	= 72 class hours	(3 × 8 × 1.5)	= 36 hours
	Question sections		= 2
	(At 15 students per session average)		
	Question sessions		= 12
	Hours per session		= 1.5
	(2 × 12 × 1.5)		= 36 hours
	Total load (36 + 36)		= 72 hours

fact, have 15 students. These sessions were felt in no way to be inferior.

Relationship to educational quality   It is felt that this course has increased the quality of education in several ways. First, students in the question sessions had a chance to follow their agenda. They could inquire about what interested them—whether or not it was part of the strict curriculum. And the students took advantage of it. Questionnaire data reflect their belief that the course was better planned and better orchestrated for them. Second, and perhaps most important, the individual students who most wanted exposure to the instructor in this particular course received it in the self-study group. Twenty-five percent of the class, on the average, attended the question sessions and received attention as if the 40-man class were a 10-man seminar. In the questionnaire, "access to the instructor" was seen to be significantly greater (.01 level) in the self-study sections than in the regular sections (Figure B-1, bottom row). Some students noted that the computer program allowed them to get an integrated understanding of that section of the material which they felt was not available in previous courses they had taken.

This particular course deals with basic material. Its decreased need for faculty time will also provide faculty availability to teach more professor-dependent material in later courses in smaller sections. Alternatively, greater faculty time will be available for curriculum development to introduce new concepts and material.

SUMMARY   The educational literature has recorded many advances in technique over the past few years. Some have stressed technology. Others have stressed more awareness of human potential and psychology in the learning process. Unfortunately, most of these advances have been applied one at a time.

This paper suggests that the strengths of each of the three major available resources in the learning process must be clearly understood and the use of these three resources carefully orchestrated in each course. The exact use of each resource will depend on previously defined course objectives, the transformation of these objectives into relevant classes of material, and the methods which are chosen to best transmit each type of material. We know a great deal about this process, but it is far from a science at present.

An illustration of the recommended process as performed for a particular course has been given. It suggested that careful use of the process, resulting in an integrated and selective use of the available resources, can result in greater academic productivity, while at the same time increasing both perceived course quality and student satisfaction with the course.

Of some importance is the fact that this educational change is implementable in today's universities. It is not a radical departure, yet it goes far toward meeting some of the currently felt needs in education as noted in the first several paragraphs of this paper.[8]

[8]See Schein (1972, pp. 97–98) for a discussion of the importance of this last factor: the need to fit educational innovation into the present system.

References

ACM SIGCUE Bulletin, vol. 6, no. 4, Association for Computing Machinery, 1133 Avenue of the Americas, New York, October 1972.

Anthony, R. N.: *Management Accounting,* Richard D. Irwin, Inc., Homewood, Ill., 1970.

Armer, Paul: "Computer Aspects of Technological Change, Automation, and Economic Progress," in The National Commission on Technology, Automation, and Economic Progress, *Technology and the American Economy: The Report of the Commission,* Government Printing Office, Washington, 1965, vol. I, appendix, "The Outlook for Technological Change."

Ashby, Eric: *Any Person, Any Study: An Essay on Higher Education in the United States,* McGraw-Hill Book Company, New York, 1971.

Blau, Peter M., and W. Richard Scott: *Formal Organization: A Comparative Approach,* Chandler Publishing Company, San Francisco, 1962.

Bork, Alfred M.: Quoted in *ACM SIGCUE Bulletin,* vol. 7, no. 4, p. 4, October 1973.

Bowen, William G.: *The Economics of Major Private Universities,* Carnegie Commission on Higher Education, Berkeley, Calif., 1968.

"Bringing Graduate School to the Plant," *Business Week,* vol. 2106, pp. 64–65, Jan. 10, 1970.

Bunderson, V.: Quoted in *ACM SIGCUE Bulletin,* vol. 8, no. 1, p. 22, January 1974.

Carne, E. Bryan: "Telecommunications: Its Impact on Business," *Harvard Business Review,* vol. 50, pp. 125–132, July–August 1972.

Carnegie Commission on Higher Education: *The Fourth Revolution: Instructional Technology in Higher Education,* McGraw-Hill Book Company, New York, 1972.

Cartter, Allan M.: "Scientific Manpower for 1970–1985," *Science,* vol. 172, pp. 132–139, Apr. 9, 1971.

Cheit, Earl: *The New Depression in Higher Education,* McGraw-Hill Book Company, New York, 1971.

Chu, Godwin C., and Wilbur Schramm: "Learning from Television: What the Research Says," in Sidney G. Tickton (ed.), *To Improve Learning: An Evaluation of Instructional Technology,* R. R. Bowker Company, New York, 1971, vol. 1, pp. 179–182.

Cohen, Muriel: "Private Colleges in State Warned Only Fittest to Survive," *Boston Evening Globe,* Dec. 21, 1972.

Coleman, James S., et al.: *Equality of Educational Opportunity,* U.S. Office of Education, Washington, 1966.

"Colleges Plug In the Teaching Computer," *Business Week,* Apr. 7, 1973.

Computing Newsletter, March 1973, p. 4.

Comstock, G. A.: "The Computer and Higher Education in California," in R. E. Levien, *The Emerging Technology,* McGraw-Hill Book Company, New York, 1972*a*, pp. 195–249.

Comstock, G. A.: "National Utilization of Computers," in R. E. Levien, *The Emerging Technology,* McGraw-Hill Book Company, New York, 1972*b*, pp. 129–194.

Dalkey, Norman C.: "An Experimental Study of Group Opinion," *Futures,* vol. 1, pp. 408–420, September 1969.

Davis, Gordon B.: *Management Information Systems: Conceptual Foundations, Structure, and Development,* McGraw-Hill Book Company, New York, 1974.

Dearden, F.: *Essentials of Cost-Accounting,* Addison-Wesley Publishing Company, Inc., Reading, Mass., 1969.

Deighton, Lee C.: "Instruments of Instruction: The Book plus the New Media," in Sidney G. Tickton (ed.), *To Improve Learning: An Evaluation of Instructional Technology,* R. R. Bowker Company, New York, 1971, vol. 2, pp. 507–510.

Demb, Ada B.: "Universities: An Analytic Approach for Understanding Change," unpublished manuscript, Harvard Graduate School of Education, Cambridge, Mass., January 1973.

Drucker, Peter: *The Age of Discontinuity: Guidelines to Our Changing Society,* Harper & Row, Publishers, Incorporated, New York, 1969.

Drucker, Peter: "The Surprising Seventies," *Harper's Magazine,* July 1971, pp. 35–39.

Education in Britain, Central Office of Information, London, September 1971.

Edwards, E. M.: "APL—The First Programming Language Suitable for Engineering Undergraduates," *IEEE Transactions on Education,* vol. E14, no. 4, pp. 179–180, November 1971.

Eisner, Mark: *A Researcher's Overview of the TROLL/1 System,* Department of Economics, MIT, Cambridge, Mass., 1971.

Ferster, C. D.: "Individualized Instruction in a Large Introductory Psychology Course," unpublished manuscript, Georgetown University, Washington, 1968.

Flory, John: "Films for Learning," in Sidney G. Tickton (ed.), *To Improve Learning: An Evaluation of Instructional Technology,* R. R. Bowker Company, New York, 1971, vol. 1, pp. 211–230.

Forsythe, Richard O.: "Instructional Radio," in Sidney G. Tickton (ed.), *To Improve Learning: An Evaluation of Instructional Technology,* R. R. Bowker Company, New York, 1971, vol. 1, pp. 241–258.

Foster, G. H.: "APL: A Natural Language for Engineering Education?" *IEEE Transactions on Education,* vol. E14, no. 4, pp. 174–185, November 1971.

Fox, Harold W.: "Two Dozen Ways of Handling Cases," *Collegiate News and Views,* vol. 26, pp. 17–20, Spring 1973.

Glenny, Lyman: "The Anonymous Leaders of Higher Education," *Journal of Higher Education,* vol. 43, pp. 9–22, January 1972.

Goldstein, Henry, David L. Krantz, and Jack D. Rains (eds.): *Controversial Issues in Learning,* Appleton-Century-Crofts, Inc., New York, 1965.

Goode, Delmar (ed.): "Editorial," *Improving College and University Teaching,* vol. 19, pp. 90–92, September 1971.

Gordon, M. J., and G. Shillinglaw: *Accounting: A Managerial Approach,* Richard D. Irwin, Inc., Homewood, Ill., 1964.

Gorovitz, Samuel: "Reflections on Campus Pessimism," *Science,* vol. 178, pp. 586–590, Nov. 10, 1972.

Gould, Samuel: *Today's Academic Condition,* Colgate University Press, Hamilton, N.Y., 1970.

Graves, Thomas A., Jr.: "Crises in University Governance," *Collegiate News and Views,* vol. 24, no. 3, pp. 1–3, March 1971.

Grayson, L. P.: "Costs, Benefits, Effectiveness: Challenge to Educational Technology," *Science,* vol. 175, pp. 12–19, Mar. 17, 1972.

Green, B. A.: *Self-Paced Course in Freshman Physics,* Occasional Paper no. 2, Education Research Center, MIT, Cambridge, Mass., Apr. 4, 1969.

Greenberger, Martin, Julius Aronofsky, James L. McKenney, and William F. Massey (eds.): *Networks for Research and Education,* The M.I.T. Press, Cambridge, Mass., 1974.

Grubb, R. E.: "Learner-Controlled Statistics," *Programmed Learning and Educational Technology,* pp. 38–42, January 1968.

Guetzkow, H. E., L. Kelley, and W. J. McKeachie: "An Experimental Comparison of Recitation, Discussion and Tutorial Methods in College Teaching," *Journal of Educational Psychology,* vol. 45, pp. 193–207, April 1954.

Hansen, D. N., W. Dick, and H. T. Lippert: *Research and Implementation of a Collegiate Instruction of Physics via Computer-Assisted Instruction,* Technical Report no. 3, Florida State University, Tallahassee, November 1968.

Harman, Harry H.: *Modern Factor Analysis,* 2d ed., The University of Chicago Press, Chicago, 1967.

Hechinger, Fred M.: Quoted in Thomas A. Graves, Jr., "Crisis in University Governance," *Collegiate News and Views,* vol. 24, no. 3, p. 4, March 1971.

Heron, W. T., and E. W. Ziebarth: "A Preliminary Comparison of Radio and Classroom Lectures," *Speech Monographs,* vol. 13, 1946. Quoted in Richard O. Forsythe, "Instructional Radio," in Sidney G. Tickton (ed.), *To Improve Learning,* R. R. Bowker Company, New York, 1970, pp. 241–258.

Hertz, David B.: *New Power for Management,* McGraw-Hill Book Company, New York, 1969.

Herzog, Eric L.: "Work Relationships in the Delivery of Health Care," unpublished doctoral dissertation, Sloan School of Management, MIT, Cambridge, Mass., n.d.

Hickey, Albert E., and John M. Newton: *Computer-Assisted Instruction: A Survey of the Literature,* Entelek, Inc., Newburyport, Mass., 1967.

The Hidden Medium: Educational Radio, Herman W. Land Associates, Inc., New York, 1966.

Hilgard, Ernest R.: *Theories of Learning,* 1st ed., Appleton-Century-Crofts, Inc., New York, 1948.

Hilgard, Ernest R., and Gordon H. Bower: *Theories of Learning,* 3d ed., Appleton-Century-Crofts, Inc., New York, 1966.

Hodgkinson, Harold L.: *Institutions in Transition,* McGraw-Hill Book Company, New York, 1971.

Hoffer, E. P.: "Experience with the Use of Computer Simulation

Models in Medical Education," *Computers in Biology and Medicine,* vol. 3, no. 3, pp. 269–280, October 1973.

Hoffer, E. P., G. O. Barnet, and B. B. Farquhar: "Computer Simulation Model for Teaching Cardio-Pulmonary Resuscitation," *Journal of Medical Education,* vol. 47, pp. 343–348, May 1973.

Hoffman, Jonathan: "Computer-Assisted Instruction Revisited," *College Management,* vol. 8, no. 8, pp. 21–23, October 1973.

Horngren, C. T.: *Accounting for Management Control,* Prentice-Hall, Inc., Englewood Cliffs, N.J., 1970.

Ikenberry, Stanley O.: "The Organizational Dilemma," *Journal of Higher Education,* vol. 43, pp. 23–34, January 1972.

In North Carolina: Computing Power for Higher Education, IBM Computing Report, pp. 2–6, Summer 1973.

Kaplan, A., A. L. Skogstad, and M. A. Girshick: "The Prediction of Social and Technological Events," *Public Opinion Quarterly,* vol. 14, pp. 93–110, Spring 1950.

"Karl Marx U. Borrows from NYU," *Business Week,* vol. 2211, p. 84, Jan. 22, 1972.

Katz, Richard: *The Self-Assessment Workshop: Instructors Manual,* Peace Corps contract 80-1531 Task Order 1, Division of Research, Washington, 1970.

Keller, F. S.: "Goodbye, Teacher . . . ," *Journal of Applied Behavior Analysis,* vol. 1, pp. 78–89, Spring 1968.

Kemeny, J. G.: *Computers in Higher Education,* Report of the President's Science Advisory Council, Washington, February 1967.

Kerr, Clark: "Foreword," in Earl F. Cheit, *The New Depression in Higher Education,* McGraw-Hill Book Company, New York, 1971, pp. vii–xv.

Kochen, M., C. Abraham, and E. Wong: *Adaptive Man-Machine Concept-Processing,* IBM, Air Force Contract AF 19(604)8446, Yorktown Heights, N.Y., 1958.

Kolb, David A.: *Individual Learning Styles and the Learning Process,* Working Paper 535-71, Sloan School of Management, MIT, Cambridge, Mass., Spring 1971.

Kolb, David A., and Marshall B. Goldman: *Toward a Topology of Learning Environments,* Working Paper 688-73, Sloan School of Management, MIT, Cambridge, Mass., December 1973.

Korn, James H.: "Promoting Good Teaching," *Journal of Higher Education,* vol. 43, pp. 123–132, February 1972.

Kornfeld, Leo L.: "The Campus as a Management Problem," *Wall Street Journal,* Dec. 9, 1970.

Levien, Roger E.: *The Emerging Technology: Instructional Uses of the Computer in Higher Education,* McGraw-Hill Book Company, New York, 1972.

Levien, Roger E., and M. E. Maron: *A Computer System for Inference Execution and Data Retrieval,* RAND Memorandum RM-5085-PR, The RAND Corporation, Santa Monica, Calif., 1966.

Madnick, S. E.: "The Future of Computers," *Technology Review,* vol. 75, no. 8, pp. 34–45, July–August 1973.

Madnick, S. E., and J. J. Donovan: *Operating Systems,* McGraw-Hill Book Company, New York, 1974.

Martinson, John L., and David C. Miller: "Educational Technology and the Future of the Book," in Sidney G. Tickton (ed.), *To Improve Learning: An Evaluation of Instructional Technology,* R. R. Bowker Company, New York, 1971, vol. 2, pp. 517–528.

Mayhew, Lewis B.: "Higher Education—toward 1984," *Educational Record,* vol. 53, pp. 215–221, Summer 1972.

Meadows, Dennis L., Donella H. Meadows, Jorgen Randers, and William H. Behrens III: *The Limits to Growth,* Universe Books, New York, 1972.

Medsker, Leland L., and Dale Tillery: *Breaking the Access Barriers: A Profile of Two-Year Colleges,* McGraw-Hill Book Company, New York, 1971.

Miles, Matthew: *Learning to Work in Groups,* Teachers College Press, Columbia University, New York, 1965.

Molnar, Andrew R.: "Critical Issues in Computer-Based Learning," *Educational Technology,* vol. 11, August 1971, pp. 60–64.

Mosmann, Charles: *Academic Computers in Service,* Jossey-Bass, Inc., Publishers, San Francisco, 1973.

National Academy of Sciences National Research Council: *Digital Computer Needs in Universities and Colleges,* Washington, 1966.

National Commission on the Financing of Postsecondary Education: *Financing Postsecondary Education in the United States,* Government Printing Office, Washington, December 1973.

Newell, Allen, J. C. Shaw, and H. A. Simon: "Empirical Explorations with the Logic Theory Machine," in Edward A. Feigenbaum and Julian Feldman (eds.), *Computers and Thought: A Collection of Articles by Armer and Others,* McGraw-Hill Book Company, New York, 1963.

Nie, Norman H., Dale H. Bent, and C. Hadlai Hull: *Statistical Package for the Social Sciences,* McGraw-Hill Book Company, New York, 1970.

Nordman, B. J.: *Teaching Machines and Programmed Instruction: An Introduction and Overview,* Report no. 260, University of Illinois, Urbana, 1962.

O'Neil, Robert M.: *The Courts, Government, and Higher Education,* A Supplementary Paper for the Committee for Economic Development, New York, 1972.

"Open University Put to the Test," Ford Foundation *Letter,* Mar. 15, 1973, p. 2.

Orlicky, Joseph: *The Successful Computer System: A Management Guide,* McGraw-Hill Book Company, New York, 1969.

Pake, George E.: "Whither United States Universities?" *Science,* vol. 176, pp. 908–916, May 28, 1971.

Patrick, Kenneth G., and Richard Eells: *Education and the Business Dollar,* Macmillan & Company, Ltd., London, 1969.

Piaget, Jean: *Language and Thought of the Child,* Harcourt, Brace and Company, Inc., New York, 1962.

Pigors, Paul, and Faith Pigors, "Learning by the Incident Process," *Technology Review,* vol. 65, no. 4, February 1963.

Pillsbury, Wilbur F.: *Computer Augmented Accounting, Compuguide One,* South-Western Publishing Company, Incorporated, Cincinnati, 1970.

Pillsbury, Wilbur F.: *Computer Augmented Accounting, Compuguide Three,* South-Western Publishing Company, Incorporated, Cincinnati, 1973.

PLATO, publication of the Computer-Based Education Research Laboratory, University of Illinois, Urbana, December 1972.

President's Science Advisory Council: *Computers in Higher Education,* Government Printing Office, Washington, 1967.

Quillian, M. Ross: *Semantic Memory,* ARPA AF 19(628)5065, Bolt, Beranek, and Newman, Inc., Cambridge, Mass., October 1966.

"Research Firm Empowered to Award Degrees," *Boston Globe,* Mar. 18, 1973.

Rivlin, Alice M.: "What Does the Most Good?" *Systematic Thinking for Social Action,* The Brookings Institution, Washington, 1971, chap. 3.

Rockart, John F., Michael S. Scott Morton, and Zenon S. Zannetos: "Associative Learning Project in Computer-Assisted Instruction," *Educational Technology,* vol 11, pp. 17–23, November 1973.

Rudberg, Donald A.: "The Applicability of APL to All Levels of Electrical Engineering Education and Research," in G. H. Foster, "APL: A Natural Language for Engineering Education?" *IEEE Transactions on Education,* vol. E14, no. 4, pp. 174–185, November 1971.

Schein, Edgar H.: "The Reluctant Professor: Implications for University Management," *Sloan Management Review,* vol. 12, pp. 35–49, Fall 1970.

Schein, Edgar H.: *Professional Education: Some New Directions,* McGraw-Hill Book Company, New York, 1972.

Schein, Edgar H., and Warren Bennis: *Personal and Organizational Change through Group Methods,* John Wiley & Sons, Inc., New York, 1965.

Scott Morton, M. S.: "On Educational Technology," unpublished paper, Sloan School of Management, MIT, Cambridge, Mass., 1970.

Scott Morton, M. S., and Zenon S. Zannetos: "Efforts toward an Associative Learning Instructional System," in *Proceedings of IFIPS Conference, Scotland, 1968,* North-Holland Publishing Company, Amsterdam, 1969, pp. 1337–1341.

Sharpe, William F.: *The Economics of Computers,* Columbia University Press, New York, 1969.

Smith, Peter J.: "Britain's Open University: Everyman's Classroom," *Saturday Review: Education,* Apr. 29, 1972, pp. 40–50.

Snyder, Benson R.: *The Hidden Curriculum,* Alfred A. Knopf, Inc., New York, 1971.

Stetten, K. J.: *The Technology of Small Local Facilities for Instructional Use,* MITRE Report no. M69-39, MITRE Corporation, Bedford, Mass., April 1970.

Stetten, K. J.: *Toward a Market Success for CAI,* MITRE Corporation, Bedford, Mass., June 1972.

Suppes, Patrick, and Mona Morningstar: *Evaluation of Three CAI Programs,* Technical Report no. W0142, Institute for Mass Studies in the Social Sciences, Stanford University, Stanford, Calif., May 1969.

Talk Back TV, Institute of Technology, Southern Methodist University, p. 5, n.d.

Toffler, Alvin: *Future Shock,* Random House, Inc., New York, 1970.

U.S. Office of Education: *Digest of Educational Statistics, 1972,* Washington, 1973.

U.S. News and World Report, Jan. 15, 1953.

Vaughan, T. R., and G. Sjoberg: "The Politics of Projection: A Critique of Cartter's Analysis," *Science,* vol. 177, pp. 142–147, July 14, 1972.

Weeg, G. P.: "Trends in Instructional Use of Computers," in *Proceedings of the EDUCOM Fall Conference,* EDUCOM, Princeton, N.J., October 1973.

Weingarten, Fred W., et al.: *A Study of Regional Computer Networks,* Computer Center, University of Iowa, Iowa City, 1973.

Weizenbaum, J.: "ELIZA: A Computer Program for the Study of Natural Communication between Man and Machine," *Communications of the ACM,* vol. 9, pp. 36–45, January 1966.

Wentworth, Eric: "No Silver Spoon for Higher Education," *Saturday Evening Review,* July 22, 1972, pp. 38–39.

Wight, Albert: *Cross-Cultural Training,* Center for Research and Education, Estes Park, Colo., 1969.

Wilcox, Jarrod: *A Survey Forecast of New Technology in Universities and Colleges,* Working Paper 585-75, Sloan School of Management, MIT, Cambridge, Mass., January 1972.

Wilkinson, J. W.: *Accounting with the Computer: A Practice Case,* Richard D. Irwin, Inc., Homewood, Ill., 1969.

Winograd, Terry: *Procedures as a Representation for Data in a Computer Program for Understanding Natural Language,* revised dissertation, originally issued as Project MAC T.R.-84., MIT, Cambridge, Mass., January 1971.

Withington, F. G.: "Will Technology Save the Day?" in Fred Gruenberger (ed.), *Information Systems for Management,* Prentice-Hall, Inc., Englewood Cliffs, N.J., 1972.

Wood, Ben D., and Frank N. Freeman: *Motion Pictures in the Classroom,* Houghton Mifflin Company, Boston, 1929.

Zannetos, Zenon S.: "Programmed Instruction in the Light of Anticipated Computer Technology," *Accounting Review,* vol. 42, pp. 566–571, July 1967.

Zannetos, Zenon S., James Beville, and John H. Wagner: *The Development of an Interactive Graphical Risk Analysis System,* Working Paper 502-70, Sloan School of Management, MIT, Cambridge, Mass., December 1970.

Zinn, Karl L.: "Computer Assistance for Instruction: A Review of Systems and Projects," in D. D. Bushnell and D. W. Allen, *The Computer in American Higher Education,* John Wiley & Sons, Inc., New York, 1967, pp. 77–107.

Zinn, Karl L.: *An Evaluative Review of Uses of Computers in Instruction,* Project CLUE, The University of Michigan Press, Ann Arbor, December 1970.

Index

Maxicomputers, 71–72
Mayhew, Lewis B., 203, 238–239
Meadows, Dennis L., 124
Meadows, Donella H., 124
Medsker, Leland L., 216–219, 223
Memory (Ebbinghaus), 12*n.*
Midicomputers, 71–72
Miles, Matthew, 19
Miller, David C., 34
Minicomputers, 71–72, 98
Minnesota Computer Time-Sharing
  Network, 70
Minority groups, 201, 210, 214
MIT Multics system, 289*n.*, 300, 308
MITRE Corporation, 95, 98–101
MITRE'S TICCET project, 95, 98–101,
  278
Mobil Oil Corporation, 50
Molnar, Andrew R., 151
Montana State University, 119
Morningstar, Mona, 87, 101
Mosmann, Charles, 126
Motion pictures, 133

National Academy of Sciences, 167–
  171
National Bureau of Economic Research
  Data Bank, 122, 123
National Commission on the Financing of
  Postsecondary Education, 206, 213,
  215
National Institute of Education, 210
National Science Foundation (NSF), 70,
  86
Neogestalt theory, 13
New England Regional Computing
  Company (NERCOMP), 70, 120
New York Times, The, 233
New York University, 125
Newton, John M., 80
Nordman, B. J., 318
North Carolina Education Computing
  Service (NCECS), 70
North Carolina State University, 124
Northeastern University, 40
Northern Virginia Community College,
  100

Ohio State Medical School, 102
Ohio State University, 113
O'Neil, Robert M., 211, 213
On-line interactive systems, 68–75
Open universities, 198, 219–222, 275
"Open University Put to the Test," 220
Operating systems, 59
Opportunity, equality of, 201–202
Organismic theory, 13
Organization, technology and, 4–5
Orlicky, Joseph, 55
Overhead transparencies, 44–45

Pake, George E., 202, 207, 235
Paper programmed instruction (PI), 49–52
Patrick, Kenneth G., 214
Pavlov, Ivan P., 15
Peace Corps, 19
Phoenix Community College, 100
Piaget, Jean, 15
Pigors, Faith, 19
Pigors, Paul, 19
Pillsbury, Wilbur, 102, 103
PLATO I project, 95
PLATO II project, 95
PLATO III project, 95
PLATO IV project, 95–98, 101, 278
PL/C, 73
PL1, 79, 289*n.*
President's Science Advisory Committee
  (PSAC), 177
Private donors, 198, 214–215
Procedures:
  acquisition of, 139
  embedding of, 141
  integration of, 143–144
  testing of, 145
Processors, 56–57, 61–64
Professional organizations, 198, 215–
  216
Programming, 79–80
Project CLUE, 80, 86, 103
Project IMPRESS, 126
Project Intrex, 126*n.*
PSSC film, 89–90
Psychology, learning process and, 12–
  13